Jacques Rancière

Published:

Jacques Rancière

Oliver Davis

polity

First published in 2010 by Polity Press

Polity Press
65 Bridge Street
Cambridge CB2 1UR, UK

Polity Press
350 Main Street
Malden, MA 02148, USA

ISBN-13: 978-0-7456-4654-1
ISBN-13: 978-0-7456-4655-8 (pb)

A catalogue record for this book is available from the British Library.

Typeset in 10.5 on 12 pt Palatino
by Toppan Best-set Premedia Limited
Printed and bound in Great Britain by MPG Books Group Limited, Bodmin, Cornwall

For further information on Polity, visit our website: www.politybooks.com

Contents

Preface

Jacques Rancière, the philosopher of equality, is now in his eighth decade and interest in his work has never been greater. His singular intellectual project, which spans a daunting range of disciplines, has been steadily and patiently elaborated in numerous books, articles, lectures and interviews since the mid-1960s. While it would be misleading to suggest that he languished in complete obscurity after his contribution to Louis Althusser's *Reading Capital* [1965],[1] it is only really relatively recently that this professional philosopher has risen to public prominence in his own right in France and that his impact has begun to be felt in the English-speaking world. Within academia the opening decade of the millennium saw several high-profile international conferences devoted to Rancière's work, a flurry of keynote addresses, an ever-diminishing time-lag between the appearance of his writing in French and its emergence in English translation, as well as translations into a number of other languages (including a recent Hindi translation of *The Nights of Labor*), a plethora of journal special issues and a growing tide of single-author studies and essay collections dedicated to aspects of his thought and his relationship with other thinkers. This, however, is the first book-length study by a single author, in any language, which is devoted entirely to Rancière's thought and engages with all of his major interventions in and across the fields of politics, pedagogy, history, literature and aesthetics. At the time of writing, we are still in that particular moment in the reception of his work in the English-speaking world when editors and authors grapple to derive an adjective from his name ('Rancierian' will be used here) and translators seek to stabilize the English versions of his key terms. Perhaps it is fitting, if only trivially so, given Rancière's critique of consensus, that little consensus has yet to emerge on these issues.

Bridging the gap between academia and the wider world are his invaluable interviews, a selection of which, running to over six hundred pages, was published in French last year, in 2009, under a title apt for an interviewee who has pursued and continues to pursue his intellectual project with indefatigable tenacity, *Et tant pis pour les gens fatigués, And Too Bad for the Weary*.[2] Outside academia rumours continue to circulate of the influence of Rancière's political thought over Ségolène Royal in particular, the former presidential candidate of France's Socialist Party. And his work on aesthetics is now displayed prominently on the philosophy shelves of many a contemporary art bookshop and is rapidly becoming established as an essential point of reference for artists and curators.

Such an explosive moment in the reception of any thinker's work is hazardous for aspiring explainers and not just because of the ordinary scholarly dangers of missing or failing to account for significant new material. The desire to promote work which one finds exceptionally enabling and transformative can easily give rise to the sort of unbalanced enthusiasm which eventually does it a disservice, particularly if that enthusiasm attracts the resentful attention of others less favourably disposed to the initial premises, the intentions and the manner of the thought in question and who, in rage, see fit to rubbish it. It then invariably takes years of painstaking sifting by fairer-minded commentators to set the record straight. This unfortunate pattern, which draws strength from the inherent conservatism of the academic establishment and the anti-intellectualism of the wider culture in Britain and the United States, has been repeated all too often in the reception of French-language philosophers from the Continental tradition whose work is taken up in the English-speaking world as French Theory: Sartre, Foucault, Althusser and Derrida, to name but four, have all shared a similar fate in this respect. If the tone in the main chapters which follow is sometimes more sober and the approach more directly contestatory than some other work on Rancière, this is my attempt to avoid the kind of overinflation which feeds that dispiriting pattern of reception. Yet at the same time I have tried to avoid replicating the no less disheartening cross-Channel division of labour identified by E.P. Thompson in his assessment of the relationship between French and English Marxism: 'they propose and we object'.[3] Nevertheless, for unalloyed enthusiasm and an unqualified statement of the importance of Rancière's work, the reader will have to wait until the Afterword.

The hazards to aspiring explainers inherent in the explosive moment in its receptional lifetime at which Rancière's thought has now arrived are compounded considerably by some of the specific asperities of a body of work which make it especially resistant to the kind of explanatory critical exposition offered in this book. I wish briefly to survey these here, in order to measure and acknowledge the particular presumptuousness of my undertaking and as a prelude to defending what I hestitate to call my method. First among those features of Rancière's work which make it resistant to explanation is its own intense and principled suspicion of the very act of explaining. According to the nineteenth-century maverick pedagogue Joseph Jacotot, the subject of Rancière's most seductive book, *The Ignorant Schoolmaster* [1987], explaining stultifies because it is premised on and perpetuates intellectual inequality between teacher and student.[4] The detail of these claims and Jacotot's radical pedagogical alternative will be examined in Chapter 1. The point I want to make here is more about the implications of the particular ways in which Rancière's work as a whole fights to avoid the explanatory mode. His philosophical style, in the main, is declarative or assertoric rather than explanatory: even when he analyses an existing body of thought or discourse, as he does in his ongoing project on aesthetics, the analysis proceeds not by explaining but by proposing theses and constructively elaborating new conceptual configurations and frameworks of understanding.

Whereas explainers have explicitly to establish hierarchies, both at macro level in their selection and presentation of the material and at sentence level in their use of subordinating and co-ordinating structures, Rancière's thinking and writing are egalitarian: parataxis, or juxtaposition, is his favoured linguistic and conceptual mode. Equality is not just declared by, but enacted in, the Rancierian sentence, which tends to eschew both hierarchizing constructions and qualifiers expressive of degree: the preponderance of on-or-off assertoric structures, notably 'it is a question of' and 'it is not a question of' (*il s'agit de / il ne s'agit pas de*), lends the thinking an impassioned drivennness at local level but makes systematization challenging, to say the least. And of course this is part of the point. Readers have responded to the very particular texture of Rancière's work differently. I have analysed it elsewhere as a productive performance of textual, conceptual and affective irritability; Hayden White has expressed somewhat puzzled appreciation of its 'aphoristic, almost oracular' tone.[5] Yet the crucial point is that the declarative approach, as practised by Rancière, differs decisively from the lecturely authoritarianism for which it can risk being mistaken in that it assumes the reader is on an equal footing and leaves him or her radically free before the thought, free to take it or leave it, free to disagree or remain unconvinced. Or free, as in my case, to rub against its grain by trying to explain it, even if the only explanation I can in all conscience hazard is one which explicitly disavows its own authority and assumes, from the outset, the equal capacity of any reader to make sense of the work, as well as his or her freedom to disagree with, or to remain unconvinced by, the reading I propose.

Explanation, in Rancière's case, is also difficult for pragmatic, as well as ethical, reasons because of the sheer range of his work over so many disciplines and debates and the particular way his thought has of lodging itself in the interstices of discussions which are often already complex in their own right. As he has said himself, his books are 'always forms of intervention in specific contexts'.[6] But what exactly is an 'intervention'? S/he who intervenes etymologically 'comes between'. In normal English usage 'intervention' is seldom far from interference and readily implies meddling with something which could have been left alone, intruding to prevent things taking the course they might otherwise have taken. In French, however, and in English uses of the term which play on its resonances in that other language, such as Rancière's in the article, first published in English, from which the above quote was taken, the scope of the verb *intervenir* and its noun *intervention* is wider in normal usage and more detached from the notion of obstructive interference. Indeed legitimate examples of *interventions* include not only short presentations at conferences and, historically, the act of speaking up for one of the parties in a courtroom, but in principle almost any act of interceding.[7] The English 'intervention', as it is ghosted by its French *intervention*, is thus a term which is wide open and so already predisposed to egalitarian uses: given application, there is no debate, or issue, or arena, which is in principle off-limits to anyone. Rancière is by no means an autodidact, and few of us who have any first-hand experience of institutional education can meaningfully claim to be one; yet in his practice of the intervention, in this augmented bilingual sense, he renews with the nineteenth-century autodidact's egalitarian (self-)confidence that, given need, desire and tenacity, knowledge is open to anyone and everyone.

   That Rancière's practice of the intervention gives rise to particular practical difficulties for would-be explainers is undeniable: often the discussions in which he intervenes are already formidably complex, particularly in the case of historiography, which I examine in Chapter 2. Moreover, his interventionary approach discourages attempts to systematize his work. I have tried in the pages which follow to strike a balance between recontextualization – resituating his work in the conceptual and political contexts with which it engages – and a recognition and exploration of the singularity of his work in its own terms. Since the practice of contextualization is itself problematized in Rancière's work and over-contextualization is certainly 'un-Rancierian', for reasons which will become clear, again in Chapter 2, this book about Rancière cannot with any confidence claim to be Rancierian. In defence of my 'method', I hazard that it would be almost impossible to grasp the real originality and interest of Rancière's singular project without some familiarity with the varied contexts in which it intervenes. Nevertheless, I make no exaggerated claims to have somehow overcome the plurality of these interventionary contexts and explained Rancière's thought as a systematic unity. What I present instead is an explanatory and critical analysis of his thought's emergence, its development and its major concerns, together with a provisional assessment of its value. I focus on what I judge to be the major texts, but part of what this means is that I focus on those texts which lend themselves to the kind of explanatory project I am undertaking: if the constraints of the task in hand mean I pass over quickly some of the more oblique or highly context-specific works, for instance *Short Voyages to the Land of the People* or *Hatred of Democracy*, this implies no judgment about either their intrinsic worth or their openness for other kinds of project than the one I am undertaking here.[8]

   Here then is a sketch-map of the ground which will be covered. Chapter 1 is concerned with Rancière's early politics and traces the emergence of his unique conception of equality from his critique of pedagogy. His break with former teacher Louis Althusser, his reflection on the egalitarian meaning of the events of May '68 and his penetratingly oblique reflection on the Marxist tradition of social criticism, in *The Philosopher and His Poor* [1983], are shown to be preparing the ground for the articulation of his distinctive conception of declarative equality in *The Ignorant Schoolmaster* [1987]. Chapter 2 discusses Rancière's historical and historiographical work, his work in the archives of French nineteenth-century worker emancipation, alone and as part of the collective behind the groundbreaking journal *Les Révoltes Logiques* [1975–81]. The multifaceted politics of his practice of the archive are explored and related to his later and ill-understood historiographical treatise, *The Names of History* [1992]. The suggestion is that this book's nuanced critique of historicism lays the epistemological foundation for the quasi-historical concepts invoked in his later and ongoing work on aesthetics. Chapter 3 tackles Rancière's mature politics and covers his ground-clearing distinction between politics and 'the police', his structural account of democracy in terms of the 'wrong' and the 'miscount', his concept of political subjectivation and his analysis of the aesthetic dimension to politics. Splitting the politics into two chapters, 'early' and 'mature', and arranging them either side of the chapter on history, does not signal either a neo-Althusserian dogmatism of the 'break' or a wish to downplay the 'early' politics, but is rather an attempt to emphasize the singular shape which Rancière's detour via the archives imparts to the developmental pattern of his thought.

Chapters 4 and 5 show how his political and historiographical writing inform his analysis of literature, art and aesthetics: Chapter 4 examines his work on verbal art, which serves both as a partial template for, and the first phase of, his ongoing project on art and aesthetics, the subject of Chapter 5. That chapter explains this project in terms of what I think are its twin aims: to provide an analytical framework for the understanding of art and aesthetic experience and to derive a non-reductive conception of the politics of art. The middle section of Chapter 5 analyses Rancière's film criticism and film theory. The Afterword returns to reflect on the meaning of the exemplary singularity of Rancière's work.

Acknowledgements

I would like to thank the University of Warwick for a term of research leave and to colleagues Emma Campbell, Siân Miles and Douglas Morrey for support both moral and intellectual. For help on specific points in relation to this book and my other work on Rancière, thanks also go to Jeremy Ahearne, Daniel Andersson, Sudeep Dasgupta, Nick Hewlett, Leslie Hill, Christina Howells, Hector Kollias and Adrian Rifkin. I am grateful to the Friedrich Wilhelm Murnau Stiftung for kindly granting permission to reproduce a still image from Murnau's *Herr Tartüff*, and to Campement Urbain for their kind permission to reproduce an image from their project *Je et Nous*. Thanks finally to Wesley Gryk for stability and sustenance while this book took shape.

1

The Early Politics

From Pedagogy to Equality

This chapter traces the emergence of the central unifying concept in Rancière's work, equality, from his reflections on pedagogy. These were shaped by his own experience of institutional education, as a student of Marxist philosopher Louis Althusser in the early and mid-1960s. He subsequently became one of his former teacher's most trenchant critics; the May '68 revolt crystallized his objections to Althusser's thought and much of Rancière's work thereafter can broadly be understood as the attempt to give discursive form to the idea of radical equality implicit in May but unrecognized, at the time, by Althusser.

Rancière's most suggestive reformulation of the concept of equality takes place in *The Ignorant Schoolmaster* [1987], a book about pedagogy. This chapter aims to show how the far-reaching positive conception of radical equality contained in that book emerges out of sustained critical reflection on, and polemical reaction against, the philosophical pedagogies (and pedagogical philosophies) of Althusser, Marx, Sartre and Bourdieu. Despite their reputation as pillars of the Left, Rancière argues that these thinkers share a repressive conception of pedagogical power and a commitment to the social privilege of intellect first articulated by Plato in *Republic*. As this chapter unfolds, Rancière's critique of the pedagogy of inequality will be related to radical thinking about education from Latin America, Britain and the United States.

Althusser's lesson

'It is impossible to choose one's beginnings,' Louis Althusser once insisted, in typically vigorous italics, with reference to, and in commiseration with, the young Marx, whose university education was steeped in the ambient philosophy of German Idealism.[1] With hindsight a similar remark could be made of the young Rancière's encounter with Althusser in the 1960s, as his student. From the moment of his first presentation at Althusser's seminar, in 1961, through his remarkably compliant contribution to *Reading Capital* [1965], the structuralist classic based on that seminar's reading of Marx's text, to the publication of his excoriating critique *La Leçon d'Althusser* (1974), *Althusser's Lesson*, Althusser was the figure of reference.[2] I cannot offer an exhaustive account of Althusser's work and its many vicissitudes here; however, because he is so decisive an influence, those features of his doctrine and philosophical style relevant to an understanding of Rancière's work will be briefly outlined.[3]

Althusser's commiserating attitude to the young Marx's intellectual upbringing was more than idle sympathy; it reflected a central point of Althusserian teaching. Althusser, who claimed to be rereading Marx 'as a philosopher', contended that Marx's early and mature work were separated by an 'epistemological break' (*coupure épistémologique*). According to Bachelard's philosophy of science, from which Althusser had adapted this concept, all sciences begin with a phase in which the world is understood from a perspective centred on human nature and concrete particular facts; only after an 'epistemological break' with this early phase does abstract and properly scientific conceptual knowledge of the world become possible.[4] Althusser argued, contrary to most other interpreters, that Marx's work after 1845, and, above all, *Capital*, was not continuous with that of the early period but rather constituted a radical break with it. *Capital*, he suggested, was a theoretical revolution which made possible knowledge of the world as it really is, or 'Marxist science'; Marx's early work, by contrast, exemplified an inferior, pre-scientific, form of understanding, which he termed 'ideology', one which sought to explain the world in terms of human nature and could therefore also be characterized as 'humanist' and 'anthropological'.[5] Belief in 'the break' is a hallmark of Althusserianism; non-Althusserian Marxists tend not to think there is so pronounced a rupture, although many would acknowledge there is a discernible general movement away from explanation in human terms towards more abstract, theoretical, formulations. For example, Marx's early account of the way in which factory workers are alienated by their work is centred on the human worker and the way in which his work gives rise to feelings of being divided from himself, from his fellow producers and from the object he is producing; 'alienation' in this early sense is a form of unhappiness, the mainly psychological quality of feeling divided from oneself.[6] By the time of *Capital*, the logic of Marx's approach, which sees him begin, in the first nine chapters, with a very abstract exposition of key economic concepts such as the commodity, value and labour, suggests he thinks that such concepts are required if the underlying mechanisms which account for the real basis of feelings of alienation are to be understood.[7] So in *Capital*, the alienating effects of work can only be properly understood in terms of the structure of economic relations in the society in question. These relations are not immediately accessible, in the sense that they cannot be intuited by the factory worker as s/he works, or by an untrained observer, because they require a developed theoretical understanding of underlying economic processes and structures.

It may sound as though Althusser had been trying to read Marx as an economist; yet he always insisted that he and his students were reading Marx 'as philosophers'.[8] What did he mean by this? Marx, Althusser rightly noted, was both a voracious and a remarkably perceptive reader. According to Althusser, in *Capital* Marx can be seen undertaking two distinct types of reading. The second type is the one which interests Althusser, and his account of it can be summarized as follows: when Marx reads the work of economist Adam Smith, for example, Marx discerns that Smith's theory had hit upon a correct answer to a question which Smith himself did not know how to formulate but which Marx is able to pose explicitly.[9] Althusser called this type of reading 'symptomatic', and, in so doing, he aligned Marx with a certain (perhaps caricaturally simplistic) kind of psychoanalyst whose therapy consists in helping the analysand formulate explicitly the problem which lies beneath the surface manifestation that is his or her symptom.[10] So to read Marx 'as a philosopher' also meant reading his text 'as a psychoanalyst', taking what it says on the surface to be a 'symptom' of its underlying meaning: Althusser's intention was to formulate explicitly, theoretically, this underlying meaning, the philosophy of Marx, which he thought was performed but not stated explicitly in *Capital*. Marx's philosophy, according to Althusser, his discovery, was a theory of history as ultimately determined by relationships of material production (a theory sometimes called dialectical materialism). *Capital* needed to be read 'symptomatically' because, while it demonstrated this discovery in practice when it analysed particular examples of material production, such as cotton-weaving in Lancashire, it contained no explicit theoretical statement of what dialectical materialism was. In *Reading Capital*, by applying Marx's symptomatic mode of reading to his own major text, Althusser claimed to be formulating Marx's philosophy in theoretical terms. The understanding of Marx's philosophy thus obtained from *Capital* was to be supplemented by an analysis of revolutionary struggle: like Marx's masterwork, revolutionary movements were thought to be practical enactments of Marxist philosophy in which it was Althusser's self-appointed task to read the theory. For Althusser, books and revolutionary movements alike were deemed susceptible to his eclectic mix of self-assertingly philosophical and notionally psychoanalytic analysis.

Rancière's contribution to *Reading Capital* followed immediately after Althusser's prefatory essay 'From *Capital* to Marx's Philosophy'.[11] Entitled 'The Concept of Critique and the Critique of Political Economy from the *1844 Manuscripts* to *Capital*', the essay is a remarkably compliant rehearsal of Althusserian doctrine.[12] Taking fidelity to Althusser's concept of the epistemological break to an extreme, Rancière even enacts the break in the very structure of his contribution, which is in two parts, corresponding to early and late Marx. He argues that in early Marx the activity of critique involves identifying contradictions and then working upwards to find the general and human meaning of the contradiction; the early Marx's approach is therefore humanist and anthropological.[13] In late Marx, by contrast, the process of critique is, to all intents and purposes, synonymous with the Althusserian practice of 'symptomatic' reading. At the heart of Rancière's contribution lies an Althusserian reading of Marx's celebrated concept of commodity fetishism. Classical political economy had succeeded, to some extent, in deriving the concept of value as the content hidden beneath the various forms of riches and in grasping that this value is realized in the exchange of goods. However, classical political economy had failed to understand that this exchange of commodities (the formula of which is given by Marx and cited by Rancière as 'x commodities $A = y$ commodities B') is impossible unless it is understood that the value of the commodity is the socially necessary labour exerted in producing it rather than a property of the object as such. A commodity only has a certain value because, according to Marx, a certain minimum amount of labour is necessary to produce it; this minimum amount of labour is itself fixed by the ways in which material production operates in the society in question. Everyday perception sees value as a simple property of objects, whereas Marxist science understands it to be a function of the overall economic and social structure, 'a metonymic manifestation of the structure'.[14] Ordinary perception is 'fetishistic' in that it takes the complex structural property, value, to be a simple property of the object; *Capital* is scientific because the relationships between commodities it describes – relationships of value – are grasped in the context of the overall economic system, as functions of the social relations of production in capitalist society. Value is a structural and scientific concept and, as such, is not accessible to ordinary perception and cannot simply be read off objects: 'We are no longer dealing with a *text* to be read in such a way as to reveal its underlying meaning but with a *hieroglyph* to be deciphered. This work of deciphering is science.'[15] Rancière's contribution is extreme in its Althusserian orthodoxy because it emphasizes the opacity of the world to ordinary perception and because it holds that only symptomatic reading can give rise to a reliable understanding of the world.

The attraction of Althusser's enterprise to Rancière and a whole generation of aspiring activists on the Left is partly to be explained by the political climate of the time: it was clear in the 1960s to all but the most ideologically self-deluding that, under Stalin, the Soviet Union had become a brutally repressive police state and 'Althusser's objective was at this stage to find in Marx's own thinking the principle of a theoretical understanding of Marxism's aberrations'.[16] Only a correct understanding of the true meaning of Marx's philosophy could serve as a reliable guide to political action and as a safeguard against those aberrations. Revolutionary political practice without correct theory was felt to be doomed to the short-sighted pursuit of ill-understood goals:

> Left to itself, a spontaneous (technical) practice produces only the 'theory' it needs as a means to produce the ends assigned to it: this 'theory' is never more than the reflection of this end, uncriticized, unknown, in its means of realization, that is, it is a *by-product* of the reflection of the technical practice's end on its means. A 'theory' which does not question the end whose *by-product* it is remains a prisoner of this end and of the 'realities' which have imposed it as an end.[17]

Althusser's enterprise held particular appeal to activists on the Left who were also intellectuals because it seemed to transcend the distinction between theory and practice by deftly redefining the kind of intellectual work undertaken in certain lecture theatres and seminars as a form of political action: 'theoretical practice'. As Rancière put it: 'We found in Althusser's work the idea that intellectuals could have a different role, one other than cultural consumption or ideological reflection: real involvement *as intellectuals* in transforming the world.'[18] That this was a false hope, and the notion of 'theoretical practice' something of a sleight of hand, did not become fully clear to Rancière until the events of May '68, as we shall see in a moment. Yet in the early and mid-sixties, Althusser's approach not only promised Marxist intellectuals a role in the revolution *as intellectuals*, it set the interpretation of Marx free from the authority of the Party, a Party which, in France, had performed a series of about-turns flagrant enough to test the loyalty of even the truest of true believers. The unqualified support by the French Communist Party (PCF) of Stalin in the fifties had given way to vigorous de-Stalinization in the sixties; simultaneously, its commitment to violent revolutionary struggle had morphed into support for the pursuit of social change by democratic means. Perhaps most damagingly of all, during the Algerian War of Independence the PCF had supported Socialist prime minister Guy Mollet's 1956 bill granting 'special powers' to the governor of Algeria, thereby effectively establishing a police state; by so doing, its traditional claim to be the party of revolution and liberation was seriously compromised.[19]

Throughout the late fifties and sixties, Althusser remained staunchly loyal, in public, to the PCF. Yet the logic of his intellectual approach was to free the interpretation of Marx from the authority of the Party, and this was undoubtedly part of his appeal to younger, 'leftist' (*gauchiste*) activists, in other words activists who positioned themselves to the left of the PCF. As Rancière put it: 'Marx's theory belonged to nobody but his readers and their only duty was to it. [. . .] Everyone could read Marx and see *what followed*. All that was required was for them to approach the text through the discipline of science.'[20] Althusser's Marxist science liberated the text of Marx from the interpretative authority of the Party, just as the Protestant Reformation had sought to free the Bible from that of the Roman Catholic Church. In *Reading Capital* Althusser defined his own 'symptomatic' mode of reading against what he castigated as the 'religious' myth of reading, a superficial approach to reading, and in so doing distanced himself still further from the church with which he had himself 'broken' at an earlier moment and, by implication, from the Party to which he remained only publicly loyal.[21]

If Althusser implicitly revoked the authority of the Party to decide on the meaning of Marx's philosophy, this proved in practice to be less emancipatory than many of his students had hoped. For behind 'the discipline of science', as Rancière terms it – parodying Althusser's grandiose rhetorical claims to scientific 'rigour', claims which he had echoed altogether more faithfully in his contribution to *Reading Capital* – lay another form of authority: pedagogical authority. The art of the 'symptomatic' reading was not open to all and sundry given sufficient investment of effort and attention, but required *instruction*: as Althusser had warned, 'We need something quite different from an acute or attentive gaze; we need an *educated* gaze.'[22] Marxist science had been set free from the authority of the Party only to become dependent instead on that of the pedagogue, Althusser. This helps explain why Rancière's repudiation of Althusserianism is entitled *Althusser's Lesson* and why, at key junctures, it frames his argument against Althusser as an argument against pedagogy. Althusserianism is 'fundamentally a theory of education', Rancière argues, and 'every theory of education strives to maintain the source of the power it seeks to shed light on'.[23] The promise of Althusser's theory – that only by a correct, rigorous, understanding of theory would a political practice be possible which avoided the aberrations of Stalinism and the compromises of democratic socialism – proved to be hollow. Because of Althusser's investment in the privileged position of the pedagogue, it would never be time for his students to fulfil the promise of political action: 'It followed from the logic of Althusserian discourse that the moment would never come: the antagonistic struggles of empirical politics would never allow philosophy the opportunity to conclude.'[24] Although Althusserianism seemed to be at the very forefront of progressive Left discourse, Rancière came to the conclusion that it functioned in accordance with a pedagogical temporality of delay: the time to act would never come, the inequalities which were to be eliminated would always remain in place. Rancière's later critique of progressive pedagogy in *The Ignorant Schoolmaster* is informed by these reflections on his experience of Althusserianism as an endlessly procrastinating process of instruction. Althusserianism served only to emphasize the gap of inequality between the instructed and those unschooled in Marxist science and hence to strengthen the authority of the teacher, Althusser, whose position in Rancière's later thought Alain Badiou has described as that of 'the master who knows', *le maître savant*, by contrast with *le maître ignorant*, the 'ignorant schoolmaster' named in the title of Rancière's book on Jacotot.[25]

Rancière's transition from compliant student to outspoken critic of Althusser did not happen in a vacuum: as Badiou has asserted, Mao's Cultural Revolution (at its height in the period 1965–8) and the near-revolution, in France, of May '68 both exerted a similar kind of pressure on the young Althusserians. The Cultural Revolution questioned – often with murderous violence – the social and institutional privileges accorded to scholars, teachers and bureaucrats by virtue of their knowledge. May '68 began as a student revolt and, whatever else it was besides, it was without doubt a questioning of the power and the processes of pedagogy. For Michel de Certeau, writing later that same year, May '68 was, in essence, a challenge to established conceptions of pedagogy in an extended sense: 'Fundamentally, it concerns the pedagogical relation in that it touches on academic, but also familial, institutions and, in a broader sense, the relation between cadres and their adherents, executive officers and those administered, those who govern and those who are governed.'[26] Moreover, May '68 saw students and factory workers engage in revolutionary action without the guidance of the Party and often to its consternation: indeed the PCF, instead of leading the revolt, was instrumental in ending it. Althusserian science and the Party to which it publicly deferred seemed similarly redundant: 'Althusserianism met its death on the barricades of May along with many other ideas of the past,' as Rancière put it conclusively.[27] The trouble was that Althusser did not seem to realize this. Before publishing his excoriating repudiation, *La Leçon d'Althusser*, Rancière had already written a sceptical book chapter and an article in which he described Althusser's work as 'reactionary' and labelled his own contribution to *Reading Capital* 'rustic' because of the crudeness with which it reproduced the Althusserian dogma of the epistemological break.[28] Rancière presents his book-length critique, *La Leçon d'Althusser*, as an exasperated reaction to his former teacher's failure to take on board the political lessons of May '68. Rancière complained that Althusser's *Réponse à John Lewis* (1973), a counterattack against the eponymous British Communist, simply restated in more accessible language the same ideas he had advanced eight years before, as though May had changed nothing.[29]

Althusser's concept of the epistemological break is easily ridiculed, yet it was a response to the legitimate question of how any new thought ever emerges. In Marx's case, the question was how his mature work emerged from the ambient German Idealism of his educational milieu. In other words it addressed the question of why pedagogy sometimes fails to produce compliant repetition of the same. Overplayed though the motif of the break was, the question it addressed is one which can be asked of Rancière's own work. Just as, for Althusser, ideology is not the opposite of science it is often taken to be but rather its necessary precondition, so Althusserianism is the contested foundation of Rancière's project.[30] It has rightly been remarked that Rancière's reaction against Althusserianism is extreme, yet it is also multifaceted.[31] Before explaining how Rancière's positive conception of radical equality emerges, I shall identify four aspects of the Althusserian legacy which are preserved in Rancière's project – two substantive and two more stylistic, in a broad sense – and reflect on the intellectual difficulty of this moment of separation.

The vestiges of one of Althusser's most distinctive and valuable early contributions to Marxism are preserved and exaggerated in Rancière's project: Althusser's critique of 'economism' and his related assertion of the relative autonomy of the superstructure. Marx and Engels had sometimes distinguished between the 'superstructure' of a given society (its concepts and cultural representations) and its 'base' (the economic relations of production). Much of Althusser's work in the early 1960s was directed against a reductive interpretation of Marx he called 'economism', according to which the cultural phenomena of the 'superstructure' could be explained directly in terms of the material relations of production, or 'base', in a given society. An economistic interpretation of Marx was a misreading, Althusser contended, because it implied that ideas were mere inconsequential froth atop the real motive forces in society, economic factors. This reassertion of the significance and relative autonomy of the superstructure went hand in hand with a revalorization of the political purchase of intellectual work, which takes place in that superstructure. Rancière will go on to exaggerate Althusser's critique of economism by turning away from economic factors altogether and focusing entirely on multiple contradictions in the superstructure. If Althusser's was an uneasy truce with economic explanation, one which allowed him to continue to call himself a Marxist while showing very little interest in economics as such, the absence of political economy from Rancière's mature work means that, although it emerged out of Marxism, it cannot itself be described as Marxist.

The legacy of Althusserianism's alluring and paradoxical promise of 'theoretical practice' is also to be found in Rancière's project. Althusser had suggested that intellectuals who were engaged in the theoretical enterprise of Marxist science and were busy clarifying the correct understanding of revolutionary struggle were, by so doing, engaged in that struggle. This promise of theory which was itself politics was the most recent, most complex and most stridently put formulation of a distinguishing characteristic of the Marxist tradition: namely materialism, the idea that theory and practice are inseparable. The question of the political character of theory, which is characteristic of the Marxist tradition, once raised, proves extremely difficult to answer conclusively. As we have seen, Althusser's theory is described by Rancière as a self-servingly pedagogical deferral of the change it promised. And when Rancière takes issue with Bourdieu's sociological analysis of education, not because it is descriptively incorrect but because it is a kind of theory which depresses rather than inspires change for the better, commentators inevitably turn to Rancière's own work and ask in what sense exactly it is capable of effecting 'change'. Even if the question of its capacity to produce effects in the real is not unique to his theory – 'the question can be asked of anyone', as he has rightly pointed out – it nonetheless still is one which he, among others, is called upon to answer.[32]

Finally, two marks of what can broadly be termed Althusser's philosophical style are reflected in Rancière's work. By reading Marx 'as a philosopher' and thereby redressing, as he proudly said, one hundred and twenty years of censorship by silence within the university, Althusser provided a model for the 'displacing' of philosophy which, as we shall see in the next chapter, Rancière would echo in the 1970s when, as a lecturer in philosophy at Vincennes, he used the academic freedom accorded him there to immerse himself and his student Alain Faure in the archives of the nineteenth-century French workers' movement and read them 'as philosophers'. For all his rhetoric of disciplinary rigour and systematicity, Althusser thus also offered an early lesson in the kind of 'indiscipline' or 'anti-disciplinarity', the intellectual and political potential of which will be demonstrated in unparalleled fashion in Rancière's work.[33] The second vestige of Althusser's philosophical style exhibited in Rancière's work is what has been called Althusser's 'declarative' conception of philosophy: the philosopher's task is 'to present theses'.[34] Some of Rancière's more schematic work, for example his assertion of the separation between politics and the police order, examined in Chapter 3, or the periodization of the history of literature and art, examined in Chapters 4 and 5, exhibits a decidedly Althusserian penchant for declaring the existence of lines of demarcation and seeing what follows.[35]

This does not prove, and I am not arguing, that Rancière's work is derivative of Althusser's in any reductive sense. It does, however, indicate that the relationship between the two thinkers is more involved than a cursory reading of Rancière and a passing familiarity with their biographies would suggest. Rancière's *Leçon d'Althusser* figures his split with Althusser precisely as a break but, in so doing, raises many of the same questions of transmission, filiation and the emergence of new thought with which Althusser (alongside Rancière) had grappled in his (in their) readings of Marx. Perhaps a break with 'the philosopher of the break', as Balibar has called Althusser, could never have been entirely 'clean', never entirely free of the suspicion that it expresses a contorted kind of fidelity.[36]

If Rancière's break with his former teacher was vexed with paradox at the time, the public revelation, some years later, of Althusser's long struggle with mental illness added, retrospectively, a further complicating dimension. Close colleagues and friends had long been aware of Althusser's condition, not least because he was allowed to reside for many years in a room in the infirmary of the École Normale Supérieure, where he taught, but it became a matter of public notoriety in 1980 after he killed his wife.[37] The question of the bearing of his illness on his work and that of his students is more easily raised than it is satisfactorily resolved. Elliott is right to urge caution on logical grounds: 'Louis Althusser became a manic-depressive murderer, no doubt about it. But not every manic-depressive murderer is Louis Althusser. The heuristic inadequacy of literary supplement psychobabble is contained in these two sentences.'[38] It is difficult not to sympathize with Elliott's assertion here of the autonomy of Althusser's work from the tragic circumstances of his life; if only the work of anyone suffering from mental illness could always be judged on its own terms. Elliott could also cite, in his favour, a well-established tradition of right-thinking professional academic contempt for the amateurish reductionism of simplistic psychobiography, one which invariably begins in literary studies with the ritual vilification of Marie Bonaparte's biography of Poe and ends with a plea for the kind of more nuanced, playful and knowing incorporation of psychoanalysis exemplified in the work of Adam Phillips or the late Malcolm Bowie.

Rancière, however, who is better placed than most to comment on Althusser, does manage to raise the unseemly question of the specific madness of Althusser's philosophy and his pedagogical practice. In his essay 'Althusser, Don Quixote, and the Stage of the Text', first published three years after Althusser's death in 1990, he observes: 'There is, in the heart of the Althusserian moment [*éclair*], something of which it is difficult to speak but that is nonetheless central: a thought of madness, a rigorous connection established between the madness of history and an intellectual's risk of madness.'[39] Rancière suggests that, for Althusser, the practice of the symptomatic reading, as outlined in his first introductory contribution to *Reading Capital*, was more than a merely philosophical, interpretative or political matter. As described by Althusser, the symptomatic reading articulates the 'question' which is latent in a text but unrecognized in the 'answers' which are contained in or constitute that text. To illustrate the way in which questions are latent or implicit in texts, Althusser inserted brackets containing ellipses and sometimes just brackets into passages from the citations of classical economists given in *Capital*. Rancière likens the former to the gaps in primary school textbooks to be filled by students: 'They are there to verify that the student knows his lesson and knows how to apply what he has been taught.'[40] Rancière goes further in this essay than in *La Leçon d'Althusser*, where, as we have seen, he had already suggested that Althusser's philosophy was an endlessly procrastinating form of schooling which served to delay rather than incite political action. In the later essay Rancière suggests that the notion of symptomatic reading turns the philosophical text and the pedagogical encounter into an intensely theatrical exchange of questions and answers.[41] The text and the pedagogical encounter become a tightly woven, almost liturgical, exchange of questions and responses, which serves to anchor Althusser's faltering spirit and to save him from lonely madness by binding him into a pedagogical relationship to others, his students.

Rancière's account is significant because it transgresses the reluctance of academic critics, well-intentioned though they often are, to raise seriously the question of the place of madness in Althusser's thought.[42] In so doing it challenges the right-thinking separation between life and work which has become enshrined as a matter of disciplinary dogma and is one example of Rancière's willingness to entertain critical concepts which defy the norms of mainstream academic practice. Yet his essay is also curious because it fails explicitly to engage with his own implication in the drama of Althusser's madness, even as it points to the apotropaic function of a pedagogy premised on the tightly knit exchange of questions and answers between master and students: Rancière suggests that Althusser sought his own security, the containment of his madness, in this pedagogical drama. Rancière's 1993 essay is striking because, like his contribution to *Reading Capital*, it is still framed largely in terms of the master's desire: it provides an arresting analysis of Althusserianism as a 'theatrical' interplay of questions and answers without ever quite going as far as to reflect on one particular student's role in that drama. Does having been involved in that drama bequeath a certain melancholia to his own work?[43] In psychoanalytic terms his involvement in that drama can be understood as 'compliance': for Donald Winnicott, compliance is the pantomime enacted by the child of the depressed mother in an attempt to placate her yet which serves only to pass down her melancholia.[44] Rancière's final gesture towards Althusser in the essay, 'to restore to his text the solitude – and I don't mean oblivion – to which it has a right', tries to perform a respectful laying-to-rest of Althusserianism.[45] Yet his reluctance to confront directly his own implication in the more insane moments of that pedagogical drama, which is analysed instead largely in terms of the needs and deficiencies of the master, is in its own way another example of compliance because it avoids posing the question of the nature of the student's desire in the presence of this overbearing influence.

For Althusser, the Marxist truth of things does not lie on the surface waiting to be intuited by the attentive reader; rather, the *'educated* reader', schooled in the art of the symptomatic reading, has to delve beneath the surface and its 'answers' to find and formulate the latent theoretical 'question'. The specialists in symptomatic reading – Althusserian intellectuals engaged in this work of theoretical practice – would then *instruct* the proletariat in correct political action; the intellectual thus stands in a one-way pedagogical relationship to the proletariat. Althusserianism's 'lesson' is one without which the proletariat are condemned to spontaneous and aberrant, rather than properly revolutionary, action:

> The 'masses' make history, no doubt about it, but not just any masses: those which *we* educate and organize. They only make history if they first understand that they are separated from it by a

thick layer of 'dominant ideology', by all of those stories the bour-
geoisie tell them and which, stupid as they are, they would always
swallow hook, line and sinker if we weren't there to teach them how
to tell good ideas from bad ones.[46]

Althusserianism is judged by Rancière to be a condescending philosophy which protects the social privilege of those institutionally
associated with it.[47] The tone in this passage is typical of Rancière's
almost visceral response to this aspect of Althusserianism; rather
than 'critique', it would perhaps better be described as a violent
allergic reaction, an inflammation of the 'epidermic' sensitivity to
pedagogical privilege which he and a generation of *gauchiste* activists inherited from May '68.[48]

Althusser's view of the instructional role of an élite vanguard of
revolutionary intellectuals, to which Rancière is taking violent
exception here, has a long history within the Marxist tradition. In
La Leçon d'Althusser Rancière especially associates the idea with the
work of Karl Kautsky.[49] Like Althusser, Kautsky had understood
Marxism as 'a "science", the outcome of a correct analysis of the
Capitalist mode of production and its consequences'.[50] The motif
is already prominent in Marx: 'As philosophy finds in the proletariat its material weapons so the proletariat finds in philosophy
its intellectual weapons and as soon as the lightning of thought has
struck deep into the virgin soil of the people, the emancipation of
the Germans into men will be completed.'[51] This motif or position
becomes a defining feature of Leninism and is taken up by
Althusser: the claim was that Marxism had been developed outside
the working class by the counter-intuitive practice of intellectuals
and subsequently 'imported' into it.[52] This way of thinking, which
is central to Althusserianism, can be described as its 'scientism' or,
as Žižek better names what he takes to be Rancière's main objection
to Althusser, 'theoreticist elitism'.[53] While the working class were
the embodiment of the future for Marxist-Leninist theorists, they
did not themselves have direct knowledge of their defining role in
the historical process. For that they depended on intellectuals: as
Rancière put it parodically, '*the workers need our scientific knowledge
[notre science].*'[54] According to Rancière, the ultimate effect of
Althusser's lengthy crusade against humanist interpretations of
Marx was to defend the privilege of intellectuals. If, as Vico had
argued, history is made by individual human subjects, then it
should, humanists assume, be immediately intelligible and require
no special schooling to grasp. This is a position Althusser had

rejected and Rancière rejects Althusser's stance in turn: 'So all chatter [*bavardage*] has just one aim: to introduce the idea, by of a false symmetry, that there are many historical illusions wh call for the *intervention* of philosophy.'[55] Was Rancière right in his substantive claim that the *sole* aim ('tout ce bavardage n'a donc qu'un but') of Althusser's attack on humanist interpretations of Marx was to shore up the institutional privilege of intellectuals and specifically the political necessity of his own work to the workers' struggle? If 'aim' (*but*) is read purposively to mean that, all along, Althusser's only intention in fifteen years of intellectual work was self-aggrandizement, then Rancière's argument is distinctly paranoid. If, however, 'aim' is taken to mean the effect, not necessarily intended, of Althusser's discourse, then there is more mileage in the claim. The latter reading is the more plausible, although it is worth noting that Rancière's point is put a lot less carefully, more ambiguously, than it might have been. May '68 had arguably demonstrated the capacity of workers and students to instigate and organize their own protests without the guidance of Marxist intellectuals; because it had in fact happened, popular revolt was eminently possible without correct theoretical understanding. Moreover, Althusserianism's overemphasis on acquiring scientifically rigorous understanding not only served to defer that struggle, by offering pedagogy, with its temporality of delay, instead of politics, but risked suppressing it by legitimating, in the endless meantime, the social and institutional hierarchies through which pedagogical power was exercised.

Platonic inequality in Marx, Sartre and Bourdieu

Rancière's exploration, in the mid- to late 1970s, of the archives of the French workers' movement was driven by the desire to refute the implicit claim of Althusserianism, that *'the workers need our scientific knowledge'*, to defeat Althusserian scientism by showing not only that workers had, time and again, organized meaningful political revolt, but also that they had demonstrated an understanding of themselves, their world and their position within it which was in no sense inferior to Marxist science. The next chapter will look in more detail at this archival work in its own right. In what remains of this chapter I shall outline the way in which Rancière's positive account of intellectual equality emerged out of his radicalization of the critique of pedagogy in *La Leçon d'Althusser* to embrace not only Marx but two other progressive thinkers in the French Marxist tradition: Sartre and Bourdieu. Rancière's encounter with the archives had bolstered his conviction that Althusserianism's understanding of the relationship between Marxist intellectual work and revolutionary struggle was wrongheaded. In *The Philosopher and His Poor* [1983], he returns to explore the contours of this motif in Marx's work, its reappearance in that of Sartre and Bourdieu and its prehistory in Plato's model of the ideal state.[56]

Rancière comes to the uncomfortable conclusion that Marx alternately disparaged and idealized the workers of his day. Rancière's reading recontextualizes Marx's work in terms of the politics of his time and what might loosely be termed his 'attitude', or the nature of his scientific gaze. Rancière describes the composite object of his scrutiny as 'Marx's very position as a scientist [*la posture même du savant Marx*]'.[57] Rancière is struck by the way Marx and Engels often distanced themselves from the working-class activists of their day, going as far in private as to refer to some of them contemptuously as jackasses hungry for new ideas but unable to engage with them other than by feeding off them like animals.[58] Marx, in Rancière's account, is guilty of a condescending view of even the most overtly politicized members of the working class as intellectually incapable and even subhuman. This contempt by Marx for the workers of his day who described themselves as Communists is juxtaposed, by Rancière, with his commitment to a theoretical position according to which the future lies with the proletariat, a new class which is strictly not a class but which would emerge with the growth of industrialization from the dissolution of existing classes, including the working class as it then was.[59] Rancière's point is not that Marx's private asides to Engels about particular workers contradict the theoretical claims of his work. Instead, Marx's private contempt seems disconcertingly consistent with the public theorizing and helps to illuminate it. Workers, as they actually are in the here and now, are the brute embodiment of a future which they are incapable of understanding:

> All the nobility of humanity may shine on the brows of Parisian workers who meet for study, but the commodity itself presents a more obtuse face. It does not have written on it that it is the 'sign of the division of labor that marks it as the property of capital', except in the form of hieroglyphics that cannot be read by workers who wear on their brows the sign of a people both chosen and condemned.[60]

So the germs of Althusserian scientism were already present in Marx's conflicted view of workers who embody a future they are unable to know. Rancière also draws attention to the way Marx is often to be found 'policing' the proletariat, particularly in *The Eighteenth Brumaire*, where he is concerned to distinguish true proletarians from their degenerate close cousins, the common criminals, colonial fortune-seekers and Bohemians, often referred to dismissively in the Marxist tradition as the 'lumpenproletariat'. What exactly are we to make of an abstract theory of the revolutionary proletarian future, Rancière asks, if, from the outset, it is accompanied by a view of large numbers of workers in the present as, at best, constitutionally unable to grasp the political reality of their own situation, or, at worst, as asinine and degenerate? Although he by no means offers a systematic and complete genealogy of Marxist 'scientism', Rancière succeeds in pointing to an uneasy combination, within the tradition, of a theory of the proletarian future with a condescendingly reductive view of concrete workers in the present and their limited capacity to understand themselves and their world. Marx assumes that, were it not for the intervention of intellectuals and their generously extended pedagogical helping hand, the proletariat would be incapable of the necessary understanding required to allow them to accomplish their historic mission, revolution: *'the workers need our scientific knowledge.'*

It is important to distinguish Rancière's precisely targeted argument against one aspect of the Marxist tradition, scientism or 'theoretical elitism', from the simplistic scatter-gun anti-Marxism of some members of a particular generation of French philosophers, the so-called 'New Philosophers', who tried, from the mid-seventies, to show that Marx's work made totalitarianism – the gulag – inevitable.[61] Rancière's target is scientism, the idea that the proletariat are incapable of understanding their political function without the pedagogical assistance of bourgeois intellectuals; May '68, its immediate precursors and its 'afterlives', at the Lip factory and in the Larzac, suggested this was a convenient fiction.[62] Scientism is associated, for Rancière, not just with a privileging of the social position of intellectuals but also with an indefinite deferral of the realization of equality: for Marx, just as for Althusser with his pedagogy of delay, the time to enact the egalitarian future would always be after the knowledge-deficit of the student-proletariat had been corrected . . . or, in other words, never now.

The bold move in *The Philosopher and His Poor* is Rancière's insinuation, by suggestive juxtaposition, an argument by parataxis, that the scientistic strand identified within the Marxist tradition – in Marx, Sartre and Bourdieu, as previously in Althusser – is rooted in a certain conception of the relationship between power and knowledge first elaborated in Plato's autocratic model of the ideal city in *Republic*. Indeed Plato, rather than Marx or Althusser, will become, in Rancière's subsequent work, the enemy number one against whom his own politics of radical equality and true democracy will be defined.[63] It is accordingly worth spending a moment outlining Plato's model before discussing the use Rancière makes of it.

Plato's perfect city in *Republic* is a political model of philosophico-pedagogical tyranny: the book is evidently a treatise on government but it is also a 'treatise on education', in which the educated rule and in turn educate their successors and, in a more limited way, those soldiers who protect them.[64] Plato allows for three social classes in his ideal city: workers, who fulfil the material needs of the society as a whole; a military class of soldier-guardians; and a governing class of philosopher-kings. Rulers must be trained, according to Plato, and tested at various stages to confirm that they have acquired the knowledge necessary to govern. This is a society in which government is the product of a selective education system and the preserve of experts. Moreover, it is a self-perpetuating system which seeks to limit movement between classes, in the sense that the current generation of philosopher-kings are charged with the education of their successors, and those to whom such education is offered are preselected from among the children of parents from the military and the ruling class; children of workers are not normally educated for government.

The hierarchy of classes in the ideal city corresponds, according to Plato, to a hierarchy of human character types. In members of the worker class, appetitive desires such as hunger and the urge to seek sexual satisfaction will predominate; in the warrior-guardians and philosopher-kings, reason and honour will prevail over appetitive desire. Plato is quite aware that this assumption is exactly that; instead of trying to justify it himself, or suggesting that the philosopher-rulers should try to justify it to those they govern, he has recourse instead to a myth he calls the myth of the three metals. He acknowledges it is a myth but suggests it be taught as though it were fact. According to this myth there are three distinct races of people in a hierarchical relationship: these gold, silver and bronze races correspond to the three social classes. There is a hereditary dimension to the myth and the social system it sanctions:

normally children will be born with roughly the same mix of metals in their soul as their parents. As Rancière notes, the main function of the selective educational system outlined by Plato is in fact to *deselect* those undeserving offspring who, by some accident of nature, have been born to parents of one of the two superior classes and thereby safeguard the (racial) purity of those classes. The greatest internal threat to the system comes from the social climber, the parvenu, the worker with ideas above his station, which is to say the worker with ideas: 'the servile worker who inflates himself to the point of claiming the freedom of the born philosopher'.[65] There is nothing especially outlandish about Rancière's commentary on Plato, but what is significant is where he repeatedly places the emphasis: on the fact that there is absolutely no rational basis for Plato's elaborate, autocratic, hierarchy. As is signalled by the title of the section on Plato, 'Plato's Lie', the entire system rests on a lie, a founding fiction.

Plato's is an anti-democratic, or autocratic, model of government; like many upper-class Athenians of his day he was troubled by the 'amateurishness' of Athenian democracy and attracted to aspects of the Spartan model of a war-state ruling over a largely servile population which provided for the material needs of the state as a whole.[66] In Plato's alternative to democracy, the ignorance and 'amateurishness' of rulers who had not been properly trained to rule and shoe-makers who thought they could philosophize as well as make shoes is replaced by a hierarchy of specialists in which each class (and within the worker class each kind of worker) would normally do one thing and one thing only.[67] Thus the shoe-maker only makes shoes and the farmer only grows crops; shoes and crops would then be exchanged for the good of all. Plato claims that only by devoting all our time to the one activity, be it shoe-making or soldiering, for which our birth equips us can the best results be achieved; the workers do not have time, Plato asserts, to do anything but work at their one specialist skill. Rancière argues that neither of the claims Plato makes to support his thesis that each worker can do only one thing in the ideal state is persuasive: neither the claim about innate character traits, nor the one about the time required to perfect a skill. Rancière recognizes that Plato is simply making an assumption that specialization is the only way to get a society's necessary work done well; workers are just assumed not to be able to do more than one thing at a time. In a real state this assumption about the worker translates into an arbitrary prohibition: 'the simple prohibition against doing anything

else'.[68] It is the 'selfishness', or *pleonexia*, of the parvenu who tres-
passes on the role or position of others that lies at the root of injustice.[69] Justice, for Plato, means staying put.

The value to Rancière of Plato's discussion in *Republic* lies in the
way in which Plato, by introducing the myth of the three metals,
admits to the arbitrariness of the distinction between those rulers
capable of philosophy and the multitude of their 'poor', the workers
judged unsuited to thought and capable only of looking after
the material needs of the society. The originality of Rancière's
reading lies not in what he says about Plato in isolation but in the
specific similarities suggested, in his argument by parataxis,
between a thinker of autocratic hierarchy and the reputedly progressive work of Marx, Sartre and Bourdieu: these thinkers become
tainted by association. All four have in common the construction
of a group Rancière calls 'the poor' (the proletariat, the workers or
the dominated), who are held to be constitutively incapable of
thought. Rancière's suggestion is that similar reasons are advanced
in each case and that these are all similarly specious; moreover, in
each case 'the philosopher' proves to be curiously dependent upon
'his poor', the poor who cannot think for themselves. Thus in the
case of Marx's proletariat, as we have already seen, individual
members of a group which is held up by the philosopher as the
embodiment of a common future are assumed to be constitutively
unable to understand that future and their role in it; such knowledge, if it comes at all, must be 'imported' by bourgeois intellectuals, who thus stand in a relationship of mutual dependence to
'the poor'.

In his reading of Sartre, Rancière concentrates on the later work
and, in particular, on the question of the relation between workers
and the Communist Party. According to Sartre, he says, workers
are unable to think for themselves and so need the Party because
'[t]hey do not have time. *They are too tired.*'[70] Rancière thus aligns
Sartre's argument in support of the Communist Party and its right
to speak for the workers with one of the specious Platonic arguments for specialization: they have no time to think because they
have no time to do anything but the work before them. In suggesting that workers are too tired to think, Sartre thus unwittingly
renews the Platonic ban on doing more than one thing at once and
rearticulates Marx's assumption that 'people "make" history but
they "do not know" they do so.'[71] At the top of Sartre's intellectual
hierarchy, above the Party which represents the workers, is the
philosopher of that Party, Sartre himself. Rancière's point is not the

simplistic and suspicious one that Sartre's apparent concern for the workers is a sham intended only to bolster his own position in the hierarchy – although he suggests that such reductionism character-izes Bourdieu's view of Sartre and of philosophy more generally[72] – but rather that Sartre's emphasis on the worker's inevitable tired-ness deprives the worker of the power of thought: 'In the realm of vulgar fatigue there is no place for vulgar freedom, the sort that is earned or lost or regained, that goes astray or loses itself in the intervals of exploitation.'[73] Sartre's workers, because of the tired-ness imputed to them, are thus constitutionally unable to think, unable to exercise the kind of self-directing intellectual curiosity of which he as a philosopher is capable. Sartre's portrayal of the risible autodidact in his early novel *Nausea* is related by Rancière to the failure in his later work to allow for workers who seize the time to elaborate their own thought, who dare to exercise their intellect without deferring to the pedagogical guidance of the Party or its intellectuals: 'What he rejects above all are the elastic intervals of autodidactic freedom.'[74] What Sartre unwittingly succeeds in doing in his late work, according to Rancière, is to deny to his tired workers, his 'poor', the same capacity for self-directing intellectual freedom which he exercises as a philosopher:

> the freedom – his own – that would be corrupted if it were refracted in the shattered time of worn-down servitudes and saved-up lei-sures, in the uncertain light of demi-knowledges and demi-cultures, in the disoriented space of pathways and dead ends where people searched not long ago for what rebellious workers and dreamers called 'emancipation' – the self-transformation of a slave into a human being.[75]

The unintended effect of Sartre's assumption that the worker is too tired to do anything other than work, Rancière argues, is to suggest that the philosopher and the worker are two different species and to underestimate the capacity of the ordinary workers, on whose behalf he and the Party speak, to think for themselves. In an intrigu-ing gesture, Rancière relates Sartre's overemphasis on the tiredness of the worker to 'the gray upon gray of the tone' of *The Critique of Dialectical Reason*, suggesting that the drabness of Sartre's well-intentioned treatise on behalf of the worker is of a piece with his implicit denial of the power of thought to those for whom he would speak.[76] In Rancière's account, the 'poor' envisaged by Marx and Sartre are far too reminiscent of those imagined by Plato: too tired to think, too busy to imagine, incapable of complexity in thought as in action. Just as, for Plato, the arbitrary prohibition on doing more than one thing at once is related to the prohibition on acting in a theatrical sense, so for Marx the demand that the proletariat embody their historical role renders them incapable of the kind of complex subjectivity associated with acting, which Rancière takes to be a necessary dimension to agency in the fuller sense:

> the question of the actor does not revolve around the art of showing but the art of living. It concerns the public only insofar as it concerns the actor himself. For in the final analysis, the pedagogy that 'raises consciousness' by unveiling exploitation and its mystifications is a very impoverished virtue. The great virtue that must be learned by the public with the actor is *humor*, the art of performing on stage where opposites never cease to interchange themselves. The art of becoming *historical agents*. No longer the simple 'bearers' of social relations [. . .].[77]

The demand that Rancière articulates here is for a recognition of the equal capacity of all for sophisticated complexity of self-understanding and self-performance which exceeds the conservative insistence that the worker must do one thing and one thing only. Marx and Sartre could respond that to the extent that they are guilty of oversimplifying, or indeed downplaying, worker subjectivity in the past and present this is unimportant because the politically significant task with which they are mainly concerned is to bring about a better future for workers. Rancière's sceptical assumption is that this deferral of the realization of equality amounts to an indefinite postponement; he asserts instead that equality must be realized in the present and, first of all, in the analytical approach we take to questions of social justice.

Rancière's dispute with Bourdieu's work on pedagogy and aesthetics is more involved than his engagements with either Marx or Sartre. I shall concentrate in this chapter on the pedagogical material and save the discussion of aesthetics for Chapter 5. Rancière's disagreement with Bourdieu is not always easy to follow, in part because while Rancière is sometimes careful to distinguish between what Bourdieu himself says and what has been done in his name by policy-makers,[78] he is not consistently careful to do so, and deliberately so since his objection, in *The Philosopher and His Poor*, is particularly to measures taken in the early 1980s by a Mitterrand government influenced by Bourdieu's work to reform the French education system, as it is implicitly in *The Ignorant Schoolmaster*. Charlotte Nordmann has argued, in a very thorough comparative textual reading, that Rancière somewhat overstates the case against Bourdieu.[79] She is right to note that Rancière's reaction against the sociologist's institutional self-interest is extreme and unforgiving.

Rancière's composite objection to Bourdieu's approach can be summarized as follows: his sociology is unduly suspicious, scientistic, self-aggrandizing, reductive, deterministic and practically (politically) ineffectual. It is suspicious and scientistic because it assumes, as Althusser did, that social mechanisms are hidden and accessible only to scientific analysis by sociologists and that surface manifestations are unreliable; it is institutionally self-aggrandizing because only sociologists are thought capable of such analysis, as opposed, in particular, to philosophers; it is reductive because it suppresses mixity of, and exchange between, high and low cultures and between oppressed and oppressors, bringing about 'the suppression of intermediaries, of points of meeting and exchange between the people of reproduction and the élite of distinction'; it is deterministic because it assumes that social milieu determines taste, thought, feeling and potential and thus, surprisingly given its progressive reputation, it renews Plato's autocratic and hereditary model of a society in which, by and large, individuals stay put in the places into which they have been born.[80] Finally, it is practically (politically) ineffective because it is 'depressing', a diagnosis of social injustice which sees this as so powerful and all-encompassing as to be beyond the redress for which the analysis ostensibly calls. It cannot inspire change. In particular, the solution advanced by Bourdieu and Passeron in *The Inheritors* and developed in their *Reproduction in Education*, 'rational pedagogy', is judged incapable of achieving its stated aim of giving students from socially disadvantaged backgrounds a better chance of success; rational pedagogy is supposed to work by making explicit in the teaching process those 'implicit norms which retranslate and specify the values of the dominant classes' and thus serve to reproduce the social status quo.[81] Rancière thinks it will be ineffective because the more privileged will always be better placed to make use of its insights.[82] Similar criticisms to some of these voiced by Rancière have been made independently by others: in particular, the idea that Bourdieu's approach is deterministic because, notwithstanding its overt 'enthusiasm' for 'resistance', his work contains 'few examples' of its 'efficacy'.[83] So too with the idea that it offers an account of domination which is so all-encompassing as to induce a sense of political paralysis.[84] Yet Rancière goes much further – Nordmann would argue too far, and sometimes this conclusion is hard to avoid – by casting doubt over the integrity of Bourdieu's enterprise and the entire discipline of which he is the exemplary representative.

So all-encompassing is Bourdieu's analysis of the repressive function of ordinary pedagogy that Rancière questions its usefulness and that of the entire discipline from which it issues: 'What can one do with a science of the school that says pedagogy is impossible? With a science of relations of power that says these are infrangible?'[85] Bourdieu is arguably more aware of the awkward paradoxes inherent in his own position than Rancière gives him credit for, not least the obvious irony of his being a teacher and researcher in the employ of élite educational institutions who has made a career out of denouncing the repressive social function of schooling. Yet perhaps the point of Rancière's disagreement is his steadfast refusal to accord Bourdieu this credit, the determination not to accept Bourdieu's display of self-awareness as mitigation for the untenable paradox of his institutional position. Indeed the allegation is that Bourdieu's work is all too easily assimilated by, and at home in, a pedagogical hierarchy of which it is overtly a critique but to which it lends new strength:

> the critique of élitism has soon become the new justification of hierarchy. The university professor analyzes the élitist methods of the suburban schoolteacher. The professor from the École des Hautes Études demystifies the élitist ideology of the university subaltern, and the national minister of Education courageously undertakes reforms aimed at suppressing the élitism of his subordinates as a whole.[86]

By virtue of its embeddedness in the institutional hierarchy – the pedagogical food-chain, so to speak – that it purports to critique, Bourdieu's work is judged to be fraudulent. Rancière's approach is to reflect Bourdieu's diagnosis back on his own practice: just as Bourdieu's analysis looks underneath education and culture to the movements of social capital which they express and disguise, discerning in institutions of learning and cultural artefacts a kind of 'fraud' which conceals oppression, so Rancière sees Bourdieu's own project as an even more sophisticated scam which preserves pedagogical privilege and inequality by purporting to analyse it. But is Bourdieu's approach really entirely wrongheaded? Perhaps not, but it does have a specific blindspot, which Rancière exposes and aligns with a distinctly conservative, Platonic, streak in the other thinkers of the Left he analyses in *The Philosopher and His Poor*: put simply, Bourdieu seems to think that he – and those instructed in his kind of sociology – know the real reasons why people are oppressed but of which they themselves are usually ignorant. Rancière thinks this view is incorrect, presumptuous and 'depressing'.[87]

Marx, Sartre, Althusser and Bourdieu: each, with increasingly sophisticated cynicism, underestimates the power of understanding and imagination of those on whose behalf they speak. Despite their intellectual standing on the Left, each is a thinker of inequality and pedagogical privilege. Each assumes, as Plato does, that the pedagogue must think for and educate those who are unable to think for themselves; only then will society change for the better. Rancière's positive conception of radical equality is an extreme, irritable, reaction against this shared investment in pedagogical power: in place of these four, each of whom embodies pedagogical power and intellectual inequality, he substitutes 'le maître ignorant', 'the ignorant (school)master', Joseph Jacotot. In the remainder of this chapter I shall explore the positive conception of radical equality which Rancière advances in his book on Jacotot and argue that it is a timely critique of schooling, which renews a long tradition of anarchist scepticism for an age which wrongly assumes that you can never have enough education.

Jacotot and radical equality

Forced into exile by the Bourbon Restoration, Joseph Jacotot (1770–1840) found himself, in 1818, teaching French literature at the University of Leuven. Because he spoke no Flemish and his students no French, he was unable to teach them anything in the ordinary way, by explaining; instead, he gave them copies of a recently published bilingual edition of Fénelon's *Télémaque* and had them recite its opening lines. When they had reached the middle of the first book, he made them repeat what they had read over and over again and then read the rest of the volume. When he asked them afterwards to write, in French, what they thought about what they had read, he was astonished to find that they were able to do so more proficiently than many for whom French was the native language.[88] Jacotot was struck by the fact that he had not explained anything to the students, and this led him to a general scepticism about the role of explanation, which Rancière articulates as follows:

> Explanation is not necessary to remedy an incapacity to understand. On the contrary, that very incapacity provides the structuring fiction of the explicative conception of the world. It is the explicator who needs the incapable and not the other way around; it is he who constitutes the incapable as such. To explain something to someone is first of all to show him he cannot understand it by himself. Before being the act of the pedagogue, explication is the myth of pedagogy, the parable of a world divided into knowing minds and ignorant ones, ripe minds and immature ones, the capable and the incapable, the intelligent and the stupid.[89]

Ordinary pedagogy, Jacotot concluded, was premised on the idea of the intellectual inequality of teacher and student. Even though its aim was gradually to bring about greater equality between the two by leading the student through a series of incrementally more sophisticated explanations, Jacotot decided that this was an unacceptably slow and hierarchical approach which misunderstood the essential character of learning and the reality of human intellect. Far better results could be obtained by presupposing from the outset that the students were the intellectual equals of each other and their teacher. Jacotot soon radicalized his experiment by teaching subjects about which he himself knew nothing: legal argument in Flemish, painting and piano-playing. His role as teacher was reduced to a relentless questioning of the students to ensure that they had applied themselves to the task at hand. Faced with performances of uneven achievement, the teacher's role was not to use these to rank the students by intelligence but rather to see weakness as evidence of a lack of application to the task. Faced with the student's protest that he cannot do better, or cannot perform the task at all, the teacher is enjoined to be 'an intractable master'.[90] Such protests are taken by Jacotot to be false modesty, expressions of stubborn pride which, Rancière adds, demonstrate a commitment on the student's part to the same logic as that of the arbitrary Platonic injunction which forbids the shoe-maker from thinking, the principle of specialization. Here is Jacotot's typically intractable response:

You must begin to speak. Don't say that you can't. You know how to say 'I can't'. Say in its place 'Calypso could not', and you're off. You're off on a route that you already knew, and that you should follow always without giving up. Don't say: 'I can't'. Or then, learn to say it in the manner of Calypso, in the manner of Telemachus, of Narbal, of Idomeneus. [. . .] You will never run out of ways to say 'I can't', and soon you will be able to say everything.[91]

Presuming the student to be equal in intelligence, the teacher thus enables him to retranslate his expression of incapacity into the very knowledge of which he thought himself incapable. This is the key point about Jacotot's method, which Alain Badiou has formalized in the following two theses:

1 Under conditions in which equality is declared, ignorance is the point at which new knowledge can emerge.
2 Under the authority of a master who lacks knowledge, knowledge can be a site of equality.[92]

Or, in other words, the radical conception of intellectual equality which Rancière derives from Jacotot is of equality which must be *presupposed*, from the outset, in the pedagogical encounter, which must be *declared* and which must be *verified* in that encounter. Jacotot's emancipatory pedagogy is not about communicating knowledge from teacher to student: 'Essentially, what an emancipated person can do is be an emancipator: to give, not the key to knowledge, but the consciousness of what an intelligence can do when it considers itself equal to any other and considers any other equal to itself.'[93]

Badiou and Todd May have both rightly insisted that the radical conception of equality that Rancière formulates in his book on Jacotot is one of the most important defining and original features of his work and has implications, as we shall see in later chapters, far beyond the field of pedagogy in a narrow sense, even though it is clearly rooted in reflection on what it means to learn and teach.[94] May usefully describes Rancière's conception as one of 'active equality', a form of equality which the oppressed presume, declare and verify for themselves and which is to be distinguished from equality as conventionally understood, the 'passive equality' which is given (or, more often, not given) by those in power. While there is much about the detail of Jacotot's (anti-)method which remains obscure in Rancière's highly seductive, enchanting, account of it, it is important to remember that Rancière is not trying to devise a new curriculum or even a pedagogical programme: the point is not that all French schoolchildren should be reciting *Télémaque* but rather that it is possible to glean from Jacotot's pedagogical experiment the political potency of a new understanding of the nature of equality.[95]

From the detail of Jacotot's approach which is spelled out, it is clear that the conception of equality Rancière derives from the maverick educationalist is also informed by his earlier critique of the pedagogy of Althusser and his caustic analysis of intellectual posturing in *The Philosopher and His Poor*. Thus, in Rancière's account of him, Jacotot is found emphasizing the materiality of the subjects (*les matières*) he is teaching and conversely the ideality, or intellectuality, of 'manual' labour: one of the principles of the method is to establish a relation of exchangeability and equivalence between the stuff of learning and the materials worked upon by the labourer: 'Each citizen is also a man who makes a *work*, with the pen, with the drill, or with any other tool.'[96] The intention is to persuade the manual worker who thinks learning is something he is unable to do that he is already exercising the same human intelligence in his work: to understand *Télémaque* takes no special gift, or no gift more special than the intellect which he is already using. This dissolves the assumptions underlying the Platonic social hierarchy, which placed the pedagogues at the summit, and posits instead the absolute interchangeability of positions and occupations: no one person is especially suited or destined for writing books any more than any other is for making shoes.

Rancière's book works hard stylistically to blur the boundaries between the conceptual and the material; it would be very misleading to describe it as an *analysis* of Jacotot and his method, or even as a *discussion* of the concepts evoked (progressivism, explanation). The book is a philosophical tale which offers material resistance to easy conceptual analysis, in part because the written texture relies so heavily on techniques more usually associated with literary writing, or writing for the stage: ventriloquism (Rancière's and Jacotot's voices often merge) and the dramatization of a conflict of ideas on education as a dialogue with a quasi-personification of traditional pedagogy as 'la Vieille', which refers semantically to 'the old (i.e. explanatory) method' and which Ross translates sensibly as 'The Old Master', yet which also means 'The Old Woman'. The more often 'la Vieille' is encountered, often distant from her semantic anchor in the old method, the more it feels as though a sinister elderly female figure is roaming through these pages, ready to prey on the minds and energies of anyone who falls into her pedagogical clutches. Moreover, the juxtaposition of dreams and historical events, as well as the dramatic interruption of conceptual discussions with strictly incommensurable stage directions ('here comes someone knocking at the door'), lend the text a complex material density which not only makes stable and precise interpretation in conceptual terms difficult but points to the principle of the exchangeability of material and conceptual, of 'manual' and 'intellectual'.[97] Given Jacotot's suspicion of explanation, it is appropriate that – because of its complex conceptual-material texture – this is an especially difficult book to explain. *The Ignorant Schoolmaster* is a skilfully crafted material object, a textured work of art and artifice, as well as a book of ideas.

In addition to the emphasis on the exchangeability of conceptual and material, Rancière's account of Jacotot's pedagogy reflects Rancière's earlier concerns in another respect: it is profoundly sceptical of the professed interest of educational institutions in equality, just as Althusserianism, for all its promise of correct revolutionary practice, seemed to Rancière, in the light of May '68, to amount to a 'pedagogy of delay' which indefinitely postponed the moment of revolution and, in the meantime, only strengthened the social and insitutional privileges of its pedagogues over those whom they tried to instruct. Although Jacotot is persuaded briefly to try institutionalizing his method, the failure, in conventional terms, of the experiment only serves to demonstrate that his egalitarian pedagogy is essentially anti-institutional: 'It cannot be propagated in and by social institutions.'[98] Whereas Jacotot's insistence is that the pedagogical encounter be a site for the realization of equality, institutions inevitably function by establishing hierarchies and inequality. This does not necessarily imply anarchism: 'The emancipated are undoubtedly respectful of the social order.'[99] Indeed Rancière emphasizes that Jacotot's students are ready to 'play the game' of political argument even though they realize that its rhetoric is more often an irrational competition for supremacy and that moments of reason are few and far between and nothing short of miraculous.[100] Rancière's profound scepticism about the interest of institutions in real equality reflects the anti-institutional tenor of the *gauchiste* experience of May '68: 'Every institution is an *explication* in social act, a dramatization of inequality.'[101] It is important to stress the extent to which this implies a pedagogy centred on the individual and driven by his or her self-belief and determination: it is the individual's desire to learn which is decisive, the individual's commitment, or lack of it, to the principle that all are intellectually equal and therefore equally capable of any activity. Rancière's wager is that if radical equality is *presupposed*, *declared* and *verified*, questions of social background, which are largely determining in Bourdieu's approach, will have little bearing. In thus emphasizing the individual student's will and need to learn and the importance of repetitive hard work, Rancière flies in the face of sociable and student-centred, 'progressive', pedagogies. Jacotot's students are almost autodidacts, so great is the emphasis placed on what they themselves are responsible for in the peda- gogical encounter, and it is clear from Rancière's interest in the self-taught worker-poets of the nineteenth century, as from his attack on Sartre's caricature in *Nausea*, that he sets considerable store by the emancipatory power of autodidactism. What is expected of the student-autodidact is nothing less than the kind of self-directing intellectual freedom which Sartre denied to the workers he felt were too tired to think and so proposed to exercise on their behalf.

Jacotot's pedagogy is extremely demanding of the individual student and very optimistic about that student's capacity, given the desire and the need, to live up to these expectations. Rancière sees Jacotot's egalitarian pedagogy as the antithesis of the progressiv- ism which promised to further the cause of equality, gradually, by way of education. Jacotot is historically significant because the 'madness' of his radical pedagogy was to presuppose equality at the outset, rather than hope for it as the outcome of the pedagogical process. His thought is thus an early challenge to the progressivism which took hold in the nineteenth century and which still domi- nates thinking about education and social equality today. Jacotot is markedly at odds with our time, just as he was with his:

> An enormous machine was revving up to promote equality through instruction. This was equality represented, socialized, made unequal, good for being *perfected* – that is to say, deferred from commission to commission, from report to report, from reform to reform, until the end of time. Jacotot was alone in recognizing the effacement of equality under progress, of emancipation under instruction.[102]

Even though *The Ignorant Schoolmaster* is not intended to be a programmatic proposal for reform of the school system, the cri- tique of progressivism which Rancière finds in Jacotot's approach has a context in the heated debates about education policy which raged in France in the 1980s.[103] I shall briefly outline this context before saying why Rancière–Jacotot's critique of progressivism continues to be pertinent today. In the early 1980s, the Socialists under Mitterrand undertook to reduce social inequalities by reforming the French education system in such a way as to give children from more disadvantaged backgrounds a better chance of success. Many of the Socialist reformers were greatly influenced by Bourdieu's work in their attempts to make the school experience more welcoming and to increase the place of popular culture in the curriculum. This quickly led to accusations of dumbing down and a contrary position emerged, which declared itself 'republican', and which maintained that the best way to reduce social inequalities was not to adapt the learning experience to the needs of the most disadvantaged but rather to teach everyone the same thing in the same way, regardless of their background. At first sight it may seem that Jacotot's approach is much closer to the 'republican' position, and for Rancière this is a source of some regret (mainly because of the reactionary turn which this republican critique would subsequently take in the late eighties).[104] Yet in fact Jacotot's egalitarian pedagogy differs from both the Socialist and the 'republican' policy positions because while these are progressivist – they seek to bring about equality gradually through education – Jacotot starts out from the presumption of equality: 'Equality is a presupposition, an axiomatic point of departure, or it is nothing.'[105] Moreover, whereas these progressivist reformers sought to change the aggregate conditions of society as a whole by modifying its institutions, Jacotot's approach is, as I have shown, anti-institutional and addressed not to society as a whole but to individuals who want and need to learn. Indeed the conception of radical equality demonstrated in Jacotot's singular pedagogy is, almost by definition, incapable of ever becoming the 'policy' of any institution, party or government.

The radical understanding of equality extracted by Rancière from Jacotot's educational practice and his own experience of, and reflection on, the logic of pedagogical privilege will be central to his mature political thought, as I shall argue in Chapter 3, and will be applied to contexts which range far beyond the narrowly pedagogical. Yet Rancière's critical reflection also has much to say about the nature and function of education in the narrower, more usual, sense and can be recontextualized within a small but vocal tradition of informed dissent which shares a scepticism of so-called 'progressive' education. Scepticism about schooling has a long history in the libertarian anarchist tradition, as Joel Spring has noted, stretching back at least as far as the seventeenth century. Robert Molesworth's *An Account of Denmark as It was in the Year 1692* took issue with the theocratic and authoritarian education system of that country, one with more than a passing similarity to the system outlined in *Republic*.[106] William Godwin, writing in the eighteenth and nineteenth centuries, voiced alarm at the way in which the modern state could use education to foster obedience and to promote political ideas such as nationalism which were more in its own interest than that of individual citizens. In the twentieth century, in the 1960s, similar criticisms were articulated about primary and secondary education in the United States by the anarchist critic Paul Goodman and other representatives of the 'de-schooling' movement.[107] In *Compulsory Miseducation*, Goodman voiced scepticism about the school system, characterizing it as a self-serving institution, 'a vast vested interest' which 'goes on for its own sake, keeping more than a million people busy, wasting wealth, and pre-empting time and space in which something else could be going on'.[108] More recently, in his *Against Schooling*, Stanley Aronowitz has attacked the conflation of mind-broadening education with results-obsessed schooling and what he considers the erroneous progressivist assumption that the extension of mass schooling into the higher education sector is indicative of progress towards greater equality. Rather than educating for critical citizenship, he argues that the vast majority of institutions of higher education are profiting from the ever-growing demand for credentials from students preparing to enter an increasingly competitive job market.[109]

Both Goodman and Aronowitz agree that the work of the leading American exponent of progressive education, John Dewey, was grossly distorted almost as soon as it was first applied. Writing in 1916, Dewey, in *Democracy and Education*, had tried to address the question of how, in the unconducive context of increasing industrialization and urbanization, the sense of community and the critical citizenship he thought vital for the survival of civilization could be fostered by education. For Dewey, the reason why schooling should develop critical thinking lay, in large measure, in the quasi-evolutionary edge which this gives over a society of conformists: progressive societies have the advantage because 'they endeavour to shape the experiences of the young so that instead of reproducing current habits, better habits shall be formed, and thus the future adult society [will] be an improvement on their own'.[110] Goodman argued that the delicate democratic balance, in Dewey's work, between critical thinking and functional efficiency broke down in favour of the latter almost as soon as his version of progressivism was put into practice: 'The practical training and community democracy, whose purpose was to live scientifically and change society, was changed into "socially useful" subjects and a psychology of "belonging."'[111] Rancière's critique of progressivism is more nuanced than that of Goodman and Aronowitz: he does not go so far as to see it as a sinister and cynical form of social engineering but he does question its understanding of the equality it is trying to further. Unlike Bourdieu, who suggested that what was needed was to reform teaching so it would be better adapted to the needs of more disadvantaged students ('rational pedagogy'), thinkers within the libertarian-anarchist tradition tend to eschew reform in favour of a partial or wholesale rejection of institutional education. While the mobile and composite character of Rancière's narrative makes it difficult to extract a single position on pedagogy and allows him to be read alternately as a reformer and a revolutionary, his work feels at home within the libertarian-anarchist tradition.

For positive experiences of egalitarian pedagogy which display marked affinities with Jacotot's method, as Rancière describes it, we can look to the work of Colin Ward, Paulo Freire and, as I have done elsewhere, to one of the pioneers of creative writing workshops in France, François Bon.[112] Ward's concept and practice of 'streetwork' was an egalitarian reconceptualization of the 'urban fieldwork' which was part of the new discipline of 'urban studies' that began to emerge in the late 1960s and early 1970s as an alternative to geography. Like Jacotot's superficially modest experiment with *Télémaque*, however, 'streetwork' was clearly intended to have much wider implications for the way we think about pedagogy in general. 'Streetwork' aimed to educate the urban child about his or her own environment by way of an encounter with the street as a site of disruption, disorder and distraction. Ward's emphasis was on fostering active, critical, citizenship by involving students in real local debates about issues which could be accessed without specialized knowledge or credentials, directly from the street. The street, with its noise and its super-saturation of sensory stimuli, rather than the controlled and hierarchized environment of the classroom, was to be the privileged egalitarian site of a very different kind of pedagogical experience:

> The emotional contact with poverty, unhappiness and general dis-
> satisfaction with which urban studies pupils are inevitably con-
> fronted seems barely represented by that bland and curious phrase
> 'urban fieldwork' and I propose 'streetwork' in its place – suggestive
> I hope of the kind of community involvement already aimed at in
> the avant-garde theatrical world through 'street theatre'.[113]

Like Rancière's Jacotot, Ward begins with a presumption of the
intellectual equality of his students and makes the pedagogical
encounter a declaration and a verification of that equality; thus
'streetwork' may involve participating directly in local disputes
over planning legislation or preparing submissions for other con-
sultation exercises. Ward, in his concept of streetwork, situates the
pedagogical encounter on the surface of shared social reality;
teacher and students share equally in the process of discovering
this reality by intervening as participants in it.

Like Jacotot's egalitarian approach, Ward's is what Paulo Freire
would have described as a 'pedagogy of hope', a method which is
sensitive to, and works to improve, the students' attitude, and
affective relationship, to learning.[114] Freire's blueprint for popular
education demands that the would-be educator first learn about
his or her students and that the pedagogical encounter be premised
on what, in a meaningful sense, is a dialogue: rather than imparting
content, Freire's teacher encourages those who have hitherto lived
in 'a culture of silence' and who had never thought of their lives
as suitable objects for commentary and thought to take them as
such. Just as Rancière's emphases on the exchangeability of material and conceptual helps to break down the Platonic hierarchy of
a society in which some were born to think and others to cater to
material needs, so Freire's emphasis is on the elaboration through
dialogue of a language of possibility which exists in the interval
between teacher and students:

> Here is one of the tasks of democratic popular education, of a peda-
> gogy of hope: that of enabling the popular classes to develop their
> language: not the authoritarian, sectarian gobbledygook of "educa-
> tors", but their own language – which, emerging from and returning
> upon their reality, sketches out the conjectures, the designs, the
> anticipations of their new world [. . .] language as a route to the
> invention of citizenship.[115]

Like Jacotot leading the locksmith to literacy by encouraging him
to relate letters to the shapes of locks, Freire's educator works with

whatever knowledge the student already has. For Rancière and Freire alike, the task of the educator is to presume, declare and demonstrate that teacher and student are intellectual equals.

In this chapter I have argued that Rancière's radical reconceptualization of equality emerged out of critical reflection on the nature of pedagogy, thinking which was informed by his own experience of studentship and his almost visceral reaction against some of the most prominent ideologues of the Left. While it may be *'impossible to choose one's beginnings'*, Rancière managed to push so tenaciously and so creatively against those whose voices filled the air in the decades of his political and pedagogical formation that something singular was bound to come of it.

2

History and Historiography

This chapter approaches Rancière's extensive historical and historiographical work by subdividing it into three moments: I examine
first his role as one of the leading members of the collective behind
the journal *Les Révoltes Logiques* (1975–81), then the book based on
his doctoral thesis, *The Nights of Labor: The Workers' Dream in Nineteenth-Century France* [1981], and finally his difficult and suggestive
theoretical work, *The Names of History: On the Poetics of Knowledge*
[1992].[1] My intention is not to cover everything but rather to discuss
a selection of significant issues and examples, ones which 'have
been chosen from the many [. . .] available either because they are
typical or because they are exceptional – as far as I can judge'.[2] The
alluring difficulties Rancière's work presents to aspiring explainers
are especially acute in the case of his historiography, largely because
of the pronounced subtlety of what, to echo again his own description of his work, I can only call his 'interventions' in a series of
what are already multiply complex conceptual, institutional and
socio-political discussions about history. The difficulty is compounded by the modulations in tone and perspective within a body
of work which ranges from sophisticated abstract conceptualizing
to an immersion in concrete detail so resolute as to have been qualified as 'heroic' methodological 'a-conceptualism'.[3]

Les Révoltes Logiques (1975–81)

Were the idea of collective endeavour not so crucial a part of the
enterprise, it could be said that Rancière was *the* leading member

of the group responsible for this journal. He was unquestionably one of its leading lights, along with feminist historian Geneviève Fraisse and his colleague at Paris VIII, the enigmatic novelist and philosopher of nomadic thought, the late Jean Borreil. The journal published fifteen ordinary issues between 1975 and 1981, as well as one special issue to mark the tenth anniversary of May '68 and two collections, in book form, after the demise of the journal proper, in 1984 and 1985. Like *History Workshop Journal* in Britain, the first issue of which appeared in 1976, *Les Révoltes Logiques* was addressed both to academic professionals and lay readers and was self-consciously partial in its political commitment to the history of the workers' and the women's movements; as in the case of History Workshop and its journal, the association between these two causes within the collective was sometimes tense, as I shall go on to show.[4] My discussion of *Les Révoltes Logiques* will, after a brief account of the journal's origins, ethos and approach, focus on a selection of Rancière's many contributions, most of which were reprinted in his *Les Scènes du peuple* (2003) and two of which appear in translation in Adrian Rifkin and Roger Thomas's *Voices of the People* (1987).[5] I shall endeavour to show how Rancière's work on the journal played an important, intellectually formative, role in the development of his later historiographical and political thought.

As Kristin Ross has argued, in her very useful discussion of the journal alongside two other French journals of radical history from the 1970s, *Le Peuple Français* and *Les Cahiers du Forum-Histoire*, *Les Révoltes Logiques* can be seen as an attempt to reflect upon and, by so doing, to further the legacy of May '68:

> By returning to the past and to a new examination of workers' speech, experience, and practices, the Utopian aspects of May could be prolonged, and the disappointments of May and its aftermath could be examined and assessed. A new renegade historical practice could continue the desire of '68 to give voice to the 'voiceless', to contest the domain of the experts.[6]

While professional historians such as Geneviève Fraisse and Arlette Farge were involved in the journal, it nonetheless situated itself at the 'renegade' outer margins of academic practice, 'where opinionated activism was articulated with the university environment and where the forms of the decomposition and recomposition of the figure of the revolutionary worker were determined'.[7] Around half the articles in the fifteen ordinary issues focus on the nineteenth-century history of the French workers' and women's movements, in particular during the period between the July Revolution of 1830 and the crushing of the Paris Commune in 1871. Of the remaining half, a few are concerned with eighteenth-century history and rather more with that of the twentieth century; there are also a number of interviews and 'documents' (presentation of archival material on a particular topic), as well as numerous review articles which help define the journal's own position by mounting a critique of major publications by established historians.

The institutional origins of the collective and its journal lay in the 'Centre de Recherches sur les Idéologies de la Révolte' at the Vincennes campus of the University of Paris (Paris VIII), where Rancière taught. It is significant that this rather imposingly titled Centre was based in a department not of history, but rather of philosophy. The institutional freedom to overlook established disciplinary boundaries was a special feature of the philosophy department at Vincennes: 'It was up to individuals to decide how they would use their position as a teacher and the time allotted for them to teach. So I took the path which led to libraries and archives and transformed my philosophy class into a research group on worker history.'[8] The freedom to experiment which this allowed its members reflected their collective determination to see perpetuated in institutional form the 'indiscipline' of May '68, and there can be no doubt that Rancière's own singular cross-disciplinary intellectual project was fostered by this unique environment, just as it in turn was nourished by his work and that of his colleagues.

At the heart of the Centre was a seminar, convened by Rancière, on the history of the workers' movement, which regrouped some of the researchers who had begun work on an aborted television documentary series which was to have told the story of the first seventy-five years of twentieth-century French history.[9] The ten-part series was to have been entitled *The Meaning of Revolt in the Twentieth Century* and its narrative framework was to have been the life of Jean-Paul Sartre, the nominal figurehead and sponsor of the project. The plan had been to tell the story through a series of 'revolts', in particular by workers and women. However, when Jacques Chirac, then Prime Minister under Giscard d'Estaing, made known his lack of enthusiasm for the project, the newly created and notionally independent state-funded second channel, Antenne 2, withdrew their backing in September 1975. Although the series was never filmed, a network of some eighty researchers had already put a considerable amount of work into the project and many of them gravitated towards Rancière's seminar and the Centre at Vincennes.

The journal's title is a quotation from a poem by Arthur Rimbaud, 'Démocratie', one of his *Illuminations*. The poem evokes the aftermath of the defeat of the Paris Commune in 1871 and, as Ross puts it, 'the wrenching emotional aftermath of the repression of revolution, the lived experience of political possibilities shutting down, the dismantling or dimming of utopian conceptions of change', which had obvious resonances in the climate of authoritarian crackdown ushered in by interior minister Raymond Marcellin after he took over at the end of May 1968.[10] The title is intended, according to Rancière, like the front cover of the first edition, to assert the 'fidelity' of the journal to the Paris Commune, 'the very archetype of revolt'.[11] It is also significant that the quotation skews the sense of Rimbaud's line. 'We shall massacre the logical revolts', declares the imperialist voice of the victors plotting the expansion of their dominion into hitherto untouched corners of France and the world; the extraction of the 'logical revolts' is a 'twisting' (*torsion*), as Rancière calls it, which salvages them from the repression they are destined to suffer in Rimbaud's line, just as the collective tried to salvage and restore the memory of past revolts, by contrast with an official history which had consigned them to the unpromising category of 'failures'.[12] The rescue operation thus envisaged was simultaneously historical and political: an attempt to set right the historical record which had too often ignored or been insufficiently curious about these events and to counteract the sense of despair prevailing in the 'après-Mai' by resituating May and contemporary political struggle in a narrative of remarkable and diverse acts of resistance. If revolts of the past could be recognized for their promise, then this would add historical depth to the political conviction that things in the present could be otherwise.

The journal's title, as Ross notes, also evoked the Maoist slogan 'On a raison de se révolter' ('It is right to revolt'), taken up by Philippe Gavi and Pierre Victor (Benny Lévy) as the title of their extended 1974 interview with Sartre.[13] Rancière has, however, distanced the journal from this staunch *gauchiste* conviction in the legitimacy of spontaneous popular uprising and emphasized instead its critical, analytical and linguistic dimensions: thus 'logiques' reflects less the inexorability of spontaneous resistance

and points more to the words, the language, involved in that resistance. The journal sought to bring complexity to the understanding
of resistance by probing the sophisticated self-understandings of
participants in particular revolts in the past, paying particular
attention to the role of language and argumentation in these struggles: 'what is known as revolt is also a scene of speech and reasons:
it is neither the eruption of a popular savagery which escapes the
disciplinary effects of power, something often glorified in those
days, nor is it the expression of historical necessity and legitimacy.'[14] Hence the emphasis in the first issue on 'the "rationaliza-
tion" of a revolt', which points forward to Rancière's insistence,
which I examine in Chapter 3, on the process of argumentation
integral to the coming into being of political subjects.[15]

Even though the journal's particular approach was more reflective than the *gauchiste* slogan which its title echoes, signs of its
proximity to the sharper end of contemporary political activism are
nonetheless apparent, for example in the one-page statement
signed by most of the collective which opens issue 7 and encourages readers to write to one Marc Sislain, a former student at Vincennes imprisoned for possessing Molotov cocktails; or in the
documents relating to the Clairvaux prison riots of May 1970; or
indeed in Olivier Roy's article on the occupation of Afghanistan
and Jean Borreil's on that of Northern Ireland.[16] Yet these pieces
are hardly representative of the journal as a whole, which strove
principally to have political effect through a careful re-examination
of revolts of the past and a purposefully inconclusive problemati-
zation of the history of the workers' and women's movements.

Although generalizations about collective enterprises are hazardous, the overarching methodological principle, or editorial
ethos, of *Les Révoltes Logiques* can broadly be characterized as the
fragmenting introduction of complication. I shall argue that this
approach will also go on to characterize Rancière's own, individual, historical work in the two later phases. Fragmentation and
complication were particularly to be introduced into established
genealogies of the workers' movement: in the manifesto printed at
the beginning of the first issue, the collective announces that it
intends to 'listen again to [*réentendre*] the findings of social history
and to re-establish thought from below [*la pensée d'en bas*] and the
issues which were debated therein'.[17] So there is an emphasis on
the complex multiplicity of 'thought from below', the understandings of self and world of the oppressed, as a dynamic site in which
issues were debated rather than as the unitary source of class

identity or subversion: 'the diversity of forms of revolt' and the 'gap' (*l'écart*) between official genealogies of resistance, 'for example "the history of the workers' movement", and the real story of the ways in which revolt is elaborated, in which it circulates, is reap-propriated and re-emerges'.[18] So from the outset the collective was explicit about its desire to complicate and fragment monolithic accounts of the history of subversion and its commitment to seeking recognition for the seriousness, the multiplicity and the dynamiz-ing complexity of 'thought from below'.

This marked a clear departure from what may, in terms of the schematic subdivision proposed in the present chapter, be called the 'pre-history' of Rancière's historiographical work: the book of archival material he edited and introduced with his former student, Alain Faure, *La Parole ouvrière* (published in 1976 but devised before the first issue of *Les Révoltes Logiques*, in the period 1973–5).[19] As its title suggests, it was premised on the assumption that there was a unitary voice of the working class which could be heard in the various writings of working-class activists in the period 1830–51. The contention both of *Les Révoltes Logiques* and of Rancière in his own later work would instead be that:

> there is no voice of the people. There are fragmented, polemical, voices which split the identity they put forward every time they speak.[20]

> The reality denoted by the terms 'worker', 'people' or 'proletarian' could never be reduced either to a positive condition or a vain imag-ining but always denoted a partial and partisan intertwining of fragments of experience and forms of symbolization, one which was provisional and polemical.[21]

An inconclusive provisionality and a critical, often polemical, breaking of received historical wisdom into fragments was typical of the journal's style of intellectual inquiry. The journal's self-appointed task was thus to reconstruct popular memory but to do so as a site of complexity and debate which fully recognized the intellectual sophistication and the heterogeneity of 'thought from below', the perspective of the downtrodden, and sought to identify and interrogate the monolithic oversimplifications of established forms of history. A negative assessment of the journal's undertak-ing would be that it enjoyed a largely parasitic relationship to its host discourse and that its interventions amounted to casually throwing a spanner in the explanatory works devised with

scholarly care by others. In my view it is important to acknowledge, however, that while a few articles (I am not thinking of any
by Rancière) were somewhat overdependent on the work they
criticized, the journal had always defined its intellectual and political mission primarily in terms of critique. The collective saw its role
as opening the space of a double questioning: 'interrogating history
from the perspective of revolt and revolt from the perspective of
history'.[22] This did mean that established mainstream history often
got short shrift, but that was consistent with the stated aims of the
journal.

Nor was the journal concerned to destabilize only mainstream
academic history; misconceptions of history in the wider culture
were also in its line of fire. One particular form of oversimplification which is rejected at the beginning of the journal's manifesto
statement is what it calls 'le rétro', not just nostalgia in an ordinary
sense but specifically the sort of prettified and depoliticized representation of the past connoted by the expression 'la mode rétro', a
mid-seventies fascination with the décor and fashion of the past
(specifically the Occupation) and epitomized by Louis Malle's 1974
film *Lacombe Lucien*.[23]

Yet it was principally with the work of academic historians that
the journal took issue. Very often the accusation was that they are
easily led astray by nostalgia or political wishfulness. The collective's polemical deployment of the nostalgia *topos* is nowhere more
forceful than in a highly critical extended review article in the third
issue, by Jean Borreil, entitled 'Some Examples of Nostalgic Politics'. Among the books gathered under this unappreciative heading
are two classics of anthropologically inflected, third-generation,
Annales-school social history: André Burguière's *Bretons de Plozévet*
(1975), a social history of the life of one Breton village in the nineteenth and twentieth centuries; and Emmanuel Le Roy Ladurie's
Montaillou, village occitan (1976), a reconstruction of life in this Pyr-
eneean village in the fourteenth century through the minutely
detailed crypto-anthropological records of the Inquisition as it
subdued an area which was one of the last preserves of the Albig-
ensian heresy.[24] Both Burguière and Le Roy Ladurie are accused of
'passéisme', nostalgia in the negative sense, in their reconstruction
of lost idylls of regional village life in which social cohesion was
achieved through omnipresent mutual surveillance.[25] Behind their
superficially progressive pleas for the preservation of authentic
Breton and Occitan cultures, Borreil detects a depoliticizing nostalgia for a society free of class conflict.

A further example of the collective's deployment of the negative nostalgia *topos* occurs in another review article, in issue 13, by Rancière, entitled 'The Factory of Nostalgia', covering works on factories, some of them by sociologists and others by former *établis*, middle-class intellectuals who had gone to work in factories for political reasons.[26] At a historical moment of rapid deindustrialization, in the late seventies, Rancière argued that continuing attachment to the older factory-based system of industrial labour, for sociologists and historians on the Left, reflected a perniciously nostalgic longing for the intellectual security of a stable object, for a working class securely and identifiably rooted, contained, in a particular location. Perhaps the most trenchant of the journal's attacks on the dangers of nostalgia for the workers' movement comes in Rancière's analysis of the way in which prominent French trade unionists were drawn to collaborate in Vichy's 'Révolution Nationale', provocatively entitled 'From Pelloutier to Hitler'.[27] Rancière examines the way in which a handful of trade unionists on the right of the CGT were too easily manipulated into supporting Pétain's regime, and in particular its notorious Charte du Travail (1941), an overhaul of French labour laws which, ironically, formally abolished trade unions as such. The article examines their sincere but misguided belief that Vichy's labour reforms enacted a faithful return to the origins of the workers' movement in the nineteenth-century workshop. The workshop of the past thus imagined to be devoid of political or proto-political conflict was, Rancière demonstrates, the product of simplificatory wishfulness. No article from *Les Révoltes Logiques* more effectively or more provocatively executes the journal's political and intellectual brief to introduce complication and difficulty into the history of the workers' movement. In choosing to focus on the spectacular misjudgments of a handful of prominent trade unionists, Rancière's purpose is not to indulge in superior hindsight but rather to demonstrate the political need for a critical understanding of the genealogy of the workers' movement. The article is thus both a justification and a consummate demonstration of the journal's approach: like the journal, the article sets out to be discomforting, to attack intellectual and political complacency. In its insistence on comprehensive and critical remembering, warts and all, rather than selective eulogizing, the journal anticipated the development in the eighties and nineties of the historico-political concept of *le devoir de mémoire*: in the words of the epigraph Rancière chooses from Heraclitus for his article on collaborating trade unionists, the journal emphasized the duty 'also to remember those who forget where the road leads'.[28]

The reader sometimes feels that the experience of admitting complexity was discomforting not just for others but for the members of the collective themselves. The journal's very first article, co-authored by Rancière and Patrick Vauday, 'Going to the Expo: The Worker, His Wife, and Machines', on worker delegations to the 1867 Paris Exhibition, is typical in this regard and illustrates the difficulties involved in reconciling two of the journal's aspirations (to restore popular memory in its complexity and to recover, from a history of 'failed' revolts, a sense of their political promise for the present) and their two principal areas of interest (the workers' and the women's movements).[29] I shall examine each difficulty in turn.

This inaugural article is concerned not with revolt in the sense of violent uprising but rather with the argued intellectual refusal, by workers, of the repressive political underside of the 1867 Exhibition. Rancière and Vauday argue that this Exhibition presented the workers who visited it with the spectacle of their own dispossession: mass-produced items bearing witness to the rapid expansion of industrialization during the Second Empire – products, in other words, of worker labour – were offered up as though they belonged to the owners of the machinery for judging by a panel of non-workers. The article focuses on the way in which the reports published by the worker delegates in the months after the Exhibition succeeded not only in grasping the meaning of this spectacle but also in contesting the underlying political reality.

Introducing their analysis of the remarkable testimony of a small number of worker delegates, Rancière and Vauday celebrate their powers of insight and draw the reader's attention to the fact that what the editors' introduction to this first issue calls their 'very concrete reflection' ('réflexion très concrète') appeared in the same year as the first volume of Marx's *Capital*: '1867 was the year when the elite workers in Paris industry took stock of what a book published in Hamburg that very year called "the separation of the worker and the intellectual forces of production".'[30] This allusive form of words is significant: while few readers would have been in any doubt as to the identity of 'the work' in question, by not naming either it or its author, Rancière and Vauday signal that they will be concerned less with the abstract theoretical formulations of middle-class intellectuals and more with the effort to validate and explore the 'very concrete reflection' of workers. Although by no means a rejection of Marx, the article repeatedly implies that the worker delegates arrived at very similar insights by a different route. Thus it is noted that all of the worker delegates, who come from highly skilled trade bodies (shoe-makers, dyers and printers), make the point that mechanization, although it lightened the burden of hard physical work, chained workers to the machine and removed their sense of mastery over and ownership of the product. The reports envisage, just as Marx did, a better future in which the machinery would be owned collectively by the workers. It could be objected that the article fails to ask whether these shrewd observations had any political effect, yet this would be to misunderstand the nature of the enterprise: the very fact that the workers demonstrate intellectual mastery of their situation in their 'very concrete reflection' was itself transgressive of the political injunction ('Plato's lie', as Rancière calls it in *The Philosopher and His Poor*) that they were destined for the life of manual labour and for that life only. To reveal in their reports the cogent intellectual and political grasp which they had of their situation rather than to read them as a series of disconnected, animal-like, grievances is, in turn, to be understood as an interpretative act with political significance.

The second half of the article speaks to the second of the journal's areas of interest, the history of the women's movement. Entitled 'Man's Mirror', it tries to show that the same delegates' reports rejected Proudhon's argument for women's natural inferiority and credits them with responding favourably to the work of nineteenth-century feminist Flora Tristan. The suggestion is that the delegates recognized that arguments such as Proudhon's were part of a logic of oppression which they rejected. This line of argument involves a certain amount of resourceful interpretation because many of the workers in question were staunchly opposed to extending the right to work to women. Rancière and Vauday argue that what they were really objecting to was cheap labour, the attempt by employers to drive down wage costs by introducing greater competition into the labour market. The article argues that if most of the worker delegates concluded that a woman's place was in the home, which was the same conclusion Proudhon had reached, the reasoning was different. The domestic sphere was construed as a place apart from state and class oppression:

> If woman's place was in the home, it was not merely so that the husband's standard of wages would be maintained; she also had the

function of participating in the defence of the workers' stand against the great offensive of capitalist disappropriation. In this power struggle women were the prize – and the hostage.[31]

Although the overriding intention of the article is to exculpate the workers by explaining their apparent sexism, in the last sentence of the above quotation there is at least a glancing acknowledgement that women suffered in the captivity of their position. So while the article overall may take too much for granted in its keenness to reconcile the workers' and women's movements and mount an argument too much driven by conviction or axiom ('From the workers' point of view inequality could never be a principle'), it is not entirely blind to the difficulty of its exculpatory task and should at least be applauded for its courage in trying to confront that difficulty.[32] While it can be argued that the article, like the journal as a whole, suffers from the relative separation of its two halves and two areas of interest – the analysis of worker and women's oppression could often be more integrated – it should be recognized that, for its time and place, France in the 1970s, the journal was at the forefront of progressive, materialist, feminist scholarship.

There are traces of tension and indeed open disagreement within the collective, just as there were in the History Workshop group, over the question of the nature of its commitment to feminism: in issue 8–9 (Winter 1979), a short review article by Rancière, in a section in this case somewhat euphemistically entitled 'debates', takes issue with the approach taken by Lydia Elhadad in her new edition of Saint-Simonian feminist Suzanne Voilquin's *Souvenirs d'une fille du peuple*. In an earlier, coauthored piece in the second issue, Elhadad and Geneviève Fraisse had attacked Valentin Pelosse's edition of the work of another nineteenth-century French feminist pioneer, Claire Demar: they contended that while Pelosse showed that the quasi-mythical figure of Woman imagined by Saint-Simonian high priest Enfantin repressed real women, he failed to recognize the dissidence and plurality of Saint-Simonian women's perspectives and thus replicated, in the process of interpretation, the oppression they had suffered.[33] Rancière, who references the earlier article, in turn accuses Elhadad of a similar thing in her edition of Voilquin, namely of presenting her as a victim of her circumstances:

a victim of men's lies [. . .] subjugated by the rationalist/progressivist discourse of colonialism in her relationship to Egypt [. . .] obliged to overplay her respectability in the very act of resisting the suffering caused by male sexual violence [. . .] recuperated, along with her sisters, in the 'socialist realism' of 1848, having renounced [. . .] the radicalism of her stance of 1832, as Free Woman.[34]

In a move which anticipates part of his argument in *The Names of History*, Rancière criticizes Elhadad's difficulty in accepting Voilquin's exceptionality, her difference from her time, and notes the ambivalence which he says characterizes Elhadad's and other feminist historians' relationship to pioneers of the past. He then goes on effectively to question Elhadad's commitment to the ethos of *Les Révoltes Logiques*: 'This approach by a woman to women's history appears to share the general attitude demonstrated towards popular memory and acts of popular revolt by intellectuals who are historians, whether professional or amateur.'[35] Rancière's article is followed immediately by a response from Fraisse, who accuses him of no less grave a crime against not just the feminist project but also that of the journal: failing to situate his analysis in the context of the developments undergone by feminism in France in the years since 1968. In the early years, she argues, the tendency in feminist scholarship, of which she cites the article coauthored with Elhadad as an example, had been to question the right of men to write about women's history at all, yet this moment had since passed: 'The real history only begins when we posit the existence of feminists of the past and the present: we are not like them, nor they like us; identifying with them is neither possible nor desirable in the slightest.'[36] So, according to Fraisse, Rancière was wrong to suggest that Elhadad's edition demonstrated a failure of proper feminist solidarity through the ages.

My narrative of the 'debate' between Rancière and Fraisse/ Elhadad has been so detailed because it raises issues which go to the heart of Rancière's historiography and historical practice: to what extent does he contextualize historically the position from which he writes? Part of his argument in *The Names of History* will be that mainstream historians tend to *overcontextualize* and, as such, are unable to recognize exceptionality and therefore to account fully for the phenomenon of revolt. Yet perhaps his own interest in revolt and his particular concentration on nineteenth-century French worker history merited a fuller historical contextualization in his own time than he gave it, as Derrida once suggested in a response to a seminar paper by him.[37] For Rancière the need for such a contextualization may not have been apparent: the choice of the period is justified by the fact that this is when 'the poor' began to write in any numbers and the range and variety of their conceptions of self and world first began to become evident. It just is the period in which today's conceptions of social class and emancipation came into being. Moreover, to have spoken in the journal about his own context and the genealogy of his interests may well have seemed to him unduly self-indulgent. Nonetheless, the reader approaching Rancière's work today, in a rather different historico-political moment, is sometimes left wondering about the balance between his interest in the problems of self-identification which his period of choice illustrates and his intellectual-political commitment to popular memory: is there a limit beyond which one can no longer pursue both objectives together, beyond which too exclusive an emphasis on the singular exceptionality of the exceptional figures works against any notion of popular memory or collective identity? This is not an exclusively theoretical issue: it relates to Rancière's own political investment in the material, and some fuller account of this might well have helped to prolong the accessibility of the work beyond its particular historical and political moment.

The 'debate' also, and more obviously, bears on Rancière's relationship to feminism. One particular point of disagreement was Rancière's rejection of Elhadad's analysis of Voilquin's horror at the harem which Enfantin had envisaged in the context of the Saint-Simonians' Egyptian adventure: Elhadad had tried to see in this harem possibilities of liberation and Rancière dismissed this as fanciful. With hindsight the attempt to re-present the harem as the space of a certain freedom for women can be seen as one extreme tendency within the psychoanalytically inspired essentialist feminism of the Psych-et-Po movement. There are few feminist scholars today who would be prepared to go nearly as far as Elhadad appears to do in extolling the emancipatory possibilities of the harem.[38] Rancière's disagreement with her here aligns him more with the tradition of materialist emancipatory feminism of the kind espoused by Simone de Beauvoir and Monique Wittig. Given the dominance of the Psych-et-Po movement over feminist scholarship in France in the late seventies, Rancière's position once again placed him at odds with his intellectual moment and also, here, with close colleagues.

The last article by Rancière from *Les Révoltes Logiques* that I shall discuss here, 'Good Times or Pleasure at the Barricades', engages with a different set of issues, but ones which are also typical of the journal's concerns and which go on to preoccupy Rancière in his later historical work: the relationship between popular culture, class identity, politics and urban space.[39] The *barrières* were cross-ing-points in the wall surrounding Paris built by the Tax Farmers of the Ancien Régime. The wall continued to serve as the boundary to Paris until the city limits were extended by Haussman in 1860. Rancière's interest lies in the way the *barrières* served as working-class meeting places where people could drink cheaply (without paying city tax) and sing subversive songs in the taverns' singing circles, the '*goguettes*', which flourished there. The *barrières* were also where the dominant imaginary of the day pictured lurid scenes of orgiastic and alchoholic excess by the urban working class, and Rancière's article begins by taking issue with the 'simple reversal' by which social historians had tried to rehabilitate them as sites of an authentic working-class culture and resistance to the discipline of factory work and bourgeois moralizing.[40] He takes issue with this simplistic and nostalgic reappropriation of the *barrières* and, in particular, with the underlying assumptions about what makes cultural practices politically subversive. This critique will be crucial in framing the orientation of his individual historical work in *The Nights of Labor*.

He begins by pointing out that the nostalgic reappropriations of the *barrières* fail to appreciate the complexity of their relationship to the world of work: in glorifying them as an antidote to the work-shop, socialist historians fail to appreciate that the *barrières* were often places in which pleasure was mixed with business, as workers were frequently hired in exchange for the price of a drink.[41] This emphasis on mixity is typical of the journal's complicating reread-ing of working-class history. Rancière also suggests that what made these places dangerous – politically subversive – was not the overtly political songs which were sometimes sung there but rather the fact that workers, who often had never learned to spell, were able to try their hand at producing verse which was indistinguish-able from that of the best taste of the day: 'A worker who had never learned how to write and yet tried to compose verses to suit the taste of his times was perhaps [*peut-être*] more of a danger to the prevailing ideological order than a worker who performed revolu-tionary songs.'[42] The form of words is tentative and the assertion hangs on a 'perhaps', as will a number of the key interpretative propositions of *The Nights of Labor*. Yet these tentative remarks of Rancière's are cautiously laying the conceptual foundations for his mature political concept of 'the division/distribution of the sensory' (*le partage du sensible*), which I examine in Chapters 3 and 5: it is by virtue of their aesthetic prowess and the intellectual grasp of the world and their position in it which their work demonstrates that this form of popular cultural production may be considered political. The songs are proof positive that the singers were not destined for the life of manual labour they led and therefore constitute a practical refutation of 'Plato's lie'. Rancière's other concern, which reflects his approach in the article coauthored with Vauday on the 1867 Exhibition, discussed above, is to turn attention to the small number of exceptional migratory figures who live at the margins of their class but who have a disproportionate effect, in part thanks to such sympathetic amplificatory social fora as the *barrières*:

> Perhaps the truly dangerous classes are not so much the uncivilised ones thought to undermine society from below, but rather the migrants who move at the borders between classes, individuals and groups who develop capabilities within themselves which are useless for the improvement of their material lives and which in fact are liable to make them despise material concerns. It was minority dreamers like these who were in turn encouraging the masses to dream as they gathered around them in the street, listening to their songs and forgetting the errand which had brought them there, buying the sheet music they sold and taking their choruses back to the workshops.[43]

Although the proposition is again put tentatively, a strong historical thesis is being advanced here: that the dreaminess of a small number and their leaning towards the aesthetic had determinate historical effects, that they succeeded in contaminating the masses, who would stop in their tracks, who would forget whatever practical errands brought them there, and who would take the songs they heard back into the workshops. The exceptional worker-singers and the *barrières* which amplify and circulate their voices are thus thought to propagate a sort of cultural disturbance which undermines the established social order. The question of the precise status of claims of this sort and the historical weight to be accorded to the phenomena they describe will also be at issue in *The Nights of Labor*: surely not everyone who passed a *goguette* forgot the errand which had brought them to the area, but if not everyone, then roughly what proportion, or in other words how significant in reality was the disruptive effect of which it constituted the idea? Rancière is just not interested in questions of this sort, either here or in his later book. Yet it is important to recognize that because the overwhelming majority of French workers of the nineteenth century left no archival traces at all in their own right, it is more difficult conclusively to resolve the question of the influence of the small minority who did on the vast majority who did not.

Rancière's concern with the *barrières* is also to probe calls by an elite of worker-writers of the time for workers to show greater sobriety and even for more vigorous policing of these spaces, which is exactly what those in power also wanted. He argues that their position is to be explained by their strategic understanding of the way in which the image of the drunk and debauched worker was used politically by those in power as a way of justifying repressive measures. Yet he cannot and does not fail to note the disturbing parallel between this elite of workers and the establishment, both of which sought to target 'a cultural space which was in the process of increasing the availability of meeting places or means of access between one class and another'.[44] While attempting to fathom the motivations which explain the alarming congruence of worker and establishment discourse, Rancière is keen to point out that both felt threatened by these spaces of multiple exchange: spaces of exchange between classes in which work and pleasure, as well as art and politics, were intertwined.

There can be no doubt that *Les Révoltes Logiques* was one of the most intellectually ambitious projects to emerge in France in the aftermath of May '68, and it remains to this day one of the most undeservedly under-recognized. What accounts for the demise of the journal in 1981? The victory of Mitterrand's Socialist Party in 1981 was, in the very early days, greeted with great optimism: perhaps it was time to build the new society of the future, and perhaps there was no longer a need for relatively obscure journals to honour the memory of revolts of the past? The desperate call for subscriptions launched by the collective in the penultimate issue, as Ross has noted, conveys a clear sense of the considerable changes not only to the political and intellectual climate since the founding of the journal in 1975 but also to the networks which permitted dissemination of politically 'marginal' material.[45] Yet there was also a sense in which the journal's approach, or ethos, as I have defined it – the fragmenting introduction of complication into accounts of revolt and worker history by mainstream historians – was always destined to prove difficult to reconcile with its other principal aim, to foster popular memory. There was also the significant practical difficulty that the highly specific and already multiply complex nature of the debates in which the journal usually intervened made it hard to sell enough copies to keep the publication going. Last, but by no means least, was the fact that, by the early eighties, feminist scholarship had established for itself something of a foothold in the academy in France, notably in departments of history, and consequently there was less need for the kind of platform which the journal had offered it in the preceding decade.

The Nights of Labor: The Workers' Dream in Nineteenth-Century France [1981]

After explaining the place of this book in Rancière's historiographical work and the way it prefigures themes in his mature politics, I shall explore what I take to be one of the most remarkable aspects of this work and some of his other contemporaneous publications but which other commentators have tended to overlook: Rancière's fascination with the secular religion of work known as Saint-Simonianism.[46] Saint-Simonianism is often referenced in accounts of the pre-history of the Marxist concept of social class and is discussed notably by Walter Benjamin, another thinker whose historiographical work is very much at odds with mainstream academic practice, as a precursor to twentieth-century conceptions of technological progress.[47] Yet the movement has seldom been thought worthy of serious exploration in its own right, and it is on Rancière's engagement with it that the latter part of this section will focus.

The work's main title is as good a route as any into some of the key concerns and complexities of the work: *The Nights of Labor*. The 'nights' in question are not, Rancière insists in the first sentence of his foreword, in any sense metaphorical.[48] Rather, they refer to the night-time in which an exceptional group of worker-writers remained awake in order to compose their tracts and treatises, novels and poems, encroaching as they did so into the time allotted for them to rest after one working day of manual labour and prepare for the next. The book is divided into three parts, and the focus in the first two sections is mainly on the writers of the 1830s and 1840s. In the first part the work of joiner-intellectual Louis-Gabriel Gauny (1806–89) is used to explore the difficulty of living the dual life, fraught with contradictions, of an intellectual and a manual labourer. In the second part Rancière explores the awkward interactions and mutual misunderstandings of middle- and working-class Saint-Simonians. In the last part he examines what he takes to be the misguided attempts to found a concept of a pure working-class culture by isolating it from what were characterized as 'alien' influences, whether by worker-writers in the journal *L'Atelier*, or by worker co-operatives founded during the Second Republic, or by Icarian and other communities of Communist inspiration founded in the United States in the later part of the century.

The book radicalizes the project to introduce complication first essayed in *Les Révoltes Logiques* and, like that journal, is pitted against the tendency of some mainstream historians to look back with simplificatory nostalgia, in this case to pre-industrial, artisanal, labour as a source of an authentic and homogeneous working-class culture. As he had in the journal, Rancière reveals a sense of the complications and contradictions and, above all, of the intellectual sophistication of the understandings of self and world demonstrated in the archival material. The message throughout is that: 'The apportionment [*le partage*] of true and false, the calculus of pleasures and pains, may well be a bit more subtle than we generally imagine it to be in the case of simple souls.'[49] It is important that most of the worker-writers chose of their own accord to write, so in other words it was they themselves who seized the freedom which nobody had thought to bestow on them; indeed it was as though the working day had been so contrived in relation to the cost of living and the level of wages that there would be no time to do anything apart from work and sleep. They thus demonstrated what Todd May has rightly emphasized is an essential feature of Rancière's unique conception of equality: that it is 'active', taken by the oppressed rather than accorded by those in power.[50] As in the case of the workers who, without any particular training or socially accredited aesthetic expertise, just composed and sang songs at the *barrières* which were as good as those to be heard in any bourgeois salon and, in so doing, transgressed the established political order by showing that they were not necessarily destined for a life of manual labour, so too these workers who chose to consume their nights with writing proved that 'proletarian workers should be treated as beings to whom several lives [are] owed'.[51] The very fact of their producing intellectual (aesthetic, literary or philosophical) work disturbed the established division of labour within the culture, demonstrated that it was arbitrary and therefore changeable. This demonstration was simultaneously both political and aesthetic, and Rancière's analysis here prefigures his mature political concept of 'the division of the sensory' (*le partage du sensible*).

Yet the book sometimes leaves room for misunderstanding, since Rancière does not always stop at this groundbreaking new understanding of the political but allows himself, on occasions, to articulate it by implication with a more conventional claim about causal influence:

> The topic of this book is, first of all, the history of those nights snatched from the normal round of work and repose. A harmless and imperceptible interruption of the normal round, one might say, in which our characters *prepare* and dream and already live the impossible.[52]

The claim that the nights of aesthetic labour of the 'several' worker intellectuals he studied 'prepared' the way for 'the impossible' comes very close to saying that later political insurrections were caused, at least in part, by nocturnal versifiers. Referring to the *goguette* of the late 1820s, he writes: 'This nighttime socialization of individual vanities *paved the way for* the three glorious days, which were followed by the nights without food or fuel in the winter of 1830–1831.'[53] These references to preparation for revolt raise again, albeit obliquely, the empirical questions – which Rancière was trying to avoid – of the extent to which these exceptional figures are representative of their class, and the extent to which their work had political influence in an ordinary sense. Thus it can seem at times as though Rancière were trying to claim allusively for these worker intellectuals a causal role in large-scale political revolt of a conventional kind which he is unable and unwilling to prove they did in fact have. This is unfortunate because what is original about the study is its attempt to assert that the politically significant events in the history of the workers' movement are not just the mass insurrections and revolutions but also all those examples of cultural production, of tentative or imitative aesthetic practice, indeed of reverie, which in themselves testify to the fact that the division of labour between manual and intellectual, with all that goes with it economically and culturally, is arbitrary and which prove that things could be otherwise. The important point about the book is the new understanding of the political which Rancière is developing in it, but unfortunately this message is sometimes obscured by allusive and unsubstantiated claims to an altogether more conventional kind of political influence.

Rancière's approach in the book is to expose and explore in their complexity the understandings of self and world of the worker intellectuals. The more complex and conflicted these understandings are, the better, and there is a special place for those who transgress the boundaries between classes, for the '[p]erverted proletarians whose discourse is made up of borrowed words' and who give the lie to fantasies of class purity.[54] Rancière's commitment to discomforting complication is also apparent in discussions of worker-on-worker violence in apprenticeship rituals and in rivalrous clashes between trades, as it is in his emphasis on the proximity and, at times, interchangeability of the roles of worker and master, as in his reference to ambivalence in the relationship between them ('the relations of intermingled collaboration and hatred with the master').[55] He emphasizes the particular embarrassment involved in workers' self-presentation as a class, drawing attention to the 'class shame' experienced by '[t]he worker journalists who must represent to others – bourgeois people, writers, politicians – a working class whose coarseness they themselves despise'.[56] All this is in an attempt to reveal a far greater degree of internal complexity to workers' self-understandings than was conventionally acknowledged, particularly perhaps by some *établis*, those middle-class *gauchiste* intellectuals of the early 1970s who had 'established' themselves in factories in search of an authentic encounter with working-class existence, which they presumed to be radically different from their own as intellectuals.

Rancière is at his most intellectually daring in this book in the seriousness with which he takes the Saint-Simonian movement and the central, broadly positive, role he accords to what is often dismissed as little more than a quirky cult of marginal significance.[57] Saint-Simonianism, the movement named after Claude-Henri de Rouvroy, Comte de Saint-Simon (1760–1825), drew its inspiration chiefly from his last, unfinished, work, *Le Nouveau Christianisme* (1821), which proposed that the heaven described in Christian scripture should be realized on earth, with the help of technology.[58] The 'messenger' of this new religion was the poorest class and the teaching was one of fraternal equality. Thus Saint-Simonianism aspired, not unambitiously (though not entirely atypically for its time), to combine three dimensions: technological advancement, religious mysticism and far-reaching egalitarian social reform. On this last point, its founder had suggested that the French Revolution was unfinished because it had failed to inaugurate a fairer social system.[59] Numbering no more than six hundred active members at the height of the movement (1831–2), the Saint-Simonians were led by two 'supreme fathers', Bazard and Enfantin, and grouped into a network of 'colleges', each numbering around fifteen lesser 'fathers', and other members of three different 'degrees'.[60] Public curiosity was aroused by some of the more unusual rituals at their base in Ménilmontant, in Paris, for example the ceremonial exchange of clothes between members of the group from different social classes. Perhaps the most notorious and ultimately ruinous of the movement's teachings was Enfantin's claim that the world was about to be saved by the advent of a female messiah and what he took to be the obligation this entailed on women members of the movement to make themselves more available than social convention deemed proper to their male counterparts.[61] Fearing widespread public disorder, a court in August 1832 decreed the dissolution of the movement.[62]

From this brief description it should be clear why to take Saint-Simonianism seriously constitutes something of a risk, yet this is a good example of how Rancière's intellectual courage and relative indifference to academic received wisdom has served him well. For his argument, informed by the testimony of worker intellectuals such as Louis-Gabriel Gauny, is not on behalf of the more bizarre precepts of the doctrine as such, but rather that we need to account for the transformative effect which an encounter with it seems to have had on the self-concept of workers at the time. In other words, looking beyond some of the more outlandish trappings of the movement, what did Saint-Simonianism mean to the workers who encountered it, and what did it allow them to think and do? Rancière argues that, in Gauny's case, the important thing was not the content of the beliefs as such, about which he seems to have remained fairly ambivalent, but rather the experience of 'conversion' and 'initiation' which his encounter with the movement afforded:

> The important thing was perhaps not the belief but the intitiation which allowed him to enter the circle of those who break the rule imposed by Plato on artisans by deciding to do something *other* than their work, by venturing onto ground reserved for others. This was not initially a matter of wealth but rather of thought, of inaugurating a different form of sociability: this friendship, or *philia*, which the practice of philosophy presupposes.[63]

The meaning of the movement evinced in Gauny's work is political in the special sense which Rancière is developing in his historiographical work: it allows Gauny a new form of life, a new way of relating to the world and other people and a new sense of self. He is coming into being as a political subject in his encounter with

– and, perhaps just as significantly, in his ambivalence towards and criticism of – Saint-Simonianism. In *The Nights of Labor* the focus falls much more on the contradictions within the movement, particularly on the difficulty which it had trying to distinguish itself from more traditional forms of religiously inspired charity: many members of the working population which middle-class Saint-Simonians set out to encounter were living in extreme poverty and were understandably interested in the material support which the movement offered.[64] Rancière also draws attention to the way in which some working-class Saint-Simonians discerned a contradiction between the overtly egalitarian message of the movement and the hierarchy within the 'colleges', in which there was a close relationship between 'degree' and social class, a hierarchy reflected in the patronizing tone of some of the lectures and teaching. Thus he once again emphasizes the capacity for critical understanding of complex phenomena by those assumed, because of their position in the social hierarchy, to be incapable of thought. If worker intellectuals such as Gauny took issue with the movement, they did so both as workers and as intellectuals, giving the lie to the Platonic division of the city. If the role of religious mysticism in working-class thought had seemed suspect to a Marxist and socialist historical tradition which sought to explain protest in predominantly material terms (working conditions, class consciousness, trade practices and so forth), then Rancière, in *The Nights of Labor* and his selection of Gauny's texts, *Louis-Gabriel Gauny: le philosophe plébéien* (1983), puts a strong case for seeking to try harder to understand the personally transformative and politically transgressive role which an encounter with such 'improper science' had in the lives of some of those touched by it. Yet the role of 'culture' in Rancière's account is by no means naïvely redemptive. Their experience of 'culture' may have transformed the lives of a minority of working-class intellectuals, but this was not always for the better: the sense of conflicted self-understanding and the feelings of being 'out of place' which it engendered led, in some notorious cases, to melancholia, indeed to suicide.[65]

The Names of History: On the Poetics of Knowledge [1992]

Let me begin with the reception of this challenging theoretical book. The historian Arlette Farge, an occasional contributor to *Les Révoltes Logiques* and one of the few French historians to have broken what she intimates was an organized silence on the book, remarked in all too brief an article that it is the work of 'a towering and penetrating intellect cutting into the flesh of the science of history with a pair of scissors'.[66] The immediate target of Rancière's alleged attack is the dominant school of twentieth-century French historiography known by the short title of its journal, founded in 1929, as the *Annales* school, or group.[67] Inaugurated by medievalist Marc Bloch and sixteenth-century historian Lucien Febvre, the school aspired to a radical reframing of the nature and proper object of the historian's craft: chronicles of the exploits of kings and generals (Hegel's 'world-historical figures') were to be replaced, in this 'New History', by an analytical approach which articulated questions, or problems, and sought to resolve them. Rather than the surface froth of political events – stories of kings and battles – the focus of the New History was to be deep social, economic and natural activities and processes, which were to be examined over long periods of time with considerable assistance from adjacent disciplines such as geography, economics, sociology and anthropology.[68]

Rancière focuses, in the first two of the seven essays which comprise this work, on the moment at the beginning of the twentieth century when the 'New History' came into being, distinguishing itself from and repudiating 'old' history by claiming to be scientific and rigorous. It is the rejection of storytelling, or narrative, in favour of problem-based analysis, which went hand in hand with the *Annales* school's claim to scientificity, a claim which Rancière calls into question by analysing key examples of how, rhetorically, New History does precisely what it claimed not to do: tell stories, in particular the story of its own scientificity.

It is entirely appropriate that Rancière, in a footnote, places his text under the tutelage of Roland Barthes's work on history.[69] The two thinkers share a love of the nineteenth-century historian Jules Michelet's passionate and voluminous historical writing and an urge to celebrate his work over and above the problem-based analytical history associated with the *Annales* school; there will be more to say in a moment about Michelet, to whom Rancière devotes two suitably lyrical chapters. Of the 'several other important texts' by Barthes on matters historical, in addition to his *Michelet* [1954], which Rancière mentions in the footnote, the most relevant is unquestionably 'The Discourse of History' [1968], 'a provocative article which quickly became infamous', in the words of historian François Hartog.[70] Barthes, too, was thought by many historians to have been hacking away at their craft in this influential article, in which he examined and categorized the different ways in which they draw attention, in their writing, to the very process of writing. Barthes observed that the real object – some thing, event or process from the past – out to which the historian's discourse reaches can only ever figure in his or her writing as a 'reality effect': 'In "objective" history, the "real" is never anything but an unformulated signified, sheltered behind the apparent omnipotence of the referent.'[71] The trouble, for serious-minded historians who want to make claims for the scientific and rigorous nature of their writing, is that novelists are no less capable of contriving such 'reality effects' in fictional texts.

It is important to recognize that Barthes is *not* saying that the real object, the past, is in any sense fictitious, but rather that it can only figure in discourse in a manner indistinguishable from the way in which events or processes figure in works of fiction; Rancière, similarly, should not be misunderstood in his essay to be making the claim typical of vulgarized postmodernism that the past in itself is a malleable effect of discourse.[72] *The Names of History* can be thought of as an analysis of some of the different forms of what Barthes called the 'reality effect' in historical writing; as the title announces, it is a work of 'poetics', or in other words a study of the way a discourse is put together. This 'poetics of knowledge' ('poétique du savoir') is defined by Rancière as:

> a study of the set of literary procedures by which a discourse escapes literature [*se soustrait à la littérature*], gives itself the status of a science, and signifies this status. The poetics of knowledge has an interest in the rules according to which knowledge is written and read, is constituted as a specific genre of discourse. It attempts to define the mode of truth to which such knowledge is devoted – not to provide norms for it, nor to validate or invalidate its claim to scientificity [*prétention scientifique*].[73]

Before we come to the detail of Rancière's argument, the question this programmatic statement begs is whether it is in fact possible to account adequately for the constitution of any discourse solely by studying the poetics of a selection of some of its prominent works. It could be argued that discourses flourish or wither in wider social, institutional and historical contexts and that not all of the 'rules' of their construction and intelligibility are necessarily legible in, or determined by, their most prominent public statements. Moreover, the articulation of a claim to scientificity, or rigour, tends to be made in specific social, financial and indeed historical contexts, for the benefit of specific audiences and with particular ends in mind: 'we are rigorous, we are scientists and our activity is a discipline', at a basic but not negligible level, often means 'we are deserving of esteem and employment'. The claim is usually made as part of a social and institutional struggle which is arguably susceptible to a more comprehensive analysis than the rhetorical, surface, textual one which the terms Rancière fixes for his own inquiry will allow him. Without looking to the insitutional and political (historical) conditions in which New History rose to ascendancy, it may just not be possible to obtain 'the rules' of its attempted self-constitution as a discourse apart from literature, or it may be possible to derive only some of these rules or factors; these may be the decisive ones or they may not. Rancière could then be criticized for failing sufficiently to acknowledge and analyse the conditioning institutional and social contexts of the rhetorical manoeuvres he discusses in *The Names of History*. I shall attempt to show that this is at least internally consistent in the sense that his dual resistance to sociological explanation and over-contextualization are important distinguishing characteristics of his historiographical thought.

If the terms of his inquiry are really as modest as Rancière says they are in the first chapter – a rhetorical reading of New History's attempted rhetorical self-extraction from literature, or, as I have put it, of its 'reality effects' – how are we to account for the feeling among historians, to which Farge and others refer, that their craft had been viciously attacked? The reaction of affronted and near-complete silence is to be explained by two factors.[74] First, by the institutional and intellectual history within French academia of friction between philosophers and historians, a history of conflict and mutual suspicion which goes back to philosopher Raymond Aron's *Introduction to the Philosophy of History* [1938].[75] Aron argued that because the historian's understanding and explanation of the past are dependent upon numerous subjective choices, historical discourse merely gestures towards a past to which it is unable to refer objectively. Historian Michel de Certeau blamed Aron for having schooled a generation of philosophers in the art of pointing out the supposed 'philosophical decisions' underlying historians' choices of how to divide up and interpret a body of material and structure their exposition.[76] Certeau suggests this led to a facile game of historians being exposed as unwitting philosophers whose practice lacked critical self-awareness by philosophers who were somehow assumed to have a magically direct relation to ideas but who were, in fact, unable or unwilling to historicize the assumption of that unmediated connection, or in other words to explain how it had come about in this particular society at this particular time that people going by the name of philosophers could enact intellectual transactions of this sort with people called historians. Although he names no names, Althusser must have been at the top, or close to the top, of Certeau's list of offenders: in his 'Outline of the Concept of History', Althusser singled out *Annales*-school historians Febvre, Labrousse and Braudel for praise as 'remarkable' but went on to criticize them for a continued reliance on an ideological understanding of time as a continuum.[77] Certeau's response, that an entire generation of philosophers failed to historicize the privileges of their own position and perspective, has been echoed by Derrida, who insisted on the need to 'pose many historical or "historial" questions about the idea of theory' and claimed that Althusser had passed over such questions far too quickly.[78]

The hostile reaction by historians to Rancière's text must be seen, secondly, as an attempt to police disciplinary boundaries in the light of what was known of his work and his affiliations prior to the publication of *The Names of History*: having been trained in philosophy in the 1960s and closely associated with Althusser, then based in a department of philosophy in the 1970s, as we have seen he then simply set about writing history. This trajectory only really made sense on the presumption that the discipline of history is not one, or is only contingently recognized as one, and that to write history requires no particular training or institutional affiliation; many historians who might otherwise have read *The Names of History* (according to Farge many refused outright even to read the book) could not but have been aware that this was the view of their subject which Rancière's trajectory implied.[79] Moreover, although Rancière asserts that his intention was neither to validate nor to invalidate the 'claim to scientificity [*prétention scientifique*]' of historical discourse, in a later interview in which he comments extensively on *The Names of History*, he remarks that 'we should not preoccupy ourselves with the question of whether what we are doing is scientific but rather with that of whether what we are doing is liable to touch upon a truth'.[80] This assertion, although made some two years after publication of *The Names of History*, sits uneasily with his denial in the first chapter of that book that he is questioning the 'claim to scientificity' of historical discourse. The difficulty with Rancière's brushing aside of the question of scientificity in this interview and his parenthesizing of it in *The Names of History* is that, if listened to with a more sympathetic ear, the wranglings over scientificity can be understood to reflect a concern to establish under precisely which conditions historical discourse is 'liable to touch upon a truth'. In other words, this can be understood as a crucial debate about what constitutes historical knowledge, rather than a self-aggrandizing bid for disciplinary-institutional supremacy by one particular school. Moreover, allowing as Rancière does for the admixture of art does not immediately resolve the matter because a similar discussion can be had in the field of art about what exactly is involved in touching upon a truth. Rancière's impatience with this whole discussion must have been informed by his repudiation of Althusser's grandiose claims on behalf of the scientificity of Marxist science. However, it could be argued that the intensity of Rancière's principled hostility to such intellectual and institutional self-aggrandizement leaves him unable to acknowledge the positive performative effects which such declarations aspired to achieve. As Peter Schöttler has observed, both Althusser in his application of the concept of the epistemological break and the *Annalistes* in their reframing of historical knowledge as the articulation and resolution of problems sought to break with teleology and to understand specific differences in a non-reductive way (between us and people in early modern times, for example, or between early and late Marx). [81] It may be that Rancière's historiography – and I return to this point in the conclusion to this chapter – is less readily able to account for global differences of the past and too inclined to concentrate on the recognizable sameness of some of its most exceptional figures.

Having surveyed some salient features of the surrounding historiographical landscape and discussed how Rancière frames his own inquiry, I turn now to the detail of his nuanced historiographical argument, which I take to consist of four principal, closely interrelated, claims:

1   History is inevitably narrative but has tended, the more institutionalized and professionalized it has become, particularly in France, to deny with ever greater vigour its kinship with literature.

2   Although the break with kings-and-battles history, inaugurated by Michelet and the *Annales* school, helped to shift the

focus of historical writing away from the rich and powerful, their authority was transferred to the historian rather than to the vanquished of history, 'the poor'.

3 Historians are prone to be uncritical in their use of the concept of anachronism and tend to overcontextualize, which means they are unable to give proper recognition to the exceptional.

4 This tendency to reduce events and ideas to their contexts leaves historians unable to account for those dynamic and revolutionary forces which by their nature exceed their contexts, in particular seditious language or 'heresy'.

I shall now examine each of the four aspects of Rancière's argument in turn.

Narrativity

Rancière takes it as axiomatic that history is narrative, or in other words that historians inevitably 'name subjects' and 'attribute to them states, affections, events', whether these subjects be individuals or, as in the case of second-generation *Annaliste* Fernand Braudel's celebrated study, entities such as the Mediterranean.[82] Rancière is asserting that history is a form of propositional knowledge. This may seem too obvious to need stating, especially, with the benefit of hindsight, given the resurgence of narrative history over the last twenty years; yet it should be understood as a response to the insistence by *Annales*-school historians that the historian's craft consisted not in the construction of narrative but rather in the framing and resolution of problems about the past. Although historian Roger Chartier has criticized *The Names of History* for focusing unduly on outdated issues, the disavowal of narrative was by no means confined to the earliest years of the *Annales* school: François Furet, in a 1975 article entitled 'From Narrative History to Problem-Oriented History', wrote of 'the possibly definitive decline of narrative history'.[83] Rancière's insistence on the inescapable narrative dimension of historical discourse aligns him with historians Paul Veyne, for whom history is 'a true novel', and Hayden White, who was the first to speak in terms of the 'emplotment' and 'poetics' of historical discourse, as well as with philosopher Paul Ricoeur and narratologist Philippe Carrard.[84]

Like Ricoeur, Rancière is intrigued by Braudel's classic of *Annales*-school historiography, *The Mediterranean and the*

Mediterranean World in the Age of Phillip II [1949], a text which performs the transition it signals in its title from an 'old history' which recounted the exploits of kings and their minions to one in which the Mediterranean Sea was the principal subject and this most powerful of kings of Spain and his accomplishments were relegated to the status of mere predicates. A few words on Braudel's book are needed to situate Rancière's reading. Braudel's study comprises three main parts. After a methodological preface, the first part surveys the geographical and climatological factors, over the long term, which shaped the Mediterranean; the second looks at economic and social factors; and only after these have been outlined does Braudel turn to the political events of Phillip's reign (1556–98). The message in this order of exposition is clear: individual people are no longer the atoms of history, and their deeds, the events they apparently initiated or in which they were involved, are no longer the basic building blocks in historical explanations of social change.[85] The main focus of Ricoeur's reading of Braudel's study is to show that, notwithstanding the *Annalistes*' rejection of narrative in favour of problem-based history, the three-part study itself constitutes a carefully structured narrative, indeed a new type of plot.[86]

Rancière takes it as given, as he is entitled to do after Ricoeur's magisterial analysis, that Braudel's study is a plotted narrative and begins his reading by drawing attention to the unusual use of verb tenses, noting in particular the surprisingly frequent use of the present and the future:

> they impose their domination, giving the 'objectivity' of the narrative the force of certainty that it needs to be 'more than a story'. The sudden event, like the fact of long duration [*comme le fait de longue durée*], is stated in the present, and the relation of an anterior action to a posterior one is expressed as the latter's future.[87]

In other words, the use of the present and future tenses, by situating the historian *in* the time he is describing, strives to reduce the room for uncertainty which past tenses allow in their acknowledgement of temporal distance within the narrative. Rancière singles out as particularly striking Braudel's account of Phillip's death, in the last main chapter, in which the historian goes as far as to place himself in the room with Phillip and to examine the papers on his desk. Rancière relates this account to a digression, in Braudel's methodological preface, which inveighs against the old narrative history, a digression in which the historian is enjoined to be wary of a form of documentary evidence which it is said became increasingly abundant in the sixteenth century, no less wary than of the missives of kings and their ambassadors which were the mainstay of the old history: the writings of 'the poor, the humble, eager to write, to talk of themselves and of others'.[88] Braudel urges caution because 'the poor are those who speak blindly, on the level of the event': being in the thick of things, they are unable to grasp the real historical forces which shape the society in which they live.[89] Rancière reads these two moments in the text together and concludes that while Braudel may well have intended the positioning of his account of Phillip's death, at the most superficial end of the explanatory sequence, to serve as an allegory of the death of the old history with its focus on kings and their exploits, the New History cannot simply inherit its authority as science from the death of the king without also regulating, or policing, the chattering voices of the poor mentioned in the prefatory digression: 'It must regulate this excessive life of speakers that has killed royal legitimacy and threatens that of knowledge.'[90] The striking use of tenses in the historical narrative which Rancière highlights thus strives to place the historian in the thick of the period he is describing, seeking thereby to co-opt for his discourse some of the authority of first-hand testimony, while at the same time allowing him to remain a historian, or in other words a professional wary of what are assumed to be necessarily short-sighted attempts to understand their period by the chattering poor who really were present in it.

Rancière is suggesting that, in Braudel's study, the denial of history's narrativity goes hand in hand with the need for the historian to assert his or her superiority over the relatively small numbers of writerly poor; if the historian's history is to be truthful, then it would appear that attempts by the poor at understanding themselves and their world must be considered suspect storytelling, perhaps containing glimpses of true understanding but necessarily short-sighted, even delusional. Rancière finds no epistemological basis for the historian's claim to superior powers of insight and seeks to place him and his account on the same footing as the vision of the period held by its poor: both are attempting, through narrative, from their own perspectives, to understand a particular period. Instead of trumpeting the superiority of their own powers of insight, historians would do better, Rancière seems to suggest, to listen to the singular voices of the poor, to recognize and explore the complexity of their own self-understandings, just as he had attempted to do in *Les Révoltes Logiques* and *The Nights of Labor.*

The poor

Seeking an answer to the question of how conventional history came to be so mistrustful of, and feel so superior to, the poor and their writings, Rancière turns to Jules Michelet (1798–1874), the prolific, passionately republican and highly literary historian, author of a monumental *Histoire de France* which ran to some nineteen volumes in the first edition, as well as of over twenty other books. Rancière argues that Michelet invented a new way of processing the testimonies of those whose social position had not destined them to think and write, but that this was simultaneously a way of making them figure visibly in the historical narrative while silencing their own voices: he 'invents the art of making the poor speak by keeping them silent, of making them speak as silent people'.[91] In Michelet's lyrical account of the foundational moment of the new democratic era, the Fête de la Fédération (the commemorations first held, across France, on 14 July 1790, of what was thought to be the end of the French Revolution), Rancière notes that Michelet repeatedly emphasizes the fact that he has held and seen contemporaneous accounts of the occasion authored by ordinary people, 'the poor', love letters in which they express their passion for the new state, often in a broken and clichéd manner. Rancière observes that even as Michelet presents us with the visible presence of these documents, he silences the voices contained therein and substitutes his own interpretation:

> The speakers never speak in vain. Their speech is always full of meaning. Simply put, they know nothing of the meaning that makes them speak, that speaks in them. The role of the historian is to deliver this voice. To do that, he must nullify the scene where the speech of the poor deploys its *blind* accents to lead it onto the scene of its visibility.[92]

Thus Michelet is a pioneer in that he contrives a way for hitherto ineligible subjects – the poor, the masses, 'ordinary people' – to enter historical narrative. Yet he is also held responsible for a procedure Rancière sees continuing to operate in the 'scientific' history of *Annales*-school historians: the price of the entry of the poor into historical narrative is the policing of their real chatter into silence. The voice which the historian 'delivers' from the poor of the past is not the voice of what they actually said but rather of what they meant to say: not the *dire*, their speech, but what the historian judges to be their *vouloir-dire*, their meaning.

After noting the way in which Michelet's narrative of the Fête de la Fédération uses tenses, Rancière zeroes in on the moment at which Michelet delivers up the meaning of the festival, in two sentences entirely devoid of verbs: 'No conventional symbol! All nature, all mind, all truth!'[93] The effect of this suppression of the verb is, Rancière claims, 'the neutralization of the *appearance of the past*'.[94] This is properly a poetic, or literary, procedure, one which Rancière notes is used both by Michelet and frequently by the *Annales* school, an example of how literary techniques are used in a paradoxical attempt to establish history's truth claim by distinguishing it from literature.

Rancière seems to be suggesting that the move to bring the poor within the scope of historical discourse, which Michelet inaugurated, could still be taken much further. If Michelet and the *Annales* school are to be credited with having displaced the deeds of kings and generals from the centre of the historical account, Rancière implies that an opportunity was lost to fill this position with the poor and their self-understandings. The double-edged seeing–silencing of their contemporaneous testimony practised by Michelet was compounded by the *Annales* school's insistence that individuals and their actions were no longer to be the atomic elements of historical explanation. This radicalization of the attempt to incorporate the poor into historical narrative is to be achieved, Rancière suggests, by way of a philosophical questioning of the historian's taboo on anachronism which will allow the value of exceptional testimony to be recognized.

Anachronism and the exceptional

In a classic of first-generation *Annales* school history, Febvre's *The Problem of Unbelief in the Sixteenth Century: The Religion of Rabelais* [1942], anachronism is characterized as the most unforgivable of all sins.[95] Febvre's study was conceived as a response to the conception of history implied in a preface to an edition of *Pantagruel* by Abel Lefranc in which he claimed that Rabelais's book was an attempt to undermine the Christian religion; a conception according to which there can be people who are ahead of their times. Febvre concludes that it was simply not possible for Rabelais to have been anything other than squarely in his time and, accordingly, a believer. In an article published four years after *The Names of History*, Rancière argues that the concept of anachronism plays a crucial structuring or regulatory role, but an underanalysed one, in Febvre's book and in the New History generally. He suggests that methodological overreliance on anachronism leaves the historian disinclined to recognize that which in any given period really is out of joint with its surroundings; in the case of Febvre's book, this means Febvre assumes far too great a uniformity of thought, world-view, or *'mentalité'* in the period in question.[96] This is problematic because, Rancière claims, it is only to the extent that ideas, institutions, people and events do not 'fit' into their surroundings that historical change is possible in the first place:

> The concept of 'anachronism' is anti-historical because it obscures the very conditions of historicity itself. There is such a thing as history to the extent that people do not 'resemble' their times, to the extent that they break with 'their' time, with the temporal line which puts them in their place by requiring them to devote their time to such and such an 'employment'.[97]

This is a big claim; in that it entirely disregards the role of longer-term geographical, climatic, economic and social factors in favour of the exceptional dynamism of the singular individual, it could be characterized as an overcorrection of the *Annalistes'* own overcorrection of the old narrative history. If we set aside the hyperbolic form of the utterance, Rancière's point is valid: concepts such as 'world-view' or *'mentalité'* can easily become falsely homogenizing and work to police out of historical intelligibility the unexpected, the atypical, the extraordinary and the exceptional and consequently to downplay the influence of individual social actors. Yet whether such exceptionality really is, as Rancière asserts in the above quotation, the general condition of historical change remains to be proven.

Rancière's criticism of the *Annalistes'* reliance on anachronism is motivated less by his interest in the question of Rabelais's belief than by his concern for the theorization of revolutionary change, in particular in the context of the French Revolution, in which the concept of anachronism has played a major role. In *The Names of History*, Rancière is concerned particularly to undermine the account advanced in Furet's *Interpreting the French Revolution*

[1978].[98] In Furet's revisionist understanding, those who partici-
pated in the Revolution and who thought they were changing their
world were essentially labouring under a misapprehension because
by 1787 France was already a society without a state: 'The Revolution is the illusion of making the Revolution, born from ignorance
of the fact that the Revolution has already taken place.'[99] Thus for
Furet the event we call the Revolution and all of the speechifying
and conceptualizing we associate with it arose from the *anachronistic* failure of participants to realize that in fighting against royal
power they were fighting against something which had expired
some two years earlier; the Revolution, for Furet, was accordingly
more 'non-event' than 'event', a huge anachronistic misunderstanding with bloody consequences but in no sense an unprecedented or foundational moment which speaks to something
essential about human nature and political organization. Rancière's
understanding of the Revolution, like that of his contemporary
Alain Badiou, is quite different. Both insist on the irreducible speci-
ficity of this event and Rancière suggests that it is the projection,
the acting-out, of something essential about human experience:
'The revolution makes an event and disruption out of the anachronism, out of the temporal distance from itself that is the nature
of the speaking being.'[100] Whereas in Furet's account the claim that
the Revolution was an anachronism implies that it was in large
measure a misunderstanding with tragic consequences in the short
term but no lasting significance, for Rancière the same claim is
precisely what establishes its significance as an event which testifies to the power of the anachronistic, that which is out of its place
in time, to function as a dynamic force for change within human
societies.

Seditious language and 'heresy'

During the second essay in *The Names of History*, Rancière digresses
from the reading of Braudel he has been undertaking to engage
with the English political philosopher and near-contemporary of
Braudel's non-subject, Phillip II: Thomas Hobbes (1588–1679), a
figure who Hayden White has rightly observed is central in *The
Names of History*.[101] Rancière's engagement with Hobbes is a particularly resourceful example of subversive close reading, a smash-
and-grab raid on one of the most celebrated arguments in favour
of sovereign power and the strong state, in Hobbes's *Leviathan*, a

work which may anachronistically be described as a dictator's handbook. Rancière interprets Hobbes's account of the causes of sedition in the modern body politic as follows:

> They are first of all opinions, affairs of poorly used words or of unwarranted phrases. The body politic is threatened by words and phrases that drag here and there, anywhere; for example, 'You must listen to the voice of your conscience before that of authority', or again, 'It is just to suppress tyrants'. These pronouncements of self-serving pastors find only too many complacent ears. The ailment of politics is first the ailment of words. There are too many words, words that designate nothing other than the very targets against which they place weapons in the killers' hands.[102]

The appeal of Hobbes's account to Rancière is nowhere more apparent than in the last line of this quotation: words such as 'tyrant' have the power to turn subjects from quiet obedience to a violent repudiation of those who govern them. For Hobbes, as Rancière notes, this dangerously non-specific and therefore readily re-deployable language arises from two sources in particular: first, from religion and above all from those Protestant preachers who appeal more to individual conscience and scripture than to the interpretative authority of any church; second, from the body of texts by classical authors and their imitators, filled with 'theories of tyranny and with its misfortunes, with stories and poems to the glory of tyrant-killers'.[103] In Chapter 29 of *Leviathan*, 'Of Those Things that Weaken, or Tend to the Dissolution of a Common-wealth', while religion and private conscience are at the forefront of Hobbes's account, the second cause Rancière cites, 'imitation of the Greeks and Romans', features in a longer list of seven or eight causes and at first sight far less prominently.[104] I said that Rancière's reading of Hobbes is resourceful because if one pays close attention to the letter of Hobbes's argument, it is clear that this cause does in fact deserve the prominence which Rancière accords it:

> From the reading, I say, of such books, men have undertaken to kill their kings, because the Greek and Latin writers, in their books, and discourses of policy, make it lawful, and laudable, for any man so to do; provided, before he do it, he call him a tyrant. For they say not *regicide*, that is, killing a king, but *tyrannicide*, that is, killing of a tyrant is lawful. [. . .] In sum, I cannot imagine, how any thing can be more prejudicial to a monarchy, than the allowing of such books to be publicly read [. . .].[105]

Taken literally, as I think the underlined phrase can only be, Hobbes is saying here that the power to name a tyrant which these texts demonstrate and thereby propagate is the single most potent cause of sedition. Although Hobbes does not say so explicitly, he must be assuming that human beings are extremely susceptible to the influence of literary exemplars. Yet if Rancière's reading of Hobbes is resourceful, it is also somewhat selective: he does not mention the institutional dimension to Hobbes's argument. For Hobbes, universities were particularly dangerous institutions because they continually exposed students to such authors' works and equipped them with just the sort of inflated sense of their own importance which might incline them to re-enact the tyrannicidal acts described therein.[106] The specific institutional context of the university exacerbated what Hobbes thought was a natural human propensity. From Hobbes's account Rancière retains only the propensity, the human susceptibility to be deviated from one's natural course by the letter. The precise nature of this propensity, which Rancière names 'literarity', will be explored further in Chapter 4. Such is the influence of Hobbes's account over Rancière that the latter displays an inverted version of the former's extreme nervousness about the power of these 'poorly used words or [. . .] unwarranted phrases'. What Hobbes feared, Rancière welcomes; but both share a very high, some would say unjustifiable, degree of confidence in the power to sway of these stories of the death of kings.

It may not be immediately apparent what Rancière's Hobbesian digression on the disruptive political power of certain kinds of language and literature has to do with the writing of history. The suggestion, in the last essay, is that historians have difficulty accepting the role which language plays not just in describing but in *making* history; what characterizes the age of democracy from the nineteenth century, is, Rancière suggests, an excess of unauthorized speech. He singles out as crucial in this regard the first rule of the London Corresponding Society, a group established in 1792 to campaign for the extension of the suffrage, with which E.P. Thompson begins his *The Making of the English Working Class*: 'That the number of our Members be unlimited.' In Thompson's words:

> Today we might pass over such a rule as a commonplace: and yet it is one of the hinges upon which history turns. It signifies the end to any notion of exclusiveness, of politics as the preserve of any hereditary élite or property group. [. . .] To throw open the doors to

propaganda and agitation in this 'unlimited' way implied a new notion of democracy, which cast aside ancient inhibitions and trusted to self-activating and self-organizing processes among the common people.[107]

Rancière's digression into Hobbes makes more sense in light of the fact that the groundbreaking conception of democracy forged by the London Corresponding Society is propagated by letter and has its roots less in particular social sites or practices than in an apparently eclectic collection of texts, including the Declaration of the Rights of Man and the Old Testament. The origins of this inherently unlimited new class born in the age of democracy thus lie, according to Rancière, in a series of acts in which human susceptibility to the letter and the errant migratory possibilities of unauthorized speech are essential, just as they are in Hobbes's account of sedition. The danger for historians of the workers' movement lies in the temptation to confine this mobile, errant, proliferating and seditious excess of speech to specific social sites and practices such as the workshop or the customs of a particular trade. Rancière here follows – indeed dramatizes – E.P. Thompson's argument that the emergence of this class cannot be explained simply as the continuation of these pre-existing social and cultural forces. For Rancière, proper recognition of the inaugural role played by the letter and human susceptibility to proliferating, errant, unauthorized, language is vital if a full and accurate account of the modern conception of democracy is to be given.

Conclusion

Like Benjamin's work on nineteenth-century French history, Rancière's historical and historiographical writing is difficult to place within existing categories and has tended to inspire mistrust and misunderstanding among professional historians. Sometimes this hostility can be accounted for, as I have suggested, by reference to the specifically French context of a long-running struggle between 'historians' and 'philosophers' since Aron. Sometimes, however, the hostility came from historians on the Left who felt, to cite Adrian Rifkin's account of the reason given by *History Workshop Journal* in 1979 for refusing articles by Rancière, that he had 'insulted the working class'.[108] Rancière's intellectual impulse in the historical writing I have examined in this chapter – which I have described as the fragmenting introduction of complication – does indeed reserve a special place for what a certain kind of Marxist-Leninist orthodoxy would term 'class traitors'. It implies a vision of how working-class consciousness develops which is very difficult to reconcile with the emphasis in politicized social history at the time on disclosing the solidarity of workers with one another and the development of their common and unified voice. Indeed all of Rancière's historical work after *La Parole ouvrière* (1976) was explicitly intended to contest the falsely homogenizing assumptions inherent in such a project by pointing to an influential minority of exceptional and hybrid figures such as the worker-poets or the bourgeois Saint-Simonians who wanted to be workers.

To say that the common purpose of the three phases of his historical and historiographical work is the fragmenting introduction of complication is perhaps just an elaborate way of saying that his work is 'critique', or in other words that its meaning depends on the body of work with which it is often in explicit, and sometimes implicit, dialogue. On occasions the reader may feel that Rancière overcorrects: in his concern to restore the agency of the individual human actor, he appears at least to sideline if not to discount altogether longer-term social, economic and geographical forces. Yet surely there are elements in the *Annales* approach which are worth preserving and which help us to understand some of the longer-term conditions, not of their own choosing, in which human subjects make their history? And how serious a danger in today's social history is the non-recognition of exceptionality in the past compared with that of the 'presentism' pervasive in our culture which occludes the difference of the past? At least, as Schöttler argues, the *Annalistes* and indeed Althusser took seriously the idea of this radical difference. Certainly Rancière's historical and historiographical interventions have to be understood, and are intended to be understood, in the light of their surrounding political and academic contexts, with which they are often engaged in polemical dialogue. The reader may accordingly regret that Rancière's work does not reflect more often, more explicitly and more *historically* on the relationship between his work and the context of its production. The question with which I end this chapter, in anticipation of Chapters 4 and 5, which examine his work on literature and aesthetics, is how the critique of overcontextualization which he mounts in *The Names of History* is to be squared with his broadly historicizing approach to literature and art.[109]

3

The Mature Politics

From Policing to Democracy

'Politics is not the exercise of power.'[1] This first of Rancière's 'Ten Theses on Politics' heralds an account of politics which is provocatively defamiliarizing: for what else could politics be but the exercise of power? This chapter explains the radical alternative vision of politics proposed in Rancière's later work through a critical analysis of what I take to be its four main elements: his opposition between politics and the 'police', his structural account of democratic politics, his theory of how political subjects come into being (political 'subjectivation') and his understanding of the aesthetic dimension to politics (his concept of the division or distribution of the sensory, *le partage du sensible*). This sequential mode of presentation is somewhat artificial because the four elements are closely interrelated in Rancière's work but I think it promises the safest route to clear understanding; the sequential treatment does mean, however, that much of the evaluation must be deferred until after the exposition of the four main elements. Unlike previous chapters this one moves relatively freely within and between the principal theoretical texts: the essays collected in the second French edition of *On the Shores of Politics* [1998], which date from 1986 to 1997, the major treatise, *Disagreement* [1995], and the 'Ten Theses' [1996]. The relationship between Rancière's political thought and the historical and philosophical context of its elaboration will be considered last of all.

Let me start by showing how the first element in Rancière's mature politics, the opposition between politics and what he calls 'the police', relates to the earlier work on politics and pedagogy

examined in Chapter 1. I noted there that 'Plato's lie' was Rancière's shorthand for his rejection of the founding justification for
the division of the city in *Republic* into a hierarchy of different
classes, each with different responsibilities and privileges. Unable
to come up with a more persuasive reason to explain to people why
they should stay in the place into which they were born, Plato suggests that the rulers have recourse to the myth of the three metals.
Plato's republic thus places a premium on people staying put, yet
its elaborate hierarchy cannot ultimately be justified in rational
terms; its rigid and autocratic social order rests on little more than
the preference of its architect and the credulity of its inhabitants.
Its hierarchical social order is contingent or arbitrary.

Joseph Jacotot's method of intellectual emancipation revealed
and exploited this contingency of the social order by demonstrat-
ing that for individual people things can be otherwise: people can
occupy different positions within the social division of labour from
the ones they do in fact hold. By showing what can be achieved by
presuming, declaring and verifying the intellectual equality of
student and teacher, the emancipating pedagogue demonstrated
that there was no reason why a locksmith should not read *Télémaque* or, for that matter, govern. Particular emphasis was placed
by Rancière on Jacotot's insistence that the emancipating pedagogue be resolutely 'intractable' in a bid to break down the resistance of the student who claims to be incapable yet who in reality
thinks that learning is not 'for them' and is thereby complicit in his
or her own oppression. But although the social hierarchy is ultimately contingent, in the eyes of Rancière's Jacotot it garners strong
support from the vested interests of educational institutions and
the self-limiting false modesty of the downtrodden. What the initial
success of Jacotot's experiments suggested was that the division of
labour and the associated social hierarchy rested much more on
personal intertia and institutional self-interest than differences in
innate ability or aptitude.

The concept of equality which lay at the foundation of Jacotot's
emancipatory pedagogy was seen, by him at least, as incommensurable with the social order: individuals could emancipate other
individuals but he denied, after the failure of a limited experiment
to do so on a small scale, that the method could ever be institutionalized. Equality and the social were held by Jacotot to be incompat-
ible almost as a matter of axiom: 'Every institution is an *explication*
in social act, a dramatization of inequality. Its principle is and
always will be antithetical to that of a method based on equality

and the refusal of explications.'[2] In Jacotot's own writing this conviction is backed by a dualistic metaphysics according to which the group or society functions by fundamentally different natural laws from the individual.[3] Although we can assume he does not share those commitments, Rancière agrees with Jacotot on the 'antagonistic' relationship between radical equality and the social order.[4] Yet unlike Jacotot, for whom this incommensurability marks the limit or terminus of his experiment in intellectual emancipation, Rancière takes this as the point of departure for his mature politics. Equality and the social order may be 'antagonistic' yet they can and they do collide, in rare moments of egalitarian politics in which the principle of equality interrupts and reconfigures the social order. The incommensurability of a contingent social order founded on inequality with a politics of equality which demonstrates that things could be otherwise becomes the first of the four main concepts of Rancière's mature politics: his ground-clearing distinction between politics and the 'police' order.

Politics and 'the police'

Rancière makes room for his alternative vision of politics by proposing that most of what is normally understood as politics be thought of as 'the police'. This includes the institutions and processes governing the organization and representation of communities, the exercise of power, the way social roles are distributed and the way that distribution is legitimated.[5] Rancière claims to be drawing here on an older and wider sense of the term 'police' than the familiar one of a repressive organ of state, one closer to that identified by Foucault in seventeenth- and eighteenth-century writings as almost synonymous with the social order in its entirety.[6] Yet despite his reference to Foucault's historical analysis and although Rancière claims that he will be using the term 'neutrally' and 'not pejoratively', to take him entirely at his word[7] and conclude that he is seriously proposing a neutral description would be to miss something important. The opposition between 'the police' and 'politics' and the renaming of most of what is normally thought of as politics as 'policing' is a *twisting* of the ordinary usage of both terms which blurs their 'proper' meanings and *dramatizes* the conflict between them. Twisting and dramatization are both characteristics of politics in Rancière's special sense, as we shall see, and so the opposition itself can be thought of as enactment of the political as Rancière understands it. And it is a twisting which also plays a game with the reader, which in its flagrant defiance of normal usage toys with his or her desire to correct, to 'police' the two terms of the opposition back to their proper meanings.

One response to the politics/police opposition would of course be to dismiss it as fanciful and attempt to restore, indeed to 'police', the terms to their 'proper' meanings; there are many who think that scholarly scrutiny should consist in precisely this sort of conceptual policing. Rancière, however, is working with a very different – more open, more creative, less 'disciplined' – view of what makes intellectual work significant. This is not a view he has settled upon merely for the sake of his own convenience but one which, as I showed in Chapter 1, emerged out of critical reflection on his experience as a once-compliant student of Althusser's:

> What were Althusser's seminars about – and what is many a seminar about? Concepts are *interrogated*, their *papers* are *checked*, they are questioned about their *identity*; those found straying without a passport beyond their *territory* are arrested, etc. [. . .] Identity checks, restraining orders [. . .] the extensive system of philosophy's policing imaginary for which Althusser is no more responsible than, in Marx's account, the capitalist is responsible for the relations of production which his existence upholds.[8]

There are many for whom this kind of assimilation of academic practice in the humanities with ideological policing epitomizes all that is wrong with the spirit of May '68: the resulting fear of doing violence to students' autonomy has left us, they would say, with teachers too anxious to teach and students too proud to learn.[9] Rancière's redescription of the structures and institutions of ordinary politics as 'policing' certainly reconnects with the sort of radical Maoist thinking legible in the above quotation, a scepticism which ironically and rather unfairly for Rancière tends to be remembered today as Althusser's legacy, notably in the theory of Ideological State Apparatuses he outlined in 1970, one year after Rancière wrote the first version of the article cited above.[10] But suppose we did try to police 'politics' and 'the police' back to their 'proper' meanings; we would then have to make a judgment about the extent of the police 'in the proper sense'. In Britain, which perhaps has the most immediately recognizable police officers of any country, and which in historical terms is the home of the modern police force, policing functions are now increasingly delegated to a wide range of other institutions: policing powers are routinely exercised by a wide range of less well-paid 'community support officers', local council workers and the like, who work alongside the police 'proper'. My point is that although Rancière's redescription of the institutions and structures of ordinary politics as 'the police' may seem far-fetched, what policing 'in the proper sense' is in today's world is by no means as straightforward a question as it may at first seem. Moreover, although Rancière seems to want to push away the ordinary meaning of the term 'police' by insisting that it is used 'neutrally' and that the men and women in uniform are just part of a much wider phenomenon, he could very easily have used a more neutral word had he so desired; by choosing to call the term antagonistic to politics 'police' he cannot avoid casting a sinister shadow of repression over the very notion of social hierarchy. His opposition between 'politics' and 'policing' does more than simply provoke us to reconsider what politics is; it also serves as a timely reminder to reflect on the slow creep of policing 'in the proper sense' into hitherto untouched areas of common life. Far from being a tired vestige of structuralism, the binary opposition between police and politics readily opens out on to a pressing contemporary discussion.

Let us turn now from 'policing in the proper sense' to Rancière's general concept of the police order. The hierarchizing and ordering work effected by this order is readily evoked by the adage 'a place for everything and everything in its place'. The police order assigns individuals to particular positions in society and assumes that their way of behaving and thinking will follow from their position: according to the police order, 'society consists of groups dedicated to specific modes of action, [of] places where these occupations are exercised, [of] modes of being corresponding to these occupations and these places.'[11] The police order expects a locksmith to think like a locksmith, which for that order means not really to think at all; similarly, if confronted by a worker who writes poetry, then it, like George Sand and other nineteenth-century bourgeois sponsors of the worker-poets, will expect him or her to write 'proletarian' poetry. The police order assumes that people have different capacities and are accordingly destined to occupy different positions in a hierarchy. The various institutions and processes of political life as we ordinarily understand it – parliamentary debate, elections, government – are thought to be just as much part of this ordering process which allocates individuals to particular places in the hierarchy. What this regulatory framework assumes is that society is a whole of which all the parts are already known – already named and counted – and have merely to be arranged in the most harmonious and productive way. What such an order specifically excludes is the possibility of a dispute over the very naming and counting of the constituent parts; we shall see that such a dispute, or 'disagreement', is for Rancière the very essence of politics.

Politics, in Rancière's sense as it is opposed to the police, occurs when people who appear to be unequal are declared to be equal and the regulatory work of the police order is shown to be arbitrary. Politics counters the police order by working to verify the presumption of equality, 'an assumption that, at the end of the day, itself demonstrates the sheer contingency of the order, the equality of any speaking being with any other speaking being'.[12] Politics offers 'the sudden [*brutale*] revelation of the ultimate *anarchy* on which any hierarchy rests'.[13] In other words politics seeks to demonstrate that since all are equal, anyone could in principle occupy a different position from the one they do in fact occupy, and shows accordingly that the hierarchizing work of the police order rests ultimately on 'an-archy', the absence of any foundational ordering principle, or *arkhe*. Politics embarrasses the police order by seeing through the imaginary garments of elaborate hierarchy which cover its naked contingency.

For all his emphasis on the scarcity of genuine egalitarian politics, Rancière's structural opposition implies that politics in this sense is always a possibility: things could always be otherwise. This does not mean that politics is in fact everywhere (it does not mean, as the slogan goes, that 'everything is political'), but rather that politics can be anywhere: it can potentially manifest itself at any time, for example in the context of a dispute over immigration and nationality, a strike by workers or an educational dispute.[14] Yet it also follows that none of these contexts or causes are intrinsically political in Rancière's sense.[15] Politics is a rare occurrence, much more so than we are accustomed to think. Politics is 'an activity of the moment and always provisional',[16] which not only interrupts the police order but reconfigures it for the better, as Žižek recognizes: 'The political act (intervention) proper [. . .] *changes the very framework that determines how things work.*'[17] I shall argue later that Rancière has more difficulty addressing the process by which the police order is reconfigured than he does the political moment which interrupts it. First, however, I must complete the theoretical picture by outlining the three remaining elements in Rancière's alternative account of politics.

Rancière's structural account of democracy: the 'wrong' and the miscount

So far it is clear that a lot of what is normally considered to be politics counts for Rancière instead as 'policing', but we know relatively little about what he thinks politics actually is, except that it involves 'active' equality. For Rancière all political struggles share a common structure, or form. Democracy for him is not just one form of political regime among others; it is the essence of politics in contradistinction to the police. For the source of this account of the essence of politics, Rancière looks back to the origins of democracy in ancient Athens.[18] Athenian democracy emerged after Solon's reforms of 594 BCE abolished enslavement for indebtedness.[19] This led to the emergence of a class of citizen called the *demos*, the people, whose members lacked any of the traditional attributes thought necessary for active involvement in the political process (wealth, birth or moral 'excellence'), yet who nevertheless claimed not only to participate in it on an equal footing with the rich, the well-born and the morally superior but to be the only source of sovereignty in the city. This usurpatory claim by the *demos* to govern is their response to the inaugural 'wrong' (*le tort* or *blaberon*) which the city does them by trying to reserve the right to govern to those with a traditional entitlement to do so, by saying that they do not 'count' in political life. Aristotle describes the members of the *demos* as those who 'had no part [share] in anything',[20] and it is in response to this 'wrong' which would reduce their political existence to nothing that they make the claim to be, in political terms, everything: 'The mass of men without qualities identify with the community in the name of the wrong that is constantly being done to them by those whose position or qualities have the natural effect of propelling them into the nonexistence of those who have "no part [share] in anything".'[21] The members of the *demos* are those the community tries to say have 'no share' in the process of government: as Rancière puts it in French, they are *les sans-part* (literally those 'without a share' in the community). Rancière thinks that this is a position within a structure which can and has been occupied by various different groups, including the poor in ancient Athens, the plebs in ancient Rome, the Third Estate in pre-revolutionary France and the proletariat.[22] In each case those whose share in the community is denied, who are 'wronged' by a status quo which refuses to recognize their political existence, respond in the name of equality that the only legitimate basis for the exercise of political power is 'the equality of anyone with anyone'. The assertion of equality, which is the same as the assertion by the *sans-part* of their existence, is for Rancière the essence of politics as opposed to the police and the very structure of democracy. The *demos* is

> an excessive part – the whole of those who are nothing, who do not have specific properties allowing them to exercise power. [. . .] Democracy is, properly speaking, the symbolic institution of the political in the form of the power of those who are not entitled to exercise power – a rupture in the order of legitimacy and domination. Democracy is the paradoxical power of those who do not count: the count of 'the unaccounted for'.[23]

The *demos*, or the *sans-part*, are thus in the difficult position of having no recognized existence within the social hierarchy of the police order: they do not count, they have not been counted. Their radical egalitarian claim seeks to highlight the contingency of this order's elaborate hierarchy, a hierarchy founded on a basic injustice, the fundamental 'wrong' of their non-recognition. Politics cannot be other than disputatious, the expression of a basic 'disagreement' or 'dissensus', because it is antagonistic towards a police order that recognizes neither the claim nor the existence of the *sans-part*, a police order which thinks it has counted all the possible members of the city and which accordingly assumes that 'there is no part [share] of those who have no part [share]' ('il n'y a pas de part des sans-part').[24] Before going on to examine the process by which the *sans-part* frame their disagreement and in so doing come into being as a political subject ('subjectivation'), I would like to put some flesh on these theoretical bones by examining two of the most developed of the illustrative examples Rancière gives of his understanding of politics which show the structural model in operation.

The first example is the story of the Aventine Secession of 494 BCE, first told by Livy writing some four hundred years later and retold by Pierre-Simon Ballanche in 1830. In a move which could be considered a forerunner of a general strike, the plebs withdrew from the city of Rome to the Aventine Hill, leaving only the small minority of power-holding patricians in a city which was accordingly unable to function. The move was in protest at the extreme concentration of power in the hands of the patrician minority. The patricians' emissary, Menenius Agrippa, told the plebs an allegorical story, which likened Rome to the human body, in an attempt to get them to return to the city. The limbs (the plebs) thought that the stomach (the patricians) was being supported at their expense without contributing anything useful to the whole so they stopped feeding it; as a result they in turn became weak. As a justification for the hierarchy, this trite little tale serves the same function as 'Plato's lie', the myth of the three metals.

What interests Rancière in Ballanche's retelling of the story is the latter's criticism of Livy for failing to see the event as anything other than a simple show of force by the plebs and political cunning by the story-telling patricians. Livy's account, according to Ballanche, shows the plebs as mutely disgruntled and, in the credence they give the allegory, gullible. Ballanche's crucial insight, according to Rancière, is that this is a struggle which bears on the very existence of the plebs as a political entity and the status of their grievances. In presenting the secession as a mere show of force by the plebs, Livy effectively adopts the perspective of the patricians, for whom the plebs are subservient animals rather than equal human beings and potential partners in government kept out of the political process within an arbitrary social order by a contingent accident of their birth. In Ballanche's retelling, much is made of the fact that the plebs make moves towards establishing their own city and political structure, with their own oracles and representatives, in which they are the source of sovereignty. They listen to Agrippa's allegory but afterwards ask for a formal agreement with the patricians. The secession is an example of politics in Rancière's sense because it is an interruption of the established order by a part of it which that order assumed 'had no part', the *sans-part* whose secession is not just a brutish revolt but a demonstration of their equality and their capacity for reason. To return to the terminology of Rancière's earlier work, this may be a revolt but it is political because it is a 'logical revolt', a revolt which involves a demonstration by the *sans-part* that they are just as capable of reasoning and argument as those who would rule over them and therefore that they deserve to participate in the city on an equal basis. Moreover, Ballanche's retelling highlights the true political significance of Agrippa's address to the plebs: it lies not in the facile allegory, which does not in any case bring about the end to the conflict, but rather in the fact that the plebs' withdrawal from the city forced Agrippa to address them in a way which presupposed their hitherto unrecognized existence as a significant entity. What Agrippa the emissary actually said matters far less in Ballanche's account; what matters is rather the significance of the fact that the plebs were sent an emissary in the first place, in other words they had behaved and were accordingly treated as though they were already participants in the political process.

For Rancière a very similar structural logic is in operation when the nineteenth-century revolutionary socialist Auguste Blanqui gives his profession as 'proletarian' during his trial in 1832. As the presiding judge remarked, this was not a recognized profession; what Blanqui's declaration designates is not an existing social group but rather 'the class of the uncounted that only exists in the very declaration in which they are counted as those of no account'.[25] What the term highlights, Rancière suggests, is the gap between the inequitable distribution of the social order and the equality of speaking beings. Like the *demos* in ancient Athens, the proletariat is the *sans-part*, those who are said to have 'no share' in the community. Like the *demos*, the struggle in the name of the proletariat will be a struggle which seeks to demonstrate the equality of those who were not counted as part of the social order. The structural logic by which the *sans-part* identify themselves with the whole of the social order in the name of the 'wrong' by which they were excluded is necessarily a matter of dispute and disagreement. The disagreement bears not just on the specific claim of the *sans-part* but also on the very existence of that subject as a subject.

Although Rancière sometimes uses language with legalistic overtones to describe the political struggle for recognition by the *sans-part*, for example by speaking of 'political litigiousness' over the 'wrong' of the miscount, one important feature of the dispute or disagreement in which politics consists is that it cannot be resolved by legal means alone, even if the law and statements of equality enshrined within it sometimes have a role to play.[26] Nor, as we shall see in a moment, is the dispute one which can be resolved by rational deliberation between the parties, even if rational argument can also have some role to play. In an important distinction, Rancière says that the 'wrong' cannot be 'resolved' or 'settled' (*régler*) but can be 'processed' (*traiter*): 'Political litigiousness reveals an irreconcilable difference which can nevertheless be processed.'[27] This 'processing' of the wrong involves the emergence and recognition of a subject. The nature of the struggle for recognition by the *sans-part* is examined in the next section.

Political 'subjectivation'

Politics, as Rancière understands it, is always disputatious or polemical. The dispute in question is not only over the content of specific claims but also, and at the same time, a struggle for recognition of the political existence of the disadvantaged party, a struggle for a 're-count' to redress the wrong of the miscount. So in the case of the proletariat:

> Before the wrong that its name exposes, the proletariat has no existence as a real part of society. What is more, the wrong it exposes cannot be settled [*ne saurait se régler*] by way of some accord between the parties. It cannot be settled [*il ne se règle pas*] since the subjects a political wrong sets in motion are not entities to whom such and such has happened by accident, but subjects whose very existence is the mode of manifestation of the wrong.[28]

Rancière calls this struggle for existence as a political subject the process of political 'subjectivation'.[29] It occurs when those who have no recognized part in the social order, the *sans-part* who do not 'count', who are invisible or inaudible politically speaking, assert their egalitarian claim, which is always also a collective claim to existence as political subjects. The process of subjectivation, as Rancière describes it, has three main characteristics: it is (i) an argumentative demonstration, (ii) a theatrical dramatization and (iii) a 'heterologic' disidentification. I shall consider each in turn.

The argumentative dimension to political subjectivation once again recalls the insistence in Rancière's historical work on *logical* revolt, on struggles which involve language and rational argument as much as they do force. In *On the Shores of Politics* he places an even stronger emphasis on the logical, or argumentative, character of revolt by referring to what he calls the 'syllogism' of emancipation.[30] As an example he gives a strike by Paris tailors, in 1833, in protest at their employers' refusal to entertain their demands for better pay, shorter working hours and improved working conditions. The major premise in the syllogism is provided by a clause from the preamble to the Charter of 1830, which resulted from the July Revolution: 'all the French are equal before the law'. In Rancière's analysis of the dispute there are three minor premises which all seem to contradict the major premise: first, in refusing even to entertain the workers' demands, the employers were not treating them as equal; second, confederations of workers and employers alike were illegal yet only the former were pursued by the authorities; third, no less a representative of the law than the public prosecutor gave a speech in which he asserted that workers were not equal members of society. While it would have been possible to conclude from this contradiction that the major premise, the equality declared in the Charter, had always been understood as a mere aspiration, this is not the approach adopted by the tailors. Instead their demand is that the major and the minor premises be reconciled, either by rectifying the inequalities described in the minor premises or by changing the major premise, the clause of the Charter, to something like 'not all the French are equal before the law'. The declaration of equality in the Charter and similar legal and political declarations of equality are thus for Rancière a powerful resource in struggles for a fairer society, but only if they are taken up confidently with a view to verifying them rather than regarded as overly optimistic aspirations or illusory misdescriptions of reality. Rancière is thus far from being a disillusioned sceptic about formal declarations of equality in legal and constitutional documents, unlike Marx, who famously saw the rights enshrined in the Declaration of the Rights of Man and the Citizen as merely an expression of the interests of the bourgeois property-owning class.[31] Rancière is not naïve enough to think such documents somehow magically produce the equality which they declare, but he does insist that they can serve as the basis for a practical verification of that equality, as part of a logical, argumentative, demonstration of the sort enacted by the tailors. Yet if there is certainly a rational, logical, element to politics as Rancière understands it, there is also rather more to it than just that: he thinks it is naïve to conceive of politics simply as a debate between subjects who disagree and negotiate over specific issues, a conception he attributes to Habermas.[32] This is because one of the subjects is 'wronged' in so fundamental a way as to place in doubt their very existence as a subject and their capacity to participate in the debate, such that their arguments tend not to be understood as rational arguments by the other party or parties. The severity of this disadvantage helps to explain why the *sans-part* must have recourse to the ruse of the theatrical, as well as sometimes to violence, to support their rational arguments.

The second characteristic of political subjectivation is, then, that it is 'theatrical' or spectacular. In the eighth of his 'Ten Theses', Rancière defines the anti-political action of the police order in terms of the denial of spectacle, the denial that there is anything to see. In so doing he reinterprets Althusser's famous characterization of ideology as interpellation. Althusser likened the way ideology takes hold of people to the response of the passer-by in the street who is hailed (or 'interpellated') by the police officer and recognizes himself or herself in that call. For Rancière, by contrast, the paradigm of the police order is provided not by the interpellative act of the officer who calls out 'Hey, you there!' but rather by another familiar gesture of ordinary policing, the instruction 'Move along now, there is nothing to see.' If the police order denies there is anything to see, politics creates spectacle: 'Politics, in contrast, consists in transforming this space of "moving-along" into a space for the appearance of a subject.'[33] Politics is thus creative and dramatic.

So intensely dramatic is Rancière's understanding of politics that Peter Hallward has described it as 'theatocracy'.[34] The term comes originally from Plato, who famously excluded theatre from his ideal city in *Republic*; not, as Hallward notes, because of the immoral content of the plays but rather because the theatre was dangerous as a place of semblance in which actors are doing two things and being two people at the same time.[35] Theatre challenges the metaphysical organizing principle of Plato's autocratic and hierarchical state, namely the principle of specialization according to which people can only do or be one thing. Theatre is connected to democracy because if actors can be themselves and someone else at the same time, then perhaps citizens can have a political existence in addition to their craft; perhaps the poor, whose one specialism is supposed to be the craft they exercise for the greater good, could also deliberate on affairs of state. In other words, perhaps one does not need to be an expert in politics, or in philosophy, in order legitimately to exercise power.

As well as this deep-level connection identified by Hallward with reference to Plato, there is a sense in which politics is axiomatically theatrical for Rancière because the emergence of the subject in subjectivation is always also an emergence into the realm of perception, of visibility and audibility: it is a manifestation. And political subjectivation resembles acting because both involve the ruse of pretending you are something you are not in order to become it: for the *sans-part* this means pretending you are already equal participants in the political process from which in fact, by virtue of the 'wrong' of the miscount, you are excluded. The strategic feigning by the *sans-part* is very similar to acting, as Rancière notes in his analysis of strikes of the 1830s, which imply 'a most peculiar [*très singulière*] platform of argument', a scene of equality which they must pretend exists already in order to create it: 'The worker subject that gets included on it as speaker has to behave *as though* such a stage existed, as though there were a common world of argument – which is eminently reasonable *and* eminently unreasonable, eminently wise and resolutely subversive, since such a world does not exist.'[36] So as well as being specifically 'theatocratic', politics for Rancière is, in a broader sense, creative or constructive in that it involves not only the manifestation of a new subject but the construction of a common space or 'scene' of relationality which did not exist previously. Moreover, in the initial requirement on the *sans-part* to act or feign, we can also discern a period of particular precariousness during which presumably their strategic 'pretence' to equality can be 'discovered' and they are especially vulnerable to being found out and policed back into their position of inequality.

The third dimension to political subjectivation is what, following Rancière's own rather elaborate description of it, I have called heterologic disidentification. This is the idea that political subjectivation always involves an 'impossible identification' with a different subject (*heteron*, in Classical Greek) or with otherness in general, the idea that subjectivation is never the straightfoward assertion of identity and always involves 'being *together* to the extent that we are *in between* – between names, identities, cultures, and so on'.[37] His two principal illustrations of the 'impossible identification' involved in subjectivation are given in the text of a lecture first given at a conference entitled 'Questioning Identity', in New York in 1991, 'Politics, Identification, and Subjectivization', and reiterated in the text of a lecture given in Paris at a conference on France and Algeria in 1995, 'La Cause de l'autre'.[38] The first example is of the impossible identification which was formative in the experience of his own generation of left-wing activists in Paris in the early 1960s: 'an identification with the bodies of the Algerians beaten to death and thrown into the Seine by the French police, in the name of the French people, in October 1961'.[39] To identify with those Algerians was impossible, yet neither was it possible to identify with the French in whose name they had been killed, and so, Rancière says, 'we could act as political subjects in the interval or the gap between two identities.'[40] The second example of an 'impossible identification' is what Rancière calls the 'assumption' of 1968, which was also a slogan, graffiti and a chant, 'We are all

German Jews.' This is a more complex example with multiple resonances.[41] However, it is clear that the identification in question is
also with a persecuted other and is 'impossible' at least in the sense
that most of the demonstrators in 1968 were not themselves German
Jews.

After presenting these two relatively thinly treated illustrative
examples, Rancière goes on in 'Politics, Identification, and Subjectivization' to stipulate that political subjectivation is never simply
the assertion of an identity but also the refusal of an identity
imposed by others, by the police order, and that it involves an
impossible identification which places the subject *between* given
identities.[42] In other words identitarian self-assertion is construed
not as politics but as policing. Rancière's emphasis on 'heterologic
disidentification' made sense in the philosophico-political moment
and location, New York, in which his 1991 paper was given: the
aim was, it seems, to articulate an account of politics in terms of
the emergence and self-assertion of hitherto unrecognized groups
while avoiding the pitfalls of US-style minoritarian identity politics. However, his emphasis on the other and the concept of otherness strikes me as an atypically compliant gesture towards the
dominant poststructuralist philosophical mood in the France of the
day, a mood novelist Joy Sorman has encapsulated with comic
matter-of-factness as comprising 'the rise of gloomy speechifying
[. . .] (the death of ideologies, etc.) and the importance of speaking
of the other'.[43] Indeed in his eagerness to distance himself from
'identity politics', Rancière's work is troublingly consistent with
the consensus of mainstream French republican universalism,
notoriously sensitive as this is to what it labels pejoratively as *le
communautarisme*.[44] If 'identity politics' is understood as the self-
assertion of a minority group gathered under the banner of a relatively stable shared identity, then it looks as though it cannot
qualify as politics in Rancière's radical alternative understanding
of the term. Yet this apparent wholesale relegation of identitarian
self-assertion to the police order is problematic, and I shall try to
explain why this is the case by referring to the example of queer
theory and activism.[45]

What distinguishes queer theory and activism from its anteced-
ents in gay and lesbian identity politics is a suspicion about the
nature and strategic usefulness of identity categories. Yet queer
theory has not been able simply to abandon or move unproblemati-
cally beyond these categories, even as it seeks to loosen their
hold, for the subject positions 'gay' and 'lesbian' continue to play

a powerful and sometimes violent role in our heterosexist societies. I am very reluctant to concede that such identity categories and all of the political projects associated with them can wholly and straightforwardly be ascribed to the logic of the police order. A few more conservative assimilationist projects and cultural manifestations evidently deserve to be, for example the already-too-much-discussed mainstream US television show and its syndicated derivatives in other countries, *Queer Eye for the Straight Guy*, which project to the world what purports to be an image of 'queerness' but in reality is the politically regressive one of entirely unthreatening middle-class, male, predominately white, American neoliberal consumerism.[46] Yet most other cases are far less clear-cut: there seems to me to be room for discussion even in the context of what many queer theorists take to be a straightforward example of conservative, assimilationist, identitarian politics, namely the demand for equal rights to the institution of marriage and the recognition of joint parenting and other family rights. Provided we attend carefully both to the often complex self-understandings of participants, as Jeffrey Weeks has argued, and to the precise political and national contexts in which the demand for equal rights to the insitution of marriage is articulated, as Eric Fassin has argued, then an arguable case can be made that gay and lesbian activist politics which draw on these relatively stable identity categories fall within the sphere of Rancierian politics.[47] In a qualified and context-specific way, such interventions can interrupt and reconfigure the police order by changing the relationship between the visible and the invisible and by bringing new subjects, new relationships and new understandings into political and social existence.

My plea for a more nuanced discussion and for careful scrutiny of the contexts in which particular identity claims are articulated echoes James Clifford's and Judith Halberstam's arguments for maintaining a critical understanding of identity politics which stops short of repudiation.[48] If queer activist projects which mobilize identity categories in framing a demand for equality must necessarily be relegated to the realm of repressive or regressive 'policing', as Rancière defines the term in opposition to egalitarian politics, then it may well be his assumptions about minoritarian identity politics which need revisiting. Seductive though Rancière's poststructuralist argument may have seemed in its day, that political subjects come into being only in the gap between identities, or in the 'heterologic fissuring' of identities and social roles which create temporary unstable 'mixed' subject positions, this cannot be allowed to mean that queer politics, to name one example, must altogether repudiate identity categories in social circulation before it can articulate its demand for equality.[49]

Although, in *Disagreement*, Rancière reiterates the insistence that politics involves heterologic disidentification, he is more cautious there about aligning identity categories with the police order and suggests that political subjectivation involves the 'transformation' of given identities.[50] This rather different emphasis allows for some minoritarian political struggles, with a critical and provisional investment in identity, to qualify as political in Rancière's sense. The key point, from his perspective, throughout this discussion of the role of identity in subjectivation, is that politics does not hinge on the properties of particular groups or communities but rather emerges from the universal principle of equality as it is put to work in the processing of particular wrongs. The principle of equality is that of the equality of 'anyone with anyone' and, as such, is an 'anonymous' requirement, one which seeks to transcend the particular attributes on the basis of which disadvantaged subjects find themselves excluded as the *sans-part*; indeed its power lies precisely in its insistence that such particularities should count for nothing. If Rancière's political thought of the early 1990s stands in danger of overcorrecting the faults of minoritarian identity politics, his account in *Disagreement*, which places more emphasis on the 'wrong' of the miscount than on heterologic disidentification, is more compatible with an identity politics with a provisional and self-critical investment in identity categories.

The aesthetic dimension of politics: the 'division' or 'distribution' of 'the sensory' (*le partage du sensible*)

One of the most distinctive features of Rancière's politics and a pivotal concept in his thought as a whole is the idea that politics has an 'aesthetic' dimension. By this he means not, in the first instance, that it is concerned with art or beauty, but rather that it has to do with perception and the sensory.[51] Part of what it means, for Rancière, to say that the *sans-part* are excluded from the sociopolitical order is that when they try to voice their grievances there is a tendency for their speech not to be heard as rational argument; one facet of the wrong of the miscount is that there is a presumption that no account will be taken of the complaints of the *sans-part*.

This does not just mean that these complaints are understood then disregarded, but rather, in a more fundamental sense, that they are not heard as meaning-bearing language. Similarly, the *sans-part*, prior to subjectivation, is invisible as a political subject. Rancière is not talking here about inaudibility or invisibility in a straightforward sense, nor is he talking about the kind of uncertainty that would give rise to doubt over whom is being referred to, to reference failure: 'Anyone can tell *who* is meant.'[52] It is a question instead of whether or not the group in question is thought to be capable of participation in the life of the community as a whole, a question of that group's share in 'the definition of the common of the community'.[53]

To become a political subject is to be heard and seen, and politics is the process of reconfiguring the ways in which subjects are heard and seen. Rancière refers in French to the way the community allocates certain kinds of share and concomitantly certain kinds of visibility or audibility to some but not to others as, in French, 'le partage du sensible', the 'division' or 'distribution' of 'the sensory'. The noun *le partage*, from the verb *partager*, meaning both to share out and to divide up, evokes simultaneously the sharing-out and the dividing-up of the sensory.[54] As Rancière has acknowledged, the concept is reminiscent of the transcendental argument as practised by Kant and 'revisited' by Foucault, in other words the argument which asks what conditions must necessarily obtain in order for x to be possible.[55] So this sharing-out and dividing-up can be understood in terms of

> the system of *a priori* forms determining what presents itself to sense experience. It is a delimitation of spaces and times, of the visible and the invisible, of speech and noise, that simultaneously determines the place and the stakes of politics as a form of experience. Politics revolves around what is seen and what can be said about it, around who has the ability to see and the talent [*la qualité*] to speak, around the properties of spaces and the possibilities of time.[56]

The way Rancière describes the possible positions in this division or distribution, as in his distinction here between 'speech' and 'noise', or in *Disagreement* between human speech or animalistic groaning, or being 'counted' and 'not counted', can sometimes make it seem as though political subjecthood were an on or off state admitting of no degrees. Yet it must follow from his account of political subjectivation as a process, one consisting in a 'series' of acts, that there is a range of intermediate positions.[57] Moreover, as

I indicated in the preceding section, there must be a period of particular precariousness during which the *sans-part* who is acting, or feigning, an equality unrecognized in the given state of things is vulnerable to being 'found out' by the police order and policed back into place. Rancière has less to say in his mature political theory about these intermediate phases of partial belonging and exclusion, of limited political subjecthood; however, as his own archival work made clear, especially *The Nights of Labor*, the intermediate positions invariably involve a tortuous interplay and infinitesimally fine balance between freedom and enslavement, between lucid self-knowledge and dreamy self-delusion. The clear-cut opposition between audibility as meaning-bearing language and animal noises is one which Rancière takes on from Aristotle's account of the origin of politics in the human capacity for language which allows for talk of justice rather than simply animalistic groaning or approbation. Rancière challenges Aristotle's account by showing that politics cannot simply be deduced from the capacity for language because the prior and properly fundamental question is always that of who, in any given social arrangement, is considered to have the capacity for language in the first place: in other words there are some subjects who are human but who are not treated as though they had the human capacity for language which they do in fact have. Yet although he successfully challenges Aristotle's account of the origins of the political, his own work tends to preserve the clear-cut opposition between human speech and animal noises. Élie During has usefully drawn attention to the range of intermediate positions determined by the political function of accent in speech: speech which is heard as accented can be understood as meaning-bearing while still serving to exclude its bearer from full recognition as a political subject.[58] In this section and the discussion below I am concentrating mainly on one side of Rancière's pivotal concept of the division of the sensory: the aesthetics of politics, or the sense in which politics is related to perception and the perceivable. I revisit the other side, the politics of aesthetics, in Chapter 5.

Overall assessment of Rancière's account of politics

Having examined sequentially what I take to be the four main elements of Rancière's radical alternative account of politics – the ground-clearing distinction between politics and the police, the structural account of democracy, the concept of political subjectivation and the exploration of the aesthetic dimension to politics – in this section I take these elements together as I discuss some of the questions the account as a whole raises.

What normative consequences follow from Rancière's view of politics? The sinister overtones of the term 'police', try as Rancière might to neutralize them, do suggest a normative requirement to engage in politics rather than policing. Yet Rancière makes one isolated but striking admission: 'The police can procure all sorts of good, and one kind of police may be infinitely preferable to another.'[59] Does it follow from Rancière's police/politics opposition that if you campaign for the fairer distribution of wealth through taxation, then the goal of what you may have considered your radical politics counts, in his terms, not as a political objective but as a commitment to a better kind of police order? It looks as though your desired outcome, a fairer distribution of wealth, is one which has to be thought of as a demand for a 'better police order', since questions of distribution are by definition matters of policing. Indeed it looks as though any campaign for a fairer or more equitable *end state* of any kind is, by definition, to be understood as a demand for a better police order. There seems to be a curious tension here between fairer end states which are, by definition, 'policing' and the processes by which those end states are arrived at, which, by definition, are 'political'. But is it not artificial to oppose the process and the end state towards which it tends? Rancière's work offers no explanation of the counterintuitive paradox it generates by placing the process of egalitarian politics in opposition to the end state of fairer distribution. This is a paradox which it would be easy not to notice because so little of Rancière's work is addressed to analysing the end state, the police order. Why is this?

Todd May in his interpretation of Rancière's politics seems comfortable with this partiality: he argues that Rancière is simply not interested in approaching the world philosophically, or politically, from the point of view of distribution and the distributors and that his work instead is 'addressed to' those disadvantaged in any given distribution or social arrangement and functions as an incitement to them to assume their equality and, in so doing, to interrupt that order.[60] May thinks that what is distinctive about Rancière's understanding of equality is that it is 'active' equality, in other words equality which the disadvantaged are not given but which they take, which they seize in a series of actions that disturb the social order and reconfigure it to better reflect the basic equality of speaking beings. In other words we are misunderstanding the police/politics opposition if we think it is intended as a descriptive or analytical tool; what the opposition, along with the rest of Rancière's politics, is trying to do in May's account is to approach the world from the perpective of those who are disadvantaged by the way things currently stand. May's interpretation makes a virtue out of what otherwise seems to be a marked one-sidedness in Rancière's account: his almost exclusive emphasis on the moment when politics interrupts the police order at the expense of the process by which that interruptive political moment is reabsorbed into the police order and reconfigures it.

May is undoubtedly right to emphasize the fact that Rancière is trying to approach the world from the perspective of the disadvantaged. Yet while this can be thought to express the ethical scrupulousness of an absolute fidelity to the struggles of the oppressed, as May would like to suggest, it also gives rise to both analytical and practical weakness. This was indeed Slavoj Žižek's main criticism of Rancière's politics: in focusing on the intermittent moments of political upsurge at the expense of the procesess by which they are reabsorbed into a police order which they reconfigure, Rancière's account neglects this vital second dimension of emancipatory politics.[61] Žižek has recently developed this charge by adding that this one-sidedness of Rancière's account allows him to avoid addressing the violence often involved in that process of reconfiguration.[62] Žižek also argues that Rancière's scrupulousness in remaining faithful to the oppressed means he fails to analyse the main obstacle to revolutionary change, namely the desire people have to be policed or mastered. Because Rancière's own theorization of politics fails to acknowledge this desire, Žižek suggests, it is itself subject to it. It is reliant on the police order it appears to want to repudiate or disrupt; it entertains 'an ambiguous attitude towards its politico-ontological opposite, the police Order of Being: it has to refer to it, it *needs* it as the big enemy ('Power')'.[63] Put most derisively, Žižek's charge is that Rancierian politics is an infantile 'game of hysterical provocation'.[64] For Žižek, who at the end of a long and approving discussion of Badiou's work concludes with this parting shot aimed implicitly at Rancière's account,

> The true task lies not in momentary democratic explosions which undermine the established 'police' order, but in the dimension

designated by Badiou as that of 'fidelity' to the Event: translating/ inscribing the democratic explosion into the positive 'police' order, imposing on social reality a *new* lasting order. *This* is the properly 'terroristic' dimension of every authentic democratic explosion: the brutal imposition of a new order. And this is why, while everybody loves democratic rebellions, the spectacular/carnivalesque explosions of the popular will, anxiety arises when this will wants to persist, to institutionalize itself – and the more 'authentic' the rebellion, the more 'terroristic' is this institutionalization.[65]

My first point in response is about the way in which this argument is framed. Žižek is right, of course, that Badiou has rather more to say about the process of inscription which follows the moment of revolt.[66] It is not clear, however, why that invalidates Rancière's analysis of the moment of political disruption. There seems to be a curiously asymmetrical assumption that because Rancière's account is more interested in some aspects of emancipatory politics than Badiou's, Rancière's, but not Badiou's, is therefore invalid because it is not a total account. In Rancière's (or Badiou's) defence, one is reminded of E.P. Thompson's rejoinder to an interviewer who implied that his work concentrated on cultural factors but neglected economics: 'I have comrades and associates.'[67] Although Rancière is now operating in a different intellectual and political climate from Thompson, one in which it may just about no longer be possible to speak of comrades, it should still be possible to acknowledge that the emphasis falls in a different place in Rancière's and Badiou's accounts of emancipatory politics – on interruption and inscription respectively – without seeking to champion one at the expense of the other.

Second, and more substantively, it is not clear on what grounds Žižek thinks that the mere fact that Rancière's concept of politics stands in structural opposition to the police order implies that it has a problematic, secret, dependency on that order or its principle, which in psychoanalytic terms Žižek expresses as the figure of the Master; Žižek presents no argument in support of his assertion that Rancierian politics '*needs*' the Master. The claim looks more like a psychoanalytically inspired universal paradox about contesting authority than an observation specifically about Rancière's theory: if in principle we all 'need', or indeed '*need*', the Master, then so, of course, do the agents described in Rancière's theory. *If.* Yet one of the distinguishing features of Rancière's account of emancipatory politics is precisely that it makes no reference to psychoanalytic concepts and, moreover, that it operates with a trust of the surface which sits uneasily with a psychoanalytic world-view of secret causes and hidden affinities; it seems contrary, to put it mildly, to try to drag it back within a psychoanalytic frame without giving a compelling reason for doing so and arguing the point. Moreover, one of the striking things about the *sans-part* in the examples of political subjectivation discussed by Rancière is their calm determination, which hardly fits Žižek's characterization of Rancière's as a politics of hysterical provocation. In the example of the tailors' strike of 1833, for instance, the calm determination with which the strikers reason their way through the 'emancipatory syllogism' has none of the feel of the kind of anxious and needy relationship to the Master which Žižek imputes to the agents in Rancière's account. Even if the equanimity and affective detachment of Rancière's disadvantaged subjects are somewhat perplexing, what he says of their disposition does not square with the mischaracterization of his politics presented by Žižek. There is no basis, other than as a matter of general psychoanalytic dogma, for asserting that Rancierian politics, specifically, is secretly dependent upon the order which it disrupts.

If Žižek fails to persuade that politics, as Rancière understands it, is perniciously dependent on the order it appears to interrupt, he is right to sense that Rancière undertheorizes the police order. Although Todd May's interpretation appears to offer Rancière a way out by arguing that his account is 'addressed to' the disadvantaged, this reluctance to probe the police order is still problematic because it means Rancière remains silent on what will inevitably be key points in any real struggle. When the process of political subjectivation is successful, from the point of view of the *sans-part*, why exactly does the police order suddenly accept their logical-theatrical demonstration of equality? How and why do struggles for subjectivation succeed? Without an analysis of the moment when the *sans-part* emerges into the daylight of recognition and presumably, in so doing, ceases to be the *sans-part*, Rancière's account is missing a crucial element.[68] It may well be that there is no general answer to the question of what makes a police order give way in the face of any particular attempt at subjectivation because all concrete conflicts are different. Yet it should still be possible to spell out, as a matter of general tendencies, the relationships between types of police order, types of subjectivation and types of logical-theatrical demonstration; in other words it should be possible to systematize the insights presented in Rancière's account in such a way as to render it more readily exploitable by the disadvantaged in particular situations.

If Rancière shies away from analysing the moment when the *sans-part* gains recognition, his account also has too little to say about the pernicious yet potentially galvanizing effects of non-recognition on the *sans-part*. While there is a coherence to the inter-related notions of being excluded from the count and the 'aesthetic' properties of being inaudible and invisible in political terms, Rancière does not appear to be interested in the powerful affective dimension which is usually involved in the experience of non-recognition. It may be partly an effect of his use of legalistic language, but Rancière's analyses of the wrong and the miscount often seem unduly rationalistic and to ignore this dimension. More importantly perhaps, they also ignore the role which affect may play as a motive force for subjectivation. Where Rancière does talk about affect is in the negative context of the 'passion' for unity which, for him, defines the politics of the French radical Right; yet affect rarely enters into his positive discussion of egalitarian politics.[69] Some insight into the affective dimension to non-recognition and the positive role these emotions can play in motivating the struggle for subjectivation is provided by the work of philosopher Axel Honneth.[70] I shall now briefly outline the way in which Honneth's work develops this undertheorized dimension of Rancière's mature politics.

Honneth's theory of recognition presupposes that there are certain core qualities which are indispensable for a liveable human life, and calls these self-confidence, self-respect and self-esteem.[71] These are modes of self-relation which are nonetheless acquired and developed intersubjectively, through being granted recognition by others who in turn are recognized. When mutual recognition breaks down, subjects are vulnerable to experiencing what Honneth calls 'disrespect' (*Mißachtung*), forms of exclusion which can range from being pointedly ignored, through insult to physical violence. Disrespect and its associated moral categories, such as humiliation, 'are used to designate behaviour that represents an injustice not simply because it harms subjects or restricts their freedom to act, but because it injures them with regard to the positive understanding of themselves that they have acquired intersubjectively'.[72] From the perspective of the *sans-part*, the experience Rancière describes of the 'wrong' of non-recognition, of being excluded from the count, must presumably involve feeling 'disrespected'. It may sound trivializing to speak of hurt feelings in the context of emancipatory politics, yet there are few examples of emancipatory political projects (except perhaps the ones Rancière describes, as he describes them) which do not involve intense emotions on the part of the dispossessed. Honneth's account is useful because it not only refocuses attention on this dimension of exclusion and so corrects Rancière's tendency to overlook it, but it also allows these emotions to be a cognitive response to the reality of injustice which can in turn motivate the struggle for redress. In other words, affect is not the froth on serious concerns but rather an integral part of the experience and knowledge of the wrong and the struggle for political subjectivation. This supplements Rancière's account and counteracts the tendency in his work to attribute to agents in the struggle for political subjectivation an implausible degree of emotional detachment. I am certainly not suggesting, however, that 'hurt feelings' can take the place of the argumentative and theatrical aspects of subjectivation that Rancière outlines. Honneth himself makes clear that the feelings alone are not enough: the feelings engendered by 'disrespect' can only translate into resistance or struggle 'if subjects are able to articulate them within an intersubjective framework of interpretation that they can show to be typical of an entire group'.[73] In that more internalized process of interpretation the notion of equality will presumably figure prominently, just as it does in the staging of the argumentative-theatrical demonstration central to Rancière's account.

If Rancière's characterization of the agents struggling for subjectivation tends to mute the affective intensity of their experience, as I mentioned it has also been suggested by Žižek that his account underplays the violence or indeed 'terror' sometimes involved in their struggles for political subjectivation.[74] If subjectivation involves rational argument, it always also involves force, though not necessarily violence in the literal sense. This is because the discussion that takes place is not a disagreement between equal parties disagreeing about particular claims but a disagreement over recognition of the political existence of one of the parties.[75] In the case of the 1833 tailors' strike, Rancière notes that the rational argument presented by the tailors in their construction of the emancipatory syllogism recalled the history of forceful uprising with which it is intertwined:

> the reasonable arguments of the strikers of 1833 were audible, their demonstration visible, only because the events of 1830, recalling those of 1789, had torn them from the nether world of inarticulate sounds and ensconced them by a contingent forced-entry [*effraction*] in the world of meaning and visibility. The repetition of egalitarian words is a repetition of that forced-entry [. . .].[76]

The word 'effraction', which does indeed mean 'forced entry', carries something of the violence of a revolutionary tradition which had already, to a limited extent, succeeded in reconfiguring the division of the sensory to allow the speech of the tailors and others like them to be heard. Yet this acknowledgement by Rancière of the violent undertones to the strikers' action is selective in that the reference to 1789 side-steps the real violence of the Revolution, which took place during the Terror (1793–4).[77] While I am not suggesting that the power of the declaration of equality in the strike of 1833 rests solely or even mainly on the Terror, it is implausible to suppose that it could have evoked the Revolution's reconfiguration of the sayable and the visible without also recalling its most violent phase. So while it would be unfair to say that Rancière avoids the issue of violence altogether, his treatment of this example is indicative of a reluctance fully to accept its role in the struggle for subjectivation.[78]

So far I have discussed Rancière's mature politics without referring to the historical, political and philsophical context of its elaboration in the late 1980s and early 1990s. I would like to conclude this chapter by briefly describing and assessing its dialogue with this context. Rancière's political work is responding to two countervailing pressures. In global terms, the collapse of many Communist regimes in, or shortly after, 1989 inspired triumphalist philosophical and political commentators to declare the 'end of history' and the 'end of politics'. In France, simultaneously, a resurgence of interest in political philosophy, particularly by neo-Aristotelians and followers of Hannah Arendt, went hand in hand with the idea that 'ideological' (emancipatory) questions could be put aside and the political rethought in ethical terms of how best to 'live together'. Rancière's determination, in *Disagreement*, to refute Aristotle's assumption that the political could be deduced from the properties of human beings (language and the power to reason) is motivated, in no small measure, by the popularity of neo-Aristotelian conceptions of politics at the time. Indeed Rancière goes much further than to attack a single philosopher's conception of politics and sets his sights instead on political philosophy as a whole, which he argues is fatally flawed and inherently conservative because it is unable to accept and think through the consequences of the basic fact that any given social order is contingent. Political philosophy, Rancière suggests, cannot help but always be looking for the most rational social arrangement; what it fails to see is that any and every social arrangement is inherently irrational and ultimately contingent. Rancière indeed goes so far as to suggest that the longstanding ambition of political philosophy is to dispense with politics altogether.

The intellectual mood-music of the 1990s, with this talk of the 'end of politics' and the return to political philosophy, was a fitting accompaniment to a trend Rancière had already discerned operating in French politics since at least the early 1980s: the growth of the idea that the aim of politics is consensus. Consensus, according to Rancière, in another characteristically emphatic reversal, is not the aim but rather the negation of politics: 'consensus politics' is effectively the transformation of politics into management, a transformation which Rancière also associates with the increasing power of élites of experts trained to undertake this managerial task.[79] The most fundamental feature of 'consensus politics', however, is its presupposition that there is prior agreement on the 'count' of the parties to any political discussion and the ways in which they count. In other words consensus politics – like all anti-political doctrines – says that 'there is no part of those who have no part'.[80]

One of the paradoxes of contemporary political discourse with which these concepts of Rancière's wrestle is that of modern democracies which think they have counted everyone, including the excluded.[81] Rancière's work invites us to entertain a certain scepticism towards the discourse of 'social exclusion', which may seek precisely to name and allocate the *sans-part* to a position within the social or police order and thus block their own attempts to make a political claim to equality. There is no doubt that positive benefits can be produced by the discourse of social exclusion; a society which entertains such a discourse may well be an example of one of Rancière's 'infinitely better' police orders. Yet the tendency inherent in such discourse is still towards a pre-emptive depoliticization of the claims to equality which could be voiced by the *sans-part*. Question it though I have, Rancière's uncompromising emphasis on politics at the expense of the police order does serve as a critical counterweight to the assumption in modern liberal democracies that every part has been counted and allocated; rather than encouraging us to plan for and institute better forms of social arrangement, Rancière reminds us that no social arrangement is likely to be good enough, that every social arrangement is in principle open to disruption by egalitarian politics.

4

Literature

Rancière may be critical of the tendency among professional historians to overhistoricize, as we found in Chapter 2, yet he is no less mindful of the different dangers posed by the opposite failing among literary critics. His account of literature and his readings of individual texts are disarming because they cut across many of the conceptual distinctions and periodizations which have become the stock-in-trade of teachers, students and other readers of literature. Neither modernism nor postmodernism is considered an especially useful notion and a number of long-established oppositions in nineteenth- and twentieth-century literary history and theory, for example between realism and Romanticism, or between 'pure' and 'committed', or political, literature, are held to be conceptually interdependent consequences of a single cataclysmic moment around the turn of the nineteenth century when, the claim is, 'literature' as we know it today came into being.

   Yet for Rancière the historically specific cultural construct 'literature' is only one part of a larger picture; he is interested, at the same time, both in the way in which literature continues to be haunted by the system which it superseded and in the relationship between literature, what he takes to be the transhistorical practice of writing (*écriture*), and the disturbance which he thinks it engenders in human individuals and communities, a disturbance he terms 'literarity' (*la littérarité*). This chapter will explain and analyse Rancière's account of the historically specific concept of literature and its relationship to the institutions and practices it superseded, as well as to 'writing' and 'literarity'. This chapter will show how

Rancière's account is elaborated in a series of vigorous rereadings of canonical works of nineteenth- and twentieth-century French literature and will focus in particular on his readings of Flaubert and Mallarmé. It will conclude by evaluating his complex reconceptualization of the relationship between literature and the political.

'What is literature?'

Rancière begins his most substantial, but still untranslated, theoretical work on literature to date, *La Parole muette: essai sur les contradictions de la littérature* (1998), or *Mute Speech: Essay on the Contradictions of Literature*, with a display of studied incomprehension in the face of prominent literary theorist Gérard Genette's desire to brush aside the question 'What is literature?', one posed perhaps most famously by Jean-Paul Sartre. Rancière concludes the same work with an insistence that it is in the nature of literature, as a 'sceptical art', for its nature to be in doubt, for it to be in question.[1] In the intervening pages he argues that the concept of literature is comprised of a set of constitutive contradictions. These contradictions can, the suggestion is, be traced back to the moment a little over two centuries ago when the age of literature, in which we still live, superseded the age of representation.

The first element of Rancière's answer to Sartre's, or literature's own, question is simple: as we know it today, literature came into being at the beginning of the nineteenth century in the 'paradigm shift' effected by early German Romanticism (*Frühromantik*).[2] The idea that the concept of literature emerged at the end of the eighteenth century was already well established in Marxist literary criticism, notably in the work of Raymond Williams and Pierre Macherey.[3] While they were concerned mainly with describing how literature emerged from interconnected social, economic and aesthetic changes over the course of the eighteenth century, Rancière is less explicitly concerned with social conditions. Although the notion of a shift from representation to literature is not unique to Rancière, he presents a detailed working-through of the relationship between the new principles of literature and the old rules of representation, as well as of the consequences of internal contradictions within the new principles.

Jean-Luc Nancy and Philippe Lacoue-Labarthe had argued in *The Literary Absolute* [1978], their edition of key texts of early

German Romanticism, that what members of that movement had invented and been the first to theorize was the overarching conception of literature with which we are still living, literature as the art of writing in an absolute sense.[4] In place of a neo-classical poetics of representation, which was comprised of classificatory principles for the division of written works into different genres and sub-genres and which stipulated normative principles for how works in each category should represent their subject-matter, the German early Romantics conceived of an overarching art of writing as such, literature. Nancy and Lacoue-Labarthe argued that even though the German early Romantics often used words other than 'litera-ture' (including 'novel', 'work' and 'poetry'), what they intended was in fact this new all-embracing concept of literature in the abso-lute sense.

Although the influence of Nancy and Lacoue-Labarthe's work is acknowledged, Rancière's analysis of the end of representation and the birth of literature takes a very different approach to the same questions. His point of departure is Victor Hugo's novel *The Hunchback of Notre-Dame* [1831], and the attack levelled against it by one hostile contemporaneous critic. Ingeniously, Rancière works backwards from a deep reading of the novel and its reception to a reconstruction of the conventions of the age of representation. Hugo's novel, Rancière argues, is emblematic of the shift from the age of representation to the age of literature. Rancière notes, as others have before him, that the central character of Hugo's novel is less the hunchback and more the cathedral named in the original French title, *Notre-Dame de Paris*: while a story of various human characters is certainly told, it is as though they and their endeav-ours were emanations from the stony substance of the building itself. Rancière concludes that the novel rides roughshod over the neo-classical poetic conventions of the age of representation, inher-ited from Aristotle, according to which the subject of a work of art should be an arrangement of human actions. In that paradigm, from the nature of the human beings represented and the kinds of circumstances in which they find themselves was supposed to flow 'appropriate' language. In Hugo's novel, however, because the central subject is a cathedral and because the idea of a kind of language appropriate to a cathedral is incoherent in terms of the poetics of representation, language is liberated from its depen-dence on the subject and does itself take centre stage. Language becomes the subject, or matter, of the work rather than merely the transparent medium of reference to a represented subject.

In the reconstruction of the poetics of representation, which Rancière develops by working backwards from Hugo's novel, there are four main principles. First, the principle of fiction: a poem is an imitation, a representation, of actions (as distinct from actions themselves). Second, the generic principle: the genre of the work (epic or satire, tragedy or comedy) depends on the nature of what is represented, in other words above all on the social standing of the characters in question and the nature of the activities in which they are involved. From this second principle follows directly the third, that of 'appropriateness' (*convenance*) in a specifically social sense: the expectation that characters' accomplishments and failures, their qualities and their defects, be suited to their position in the social hierarchy and the social contexts in which they find themselves – shepherdesses, for example, must speak and act as shepherdesses are thought to do. Rancière asserts that it is this principle of appropriateness in a social sense which is the cornerstone of French poetics of the sixteenth, seventeenth and eighteenth centuries rather than the often-cited principles of the 'three unities' and catharsis.[5] Thus in Voltaire's commentaries on Corneille's plays, Rancière maintains that 'the fault is always found to lie in a lack of appropriateness'.[6] He argues that it is clear from these commentaries that the principle of appropriateness implies that the playwright, the character and the members of the audience are on an equal plane as individuals of a certain social standing whose sphere of action is language. Moreover, one reason for going to see a play for such a person would have been to learn how to speak better. And this leads Rancière to the fourth and last element in his reconstruction of the poetics of the age of representation, that of language as action, 'the ideal of word as deed' ('l'idéal de la parole efficace').[7] In other words, the play, the playwright and the audience are assumed to inhabit a world in which social standing and agency were closely allied to rhetorical ability.

The 'cosmological change' which the transition from representation to literature constituted can be understood, Rancière suggests, as the term-by-term reversal of the four principles of representational poetics which he has identified (see the table opposite – invidious though tables are).[8] Rancière suggests that Hugo's novel was emblematic of the collapse of the old poetics of representation in which the work was a well-constructed story of men of action who explained themselves in pleasing and, above all, appropriate language. The subject of Hugo's novel is a cathedral and to the extent that it has a genre at all, as a novel, this genre is what

Rancière calls 'a false genre, a genre that is not one'; in other words, the novel is not a genre in the old (representational) sense of a distinct kind of writing determined by its subject-matter.[9]

Representation	Literature
. . . is fiction, i.e. an imitation or representation of actions	. . . is language
. . . is of a genre determined by its subject	. . . lacks genre (all subjects are equal)
. . . is characterized by words and deeds that are 'appropriate' to the represented subject	. . . is characterized by the independence of style and subject
. . . is governed by the ideal of the spoken word as deed	. . . is based on the model of writing

The changes undergone by the work of verbal art in the shift from the age of representation to that of literature will later be theorized by Rancière as part of a wider movement across all the arts, as we shall see in the next chapter, a shift from the age, or as he will prefer to say the 'regime', of representation to what he will call the 'aesthetic regime of art'. Under the aesthetic regime of art, in the vanguard of which is literature in the historically specific sense, the work of art is conceived as adhering to 'a specific regime of the sensible, which is extricated from its ordinary connections and is inhabited by a heterogeneous power, the power of a form of thought that has become foreign to itself'.[10] In other words the work of art under the aesthetic regime, in the age of literature, is thought alienated in matter and which, in turn, alienates matter. So the new work of literature must be understood as thought alienated in the material stuff of language. As it happens, the novel of 'Hugo the innovator', with its stony material protagonist, the cathedral, is almost too good an example of the new work of verbal art and encapsulates the transition far more neatly than would any other contemporaneous novel with a human main character.[11] It is probably for this reason that Rancière says that the novel is 'emblematic' of the new work of art rather than that it is merely an example of it.[12] This emblem is *doubly* exemplary, a 'super-example': for the new work of art resembles the cathedral itself in the sense that it is thought alienated in the stuff of language (or stone, or painting), just as the cathedral is thought alienated in the architecture and the ornamental carvings. Hugo's novel is thus not only

itself an example of the new work of art but also takes as its subject
a building which *resembles* the new work of art. Leaving aside the
complexity of this emblematization, the main point is that, like the
cathedral, the new work of art is a monument in language which
is self-sufficient rather than a representation, or imitation: 'it makes
no reference to any system specifying the appropriateness of the
representation to the subject. It builds, from the material substance
of words, a monument. We have simply to appreciate the magni-
tude of its proportions and the profusion of its figures.'[13]

The trouble is that the new work of art, of which *Notre-Dame* is
the consummate embodiment, this anti-representational 'monument' which aspires to self-sufficiency, is built out of ordinary
language which, according to the third principle of the new poetics,
has no necessary relation to its subject. Rancière's reconstruction
of the four principles of the old poetics and their reversal into those
of the age of literature thus provides him with two important elements for his argument on literature: foremost among the 'contradictions' of literature is the productive tension between the first
and third principles of its new poetics. The idea that the substance
of the work of art is language is difficult to reconcile with the idea
that style and subject-matter are independent of each other: 'If
poetry and art are forms of language and thought, they cannot be
subject to the principle of indifference. Language is art in so far as
it articulates a necessary relationship [. . .] between thought and its
object. It ceases to be when this relationship is one of indifference.'[14]
Unlike Hegel, Rancière does not declare this to be an irresolvable
incompatibility which invalidates the new poetics, but sees it rather
as a structuring contradiction which defines literature in the historically specific sense and which has conditioned debate about its
norms and value ever since: 'The history of "literature" is the con-
tinual replaying of the drama of this problematic compatibility.'[15]
If the new work of art is, in essence, language rather than a representation, a monument rather than an imitation, but if the choice
of language or style is in principle entirely independent of the
subject, what is to stop this supposed monument being an entirely
arbitrary confection? What is to stop the author arranging any old
words any old how? Is such a conception of an artwork coherent?
Is there anything to distinguish a work of this kind from ordinary
everyday speech as the utilitarian medium of social transactions,
what Mallarmé called 'l'universel reportage'?

In short, Rancière's answer is that not only is there is no way of
finally resolving this paradox, but moreover that it is constitutive

of literature: what the works by Hugo, Balzac, Flaubert, Mallarmé and Proust which he reads try to do is to respond to this paradox in their own singular ways. Literature, for Rancière, as Hector Kollias observes, is in essence 'agonistic': it is a struggle with this constitutive paradox.[16]

In the remainder of this chapter I shall argue that what is remarkable about Rancière's analysis is perhaps less his not unprecedented conception of literature as struggle and more his attempt to revalorize, politicize and reposition the traditionally scorned and externalized second term, namely the ordinariness of ordinary written language against which the work of literature struggles to define itself as art. Rancière's analysis suggests that ordinary written language is fundamentally allied with democracy, and he will argue that although the work of verbal art struggles to distinguish itself against the ordinariness of that ordinary language, in so doing it *carries* the democratic promise inherent in the wayward formlessness of ordinary writing.

Writing, 'literarity' . . . and literature

Rancière describes written language (*écriture*), in a transhistorical sense, by contrast with literature in the historically specific sense outlined in the preceding section, as 'an-archic': it lacks an *arkhe*, or ordering principle.[17] What he means by this becomes clearer in the course of his reading of a short section from Plato's *Phaedrus*, which presents a myth about the origins of writing, a dialogue which is also the main focus of Jacques Derrida's celebrated earlier essay 'Plato's Pharmacy' [1972].[18] After recounting what is presented as a myth of the origins of writing in ancient Egypt, Socrates offers the following commentary:

> There's something odd about writing, Phaedrus, which makes it exactly like painting. The offspring of painting stand there as if alive, but if you ask them a question they maintain an aloof silence. It's the same with written words: you might think they were speaking as if they had some intelligence, but if you want an explanation of any of the things they're saying and you ask them about it, they just go on and on for ever giving you the same single piece of information. Once any account has been written down, you find it all over the place, hobnobbing with completely inappropriate people no less than with those who understand it, and completely failing to know who it should and shouldn't talk to. And faced with rudeness and

unfair abuse it always needs its father to come to its assistance, since it is incapable of defending or helping itself.[19]

Derrida and Rancière agree that only a naïve reading would see this as a blanket condemnation of written in favour of spoken language; a straightforward condemnation of this sort would, after all, be incongruous in a written dialogue.[20] As David Bell has noted, Rancière's reading of this passage is more directly political than Derrida's: Rancière focuses on the way in which writing is said to be found 'all over the place' and to mix with 'completely inappropriate people'.[21] What he takes from Plato is the idea that there is something intrinsically anarchic, or democratic, about writing: it is a form of language which makes no distinction between those to whom it 'should' and those to whom it 'should not' speak.[22] Writing is promiscuous and lawless whereas spoken language is a facet of controlled, hierarchized, social situations.

The stark contrast between speech and writing, as Rancière characterizes it in Chapter 6 of *La Parole muette*, leaves room for doubt about the treatment of more complex examples. Presumably recorded speech, for instance, could be thought, under certain circumstances, to function in the same way that writing does: a digital recording of a lecture posted as a podcast on a website, for example, assuming enduring equality of access to electronic resources over time (a big but a conceivable assumption), would surely be 'anarchic' in exactly the same way as writing is without being writing in the ordinary sense. Although his way of proceeding is not to contemplate such limit cases, Rancière is careful to insist that there is more to the contrast between speech and writing than the common-sense understanding of both terms would suggest and careful to allow for the possibility of spoken language which functions as writing does in this respect.[23] The limit case is helpful because it suggests that what may really be at stake in the contrast between speech and writing is the degree of availability for reappropriation of the language in question: language is anarchic or democratic if, in principle, it is available to be reappropriated by anyone. This availability seems in turn to be conditioned both by the degree of fixity of the language in question and the capacity of those in a given society to gain access to it. Although Rancière is not especially concerned with such matters in the context of his discussion of writing, presumably here questions of literacy, both in the basic sense of the capacity to make sense of written characters and in the extended sense of reading competence, would be relevant, as would repressive social practices such as censorship. It is 'availability' (*disponibilité*) for reappropriation which is the crux of the contrast between speech and writing in Chapter 6 of *La Parole muette*, where Rancière remarks that: 'The specific form of visibility and availability proper to written language disrupts any notion that the discourse could legitimately belong to the source of its enunciation, or be destined for the person who in fact receives it, or determine the ways in which it should be received.'[24] My suggestion is therefore that in order to qualify as writing for the purposes of Rancière's account, what is required is that the language in question be available for reappropriation – in a relatively stable form which is accessible over time – but not that it necessarily be traced in characters on a page. So 'writing' in Rancière's sense could in principle exist in oral cultures: a set of fixed social rules or laws to which members of the culture could appeal would be an example.

The relative stability of writing, as opposed to speech, in a form independent of its initiator, the 'father' from whom Plato says it has been 'orphaned', is what makes it 'available' for reappropriation. For Rancière the fact that it is available for reappropriation by anyone, in principle if not always in practice, makes it not only indifferent to social hierarchy but actively disruptive of the kind of harmonious social order, first envisaged by Plato in *Republic*, in which individuals of each caste stick to their allotted roles and activities. It is in this sense that 'writing' is lawless, anarchic or democratic. The 'disturbance' or 'disordering' (*dérèglement*) which 'writing' produces in individuals and communities is what Rancière terms 'literarity' (*littérarité*).[25] We are 'literary' animals in the sense that we are susceptible to being disrupted, to deviate from our natural course, under the influence of writing: 'Man is a political animal because he is a literary animal who lets himself be diverted from his "natural" purpose by the power of words.'[26] Similarly, human communities are 'literary' in the sense that they are forged and shaped, but more often riven and destroyed, by the disordering effects of writing which Rancière terms 'literarity'.[27]

It is rather unfortunate that Rancière's chosen term for his transhistorical concept of the disruptive effect of writing is 'literarity' (*littérarité*), because of the confusion this encourages, and which he has recently sought to dispel, with the same or a very similar term employed by translators of Roman Jakobson (rendering his *literaturnost* with either 'literarity' or 'literariness') and taken up later by some Structuralist critics to mean the property which makes a

given work a work of literature, literature: the 'essence of literature', which for Jakobson lay in poetic language.[28] However, the
important feature of Rancière's account is not the term 'literarity'
but the underlying notion, namely that writing disrupts the settled
social order by virtue of its 'anarchic' tendency to 'speak to anyone'.
Writing will speak to the worker just as readily as it will speak to
the philosopher-ruler of Plato's *Republic*: unlike speech, which is
discriminating, writing is, in principle, open to be reappropriated
by anyone, irrespective of their allotted social role or standing; in
this sense it is allied with democracy.

One striking feature of Rancière's concept of 'literarity' is the
extent to which, like Socrates in *Phaedrus*, he too endows the written
word with a kind of agency normally reserved for human beings.
Rancière often describes writing as both 'mute' and 'talkative' and
frequently insists on its errancy, its tendency to wander waywardly:
'it sets off anywhere at all [*elle s'en va rouler n'importe où*], without
knowing to whom it should and should not speak.'[29] It could be
said that these are merely figurative expressions, taken up from
Plato's dialogue, which have little bearing on the underlying argument. In *Phaedrus* these personifications of the letter do indeed do
little or no conceptual work, but is the same true of their role in
Rancière's account? There are three aspects to the Platonic personification of writing, which Rancière adopts, and I shall examine each
in turn: its speaking, its wandering (or errancy) and its status as
'fatherless' or 'orphaned'.

The first element in the personification can be quickly dispensed
with: in reality, of course, writing does not speak – human beings
read it in specific circumstances – yet this is patently a mere figure
of speech. The second element in Rancière's personification of
writing, the errancy of the letter, is more problematic: writing
'wanders' and makes no distinction between those to whom it
should and should not speak. If the anarchic disordering which
writing is said to be capable of effecting in human individuals and
communities rests on its capacity to 'wander freely' and in principle to speak to all, how are we to understand this potential to
disrupt 'in principle' in a world in which, in practice, the accessibility of the written word for democratic reappropriation is, and
almost always has been, circumscribed by established formations
of social power, which include the control of literacy and access to
texts, books and libraries, or to electronic resources, as well as
censorship? While writing may, in principle, tend to make no distinction between those to whom it should and should not 'speak',

its principled tendency in this regard will surely be irrelevant if institutional and social structures have already been put in place which keep those to whom it 'should not speak' well away from the ambit of its peregrinations.

Is, then, the asserted connection between writing and democracy anything more than philosophical wishfulness? One ready, but inadequate, response is that the enormous expense lavished by governments of all persuasions on the policing (monitoring, tracing, storing and censoring) of written electronic communications between their citizens would suggest that there is more to it than this. The conceptual difficulty with the personification implied in the notion of the wandering letter is that it introduces a degree of circularity into Rancière's argument which such concrete examples do nothing to dispel. If writing is disruptive to the extent that it is available for reappropriation and if, as I have suggested, one of the conditions of its availability for reappropriation is that people in a given society have access to it, then this amounts to saying that writing's disruptiveness is coextensive with the degree of agency of the human subjects in that society. In other words, writing as such is not disruptive in the way in which the personification Rancière inherits implies; rather, the extent to which it is able to be reappropriated simply expresses the degree to which the society in question is free and democratic and accordingly capable of tolerating the disruption, which is not one, of 'literarity'. The capacity for disruption imputed to 'writing' as a transhistorical function, its 'literarity', obscures the question of the specific social conditions in which examples of it are encountered: the effect of the circularity is to conceal social conditions.

Rancière goes too far in the direction of attributing agency and disruptiveness to writing itself, as opposed to the human subjects who produce, consume and circulate it, who read and disrupt with it. This sits uneasily with the attempt in his historiographical writing to reserve a place for human agency in historical change, as it does with the idea examined in the preceding chapter that political subjects come into being when people deploy language and argument in a simultaneously reasoned and forceful disruption of the status quo. I have suggested that the difficulty arises from the way he incorporates the personification of writing in the *Phaedrus* into his account in *La Parole muette* and *The Flesh of Words* and relies more heavily on aspects of it than Plato does. In particular, what looks like an intrinsic property of writing in those works – the disruptive potential Rancière names literarity – may in fact be a convoluted way of describing the social conditions which affect the availability of that writing for reappropriation. One of the two introductory theoeretical essays in his more recent *Politique de la littérature* [2007], *The Politics of Literature*, does indeed move closer towards such an understanding:

> The democracy of writing is the regime of the letter which is free for anyone to take up for themselves, whether to make their own the life of the heroes or heroines of a novel, or to become a writer, or as a way of joining in the discussion about affairs of common concern. This is not a matter of irresistible social influence, but rather of a new division of the sensory [*partage du sensible*], of a new relationship between the speech act, the world it configures and the capacities of whose who inhabit that world.[30]

In this passage, then, is an explicit denial that writing's transhistorical potential to disrupt – its 'literarity' – is to be understood as an 'irresistible' power of the letter to disturb the organization of society: writing's capacity to disrupt and the social conditions which allow that power to be exercised are here seen correctly as interdependent. Even though there is no explicit qualification of Rancière's earlier discussion of literarity, this goes some way to redressing its imbalance by restoring a sense of the social contexts in which writing intervenes. In that earlier account his incorporation of the contrast between speech and writing from *Phaedrus* elided the specific social context which, at the time in which Plato wrote, informs the association in his text between writing and democracy. In ancient Egypt, from where the myth is said to hail, writing was the preserve of a priestly caste; by contrast, in Plato's Greece, as J.P. Vernant notes, 'instead of being the exclusive privilege of one caste, the secret belonging to a class of scribes working for the palace of the king, writing becomes the "common property" of all citizens.'[31] In other words the characterization of writing as inherently anarchic, or democratic, in its errant pattern of circulation, which Rancière takes from Socrates' commentary on the myth, and which he assumes to be foundational, was itself the product of a specific set of social and cultural circumstances.

The third element in Plato's personification of writing, which Rancière adopts, is the description of writing as 'fatherless' or 'orphaned'. Socrates, in the dialogue, seems to mean by this simply that writing, because it is inscribed in a material medium, is detached from its author. Yet it is tempting to see Rancière's taking up of this reference to the 'fatherlessness' of writing as a clue to the repressed attachment of his concept of 'literarity' to psycho-analysis; it is telling that the 'anarchic' disordering effect of writing, 'literarity', is described on one occasion by Rancière as 'the perversion of the letter'.[32] The fatherlessness of writing is here allied to its 'perverse' mode of circulation, its ignorance of the laws conducive to harmonious social order. This network of associations suggests there is a suppressed psychoanalytic dimension to Rancière's thinking about literarity. Elaborating on Freud's hypothesis that the principle of negation is inoperative in the unconscious, psycho-analyst Jacques Lacan argued that the unconscious is structured like a language in which signifiers – words considered in their sonic or graphic materiality rather than as their meanings – circulate in ignorance of the law which is closely associated with the idea of the father, the principle of negation he called 'the Name [No] of the Father' ('le Nom [Non] du Père'). Even though Rancière's thought tends on the whole to mark a careful distance from psychoanalysis, the connections between the 'fatherlessness' of writing and its perverse or lawless mode of circulation make conspicuously good psychoanalytic sense: writing, as Rancière conceives it, moves with a perverse disregard for those regulatory principles which strive for harmonious order in the psyche and in society.

The comparison between Rancière's concept of literarity and Lacanian psychoanalysis also points to a missing element in Rancière's elaboration of the concept of 'literarity'. He tells us almost nothing of *how* writing takes hold of the human animal and forces it to deviate from its natural course. Rather than asking, as Jean-Luc Nancy has, whether the very notion of a 'natural course' for the human animal is intelligible in the first place, my question would be whether Rancière says enough about the process, or mechanism, by which this animal is captivated and propelled in new directions by the letter.[33] In Lacanian psychoanalytic theory there is at least an attempt to explain this process: the agency of the letter is intelligible because the unconscious functions like a language.

The contrast with Lacanian psychoanalysis also makes clear the extent to which, unlike that theoretical paradigm, Rancière's theory of literarity is distinctly optimistic in political terms. The connection between writing and democracy which he establishes emphasizes the disruptive, anarchic, effects of writing in its impact on human individuals and communities. Particularly in the case of communities, as has been mentioned, Rancière's conviction is that writing tends to inscribe 'lines of fracture and disincorporation',

rather than to unify.[34] This conviction seems to be rooted, as I suggested in Chapter 2 in relation to his reading of Hobbes, in an
inverted and perhaps somewhat exaggerated estimation of the fear
which writing arouses in those who wield or counsel sovereign
power. In Lacanian psychoanalytic theory, by contrast, the 'agency
of the letter' more often works to conservative psychic, political
and social ends and even more so in Žižek's reworking of Lacan.
One striking example of the authoritarian potential of the letter to
hold individuals and communities in its grip is provided by the
discourse and politics of ethnic and racial hatred. A Lacanian
account of this discourse would stress the ways in which the hating
subject is already caught up in myriad pre-scripted social-psychic
'texts' which condition his or her responses in ways s/he is not
even aware of. Lacan and, especially, Žižek are very good at
accounting for the tenacity and prevalence of, for example, anti-
Semitism, but rather less compelling in their account of the conditions under which sometimes its 'text' can be blocked and become
inoperative. Conversely, Rancière's optimistic insistence on the
'democratic' mode of writing's circulation and its inherently disruptive, liberatory, potential is difficult to reconcile with numerous
real examples of its hierarchizing, homogenizing and oppressive
effects.

Leaving aside now the difficulties generated by Rancière's adop-
tion of Plato's personification of writing, what can be deduced from
his account about the tripartite relationship it posits between literature, writing/literarity and democracy? The significance of the
transition from the age of representation to the age of literature (or
aesthetics) is that in the latter the disruptive potential of writing is
more fully realized because the work of verbal art is modelled not
on spoken language, which corresponds in the age of representation to strongly hierarchized social structures, but on writing,
which is democratically open to reappropriation by anyone:
although works of literature struggle to distinguish themselves, as
art, from the democratic banality of ordinary writing, in so doing
they *carry* something of that disruptive ordinariness and *instantiate*
it in the social world, in the real. Zones of democratic disturbance
perforate the seamless plenitude of the ordered social field: 'Democracy is first of all the invention of words, words with which those
who do not count make themselves count and, in so doing, confuse
the ordered division between speech and silence which made the
political community a "beautiful animal", an organic totality.'[35]
The waywardness of ordinary writing threatens to negate works

of literature as verbal art: 'Democratic literarity is the precondition of literature in the [historically] specific sense. At the same time, however, this precondition threatens to destroy literature because it implies that there can be no distinction whatsoever between the language of art and that of everyday life.'[36] And yet in the singularity of their struggle against ordinary writing, works of literature give material form, which is to say being, to its potential for democratic disturbance.

How exactly do works of literature give material form to democratic disturbance, and how does this in turn have effects which may be described as political? By contrast with works of verbal art produced in the age of representation, works of literature are less firmly anchored to the world in which they were produced: no longer tied to a represented object which they must imitate and no longer under the related obligation to conform to generic codes dictated by this object, they have a radical freedom both of form and content which allows them to anticipate new kinds of social arrangement.[37] As Rancière put it in an interview: 'The political dimension of the arts can be seen most clearly in the way that their forms materially propose the paradigms of the community.'[38] What works of literature and indeed other works of art are capable of doing is inventing 'sensible forms and material structures for a life to come'.[39] It is in Rancière's reading of Mallarmé, which I discuss in the next section, that this anticipatory dimension of the literary work is most clearly articulated.

Rancière as reader

The most extensive and significant of Rancière's readings of particular works are of a set of canonical texts of nineteenth- and early twentieth-century literature, mainly French, in particular by Balzac, Hugo, Flaubert, Mallarmé and Proust; there are also shorter pieces on authors including Wordsworth, Mandelstam, Borges and Melville. If the choice of authors is, in the main, anything but surprising, Rancière's readings often astonish by the novelty of the questions they pose of these canonical works and the insouciant dexterity with which they side-step long-established critical consensus. In what remains of this chapter I shall examine how his readings of the work of two of these authors, Flaubert and Mallarmé, both conform to and strain against the theoretical framework outlined earlier. In Rancière's analysis of the literary politics

of their work, they are contrasting figures. Mallarmé's work is shown to be anticipating a new democratic readership. Contrary to his reputation, in some quarters, as an élitist, his work is shown to carry most successfully the democratic promise of writing. Flaubert's work, by contrast, struggles hardest to smother the democratic promise of the age of literature, to strangle the political disturbance it carries in spite of itself.

Flaubert

For Rancière, as for Sartre before him, Gustave Flaubert (1821–80) is a fascinating and troubling figure; it is Flaubert's work as a writer of novels, and most particularly of *Madame Bovary*, which principally preoccupies him. Flaubert's celebrated conception and practice of literary style as 'an absolute way of seeing things' implies, Rancière argues, that the status of the text as verbal art is rigorously independent of its subject-matter. Flaubert's work thus effects a radical realization of the third principle of the new poetics of literature. The stuff of the new verbal art is language rather than likeness, the likeness of the work to its represented content, so anything can be the subject of a work of literature, including the most inconsequential of conversational exchanges at a provincial agricultural fair, as in *Madame Bovary*: 'Flaubert made every word equal in the same way that he did away with any notion of a hierarchical relationship between noble and base subjects, between narration and description, between foreground and background, or ultimately between people and things.'[40] Moreover, by welcoming into his novels a plethora of apparently 'inconsequential' details and 'unmotivated' descriptions of 'incidental' objects (the barometer in 'Un coeur simple', which so preoccupied Barthes, is an example of one such 'useless' object) and organizing the text such that these details, objects and descriptions make an equal claim on the reader's attention as the characters and the plot, the novel reflects in its form the absence of hierarchization characteristic of democratic space.[41] In its refusal to hierarchize, Flaubert's work embodies 'that equality of writing which attributes equal importance and the same language to being itself and to all things'.[42] Of the various objections made by hostile contemporaneous critics to Flaubert's work, Rancière singles out for comment the common feeling that his novels were cluttered with a profusion of 'unnecessary' detail: 'The cluttered space of *Madame Bovary* stands opposed to [. . .] the freed-up space which the orderliness of aristocracy lent to the novels in the time of *La Princesse de Clèves*.'[43] Rancière argues that Flaubert's work, in its modelling of the cluttered profusion of a democratic space in which subjects and objects are juxtaposed according to a principle of equality, was correctly perceived by hostile reactionary critics to be 'democracy in literature'.[44]

In the non-hierarchizing egalitarianism of his prose and the cluttered space of democracy which it reflects, Flaubert's work carries the democratic disturbance of literarity. Yet at the same time Rancière discerns in the concept and practice of 'absolute style' a powerful counterattack against literarity which makes Flaubert's work the site of the most bitterly contested of all the singular 'agonistic' struggles in the age of literature. Style understood as 'an absolute way of seeing things' was a radical or revolutionary break with the poetics of representation. Rancière asserts, however, that this new conception of style was both 'a revolution and the contradiction of that revolution'.[45] He does not mean by this that Flaubert's work enacts a straightforward return to representational poetics, but rather that it seeks to counter the democratic promise it carries by constantly seeing through the world of human activity to the pre-individual world of impersonal sensations and fragments. The egalitarianism of 'absolute style', which places a profusion of details in non-hierarchized juxtaposition, and thereby instantiates a democratic ordering of things within the text, is an egalitarianism of parts and fragments, an equality of a sub-personal, or impersonal, kind, and will not translate into democratic or egalitarian relationships between individual people. Flaubert's absolute style dissolves the familiar world of people and actions into its pre-individual atomic constituents. His is a

> way of seeing which entirely dispenses with the affirmation of any particular point of view, which reverts from point of view to an impersonal world in which individuation is only the random disturbance of substance. The power of style which 'holds' the book is, for Flaubert, the ability to reveal this vibration, this power of deindividualization which reduces every story and every struggle of wills to the dance of atoms which 'become intertwined, split apart and recompose themselves again in perpetual vibration'.[46]

So when Charles and Emma first meet and Flaubert shows us Charles watching Emma, who is herself gazing out of the window at the fallen beanpoles in the garden, when he interrupts her gaze with an unmotivated and inconsequential question and then shows us Emma blushing, this is not a prudishly discreet or artfully oblique evocation of their falling in love, or merely an example of Emma's reverie suspending the narrative flow, but rather an undoing of the human meaning of the encounter. Flaubert's absolute style undercuts the human meaning of the scene and transports the reader to the pre-human or sub-personal level by presenting 'love which is made up entirely of a combination of affects and percepts'.[47] At sentence level, Flaubert's prose gives, with one hand, the narrative elements of a conventional story and takes, with the other, by dissolving these into 'the indifferent dance of atoms'.[48]

The pre-individual flux revealed by this dissolution of the world of human meaning into sub-personal affects and percepts is, Rancière suggests, the world of what Deleuze and Guattari termed the 'hecceity', the singular quality of, for example, 'a season, a winter, a summer, an hour, a date', the irreducible 'thisness' which it has by virtue of being a particular movement of some particular atoms and particles rather than others.[49] In Rancière's reading, the dissolution of human meanings into pre-individual affects and percepts, which Flaubert's 'absolute way of seeing' brings about, bears a political meaning. This is the singular way in which his works strive to establish themselves as literature by fighting against the democratic disturbance of literarity: 'he counters the equal right of every individual to enjoy every pleasure with the radical equality which rules at the pre-individual level of the hecceity.'[50] Rancière insists that this is to be understood not as a consequence of Flaubert's own political convictions, even though he was a notorious anti-democrat, but rather as the way in which his work constitutes itself as literature in a violent struggle against the democratic promise of its own 'absolute style'. The democratic promise of 'absolute style' as a model for the relations between whole persons is thus blocked by the way Flaubert's prose sees straight through the world of human actions and meanings to the sub-personal or pre-human.

Emma Bovary's 'crime against art', as Rancière puts it in a highly engaging reading of *Madame Bovary*, the crime for which she is 'put to death' in the novel, is her attempt to live as though the equality between impersonal and pre-individual affects and percepts enacted in the writing could be translated into equality on the personal level.[51] Emma Bovary is 'put to death', as Rancière rather dramatically characterizes her suicide in the novel, not exactly because she confuses art with life, as conventional critical wisdom would have it – not because her girlhood readings led her to have unrealistically high expectations which her mediocre provincial life fails to satisfy – but rather because the kind of art which she has tried to incorporate into her everyday life is one of human meanings which operate in the representational world of fully formed human subjects and their actions rather than literature's world of the pre-human or sub-personal. Flaubert's work thus appears to Rancière to be the site of a particularly hard-fought battle between the democratic principle inherent in its practice of 'absolute style' and a countervailing embrace of the pre-human. Flaubert's work emerges as both 'political' and 'pure' art: 'Flaubert's work is pure art and democracy in literature.'[52] Flaubert thus appears to defy a commonplace opposition in the history and theory of art, to which I shall return in the next chapter.

Mallarmé

Stéphane Mallarmé (1842–98), a figure by reputation synonymous with pure literature, is an ambitious but necessary target in Rancière's attempt to unfold the political meaning of literature. His work is the object of one of Rancière's most sustained, incisive and impassioned literary-critical performances: *Mallarmé: la politique de la sirène* (1996), or *Mallarmé: The Politics of the Siren*.[53] Rancière's reading sets out to contest what is still a widely held view of Mallarmé's work – one which has been espoused by Tolstoy, Sartre and numerous lesser critics – of the poet as an aloof contriver of elliptical textual objects which seek through obscurity or incommunicative silence to repudiate the public space of democracy and its utilitarian language of social interaction.[54] According to this view, the poems, in particular, seek through their pursuit of lexical and syntactic complexity and their linguistic and thematic self-referentiality to demonstrate the superiority of a pure literary art which lies beyond politics and history. It is important to stress, lest its originality be in doubt, that Rancière's is primarily an argument about Mallarmé's *poetry*, including his prose poems. It has always been acknowledged that his pseudonymous contributions to the fashion journal *La Dernière Mode* engaged with the relative banalities of ordinary everyday existence, and the disparity between the accessibility of these pieces and the poetry has usually been accounted for by trivializing the journalism as a money-making enterprise.[55]

So Rancière's target is what Damian Catani, in a book which engages directly with Rancière's reading, has called 'the myth of Mallarmé', the critical caricature of 'the ivory-tower poet unconcerned with social inequalities and life's economic imperatives'.[56] Rancière's insistence on the socio-political dimension of Mallarmé's poetic art is in step with current fashion in Mallarmé studies, which is to stress the poet's engagement with the everyday, yet he goes further than most Mallarmists would be prepared to in emphasizing the political meaning carried by the poetry.[57] Rancière's contention is that the difficulty of Mallarmé's poetry must be understood as the product of 'a demanding poetics which itself corresponds to an acute awareness of the complexity of the historical moment'.[58] The complexity of that historical moment, according to Rancière, has closely interrelated literary, religious and socio-political dimensions, and I shall explore these in turn in the remainder of this section. Central to Mallarmé's own perception of the poet's role in responding to this moment of historical complexity and central to Rancière's reading, as Catani rightly recognizes, is Mallarmé's sense of his living in what he called an 'interregnum', an uncertain between-time after the collapse of the old representational and metrical order, in which the poet's task is to anticipate the new social and literary conditions to come.[59]

The siren of Rancière's subtitle, the last word of Mallarmé's sonnet 'À la nue accablante tu', is taken to be emblematic of poetry in this 'between-time'. Sirens, from the *Odyssey* on, have an existence which is purely poetic. The poems, unlike works of verbal art in the age of representation, are no longer premised on their reference to the extra-textual reality they represent. Like the poem, the sirens traffic in sound: their song draws boats to the rocks if sailors are unable to prevent themselves listening. Yet in the age of literature the sirens and their song cease to connote death-dealing deceptiveness (the poem is not *merely* a mortifying self-referential play of sound patterns) and figure instead the new, evanescent, reality of verbal art: 'Mallarmé transforms them into emblems of the poem itself, of the power of a song which is capable both of making itself heard and, at the same time, falling silent. The siren is not a deceptive fictional being but the suspensive act of fiction itself, the transformation of the narrative into a disappearing hypothesis.'[60] If the stuff of verbal art in the age of representation was first and foremost the imitation of a series of human actions, in the age of literature and quintessentially in Mallarmé's poetry it is language itself. The reading process, too, has changed: rather than reconstructing the story, the poem forces the reader to formulate hypotheses and often to entertain conflicting hypotheses simultaneously. Reading Mallarmé is an encounter not with imitation but with virtuality, not with the story but with competing possibilities held suspensively, simultaneously, in play: an experience of 'the virtuality of story'.[61] Despite the many references to the 'Idea', capitalized in Mallarmé's work, Rancière is adamant that what he means by the Idea is staunchly anti-Platonic. Behind the 'anecdotal' crisis apparently provoked by the decline of the alexandrine and the advent of free verse (Mallarmé's so-called 'crise de vers') lay, according to Rancière, Mallarmé's recognition of the disappearance of the Platonic world of ideal forms, the types which had served as models for moral behaviour and indeed for the craftsman's creations.[62] Instead of representing, or imitating, the poet in the age of literature is someone who seizes and preserves unforeseen and evanescent relations. The Idea is no longer the Platonic model to be imitated but rather a pattern of relations discerned in the world, often in a fleeting moment, 'tracing in a sense datum the outline of an entirely new figure'.[63] For example, in the prose poem 'An Interrupted Spectacle' ('Un spectacle interrompu'), a clown is making a bear perform tricks at a fair when the bear suddenly rears up and places his paws on the clown's shoulder and arm. The composite figure as the two are briefly conjoined suggests, to the poet, a questioning of what makes human action meaningful and also reflects the constellation of the Great Bear.[64] The bear-clown composite is an 'emblem of the ideality of the sensory [le sensible]': the poem which captures this Idea is not an imitation but rather 'a tracing of schemas, of the virtuality of events and figures, describing a game of correspondences'.[65] And because there is no model lying 'behind' the Idea and giving it depth, Mallarmé's art is characterized by Rancière as quintessentially an art of the surface.[66]

The pattern discerned by the poet on the surface of things, but missed by the spectators in their sudden terror at the prospect of an animal on the rampage, figures a series of relationships between human beings and their worldly surroundings (their 'séjour', as Mallarmé sometimes calls it, their 'sojourn', 'abode', or 'dwelling place' on earth), in this case between a clown and a bear. While the Mallarmean poem is no longer representational in the old sense, in

its 'anti-mimetic imitation of the Idea', in its 'play of correspondences', it reflects the process of human thought in a world devoid
not only of ideal forms as Plato conceived them but also of the
divine:

> It is the way of proceeding of the human spirit itself [*le procédé même
> de l'esprit humain*]. By which let us understand the human spirit in
> its humanity, the human spirit in so far as it lacks a god to guarantee
> any truth [. . .]. In place of any notion of a realm of Ideas, fiction
> establishes the conditions of human experience in general, the condi-
> tions under which the human abode can be consecrated.[67]

This brings me to the place of the religious or spiritual dimensions
of Mallarmé's project in Rancière's reading. In a loosely contextual-
izing move, Rancière argues that Mallarmé is no stranger to the
nineteenth-century preoccupation with establishing the spiritual
basis for a new community on the ruins of the old order. For Mallarmé, just as for Hegel, Schelling and the Saint-Simonians, this
meant establishing a new form of religion which would provide
the socio-spiritual bond (*religio*) to supplement the political and
economic dimensions of the post-revolutionary social order.[68] Rancière argues, however, that the way in which Mallarmé sought to
harness the power of religion to sacralize the human community
differed markedly from what he characterizes as the dominant
tendency in the nineteenth century, as represented typically by the
Saint-Simonians. Whereas they had attempted to bring religion
back to earth from the transcendent and otherworldly in their 'New
Christianity', a cult of work and industry, of trains and canals,
Mallarmé sought instead to renew what he took to be the essential
revelation of Christianity, as expressed particularly in the ritual of
the Eucharist: that what is distinctive and sacred about the human
is the capacity to glorify absence.[69] Mallarmé's humanization of
religion was not, like the Saint-Simonians', a cult of the material
and its manipulation but rather a glorification of absence through
artifice: 'The poem is not just a "work of art". Fiction is not just the
work of the imagination. Its proper role is to succeed religion, both
in raising the human to its true greatness [*grandeur*] and in providing the principle of a community in proportion to this greatness.'[70]
Mallarmé's conception of the work of verbal art as artifice, as
opposed to the Saint-Simonian intellectuals' cult of labour and the
material, also implies for Rancière a very different relationship
between the poet and the worker. In the rituals enacted by the
Saint-Simonians at Ménilmontant in the early 1830s and mentioned

above in Chapter 2, bourgeois 'apostles' abandoned their books for shovels and wheelbarrows and joined together with working-class members of the movement to produce a spectacle intended to enact the fraternity across classes of the new religion of labour. This spectacle of the 'New Christianity' was supposed to bring 'mind' back to 'matter', to bring the spiritual back to the earthly, in a fraternal display of equality in labour. If the Saint-Simonians tried, often crudely and with limited success, to instantiate in the present the new egalitarian community, Mallarmé's attitude and that of his poetry to the democratic community of equals is, by contrast, one of anticipation and implies a paradoxical solidarity-through-separation with workers in the present. It is the paradoxical, easily misinterpreted, character of this solidarity with 'the Crowd' ('la Foule'), ordinary people, which Rancière intimates lies at the basis of of the 'myth' of Mallarmé's aloof and élitist aestheticism.[71]

Rancière's readings of two prose poems, 'Conflit' and 'Confrontation', in a key section of his study, subtitled 'The Poet and the Worker', clarify the precise nature of the paradox of the poet's solidarity-through-separation with 'la Foule' in the present and the nature of the anticipatory attitude which his poems adopt as they 'chant the splendour of the crowd to come'.[72] Both prose poems stage encounters between the worker and the poet. In 'Conflit', the poet watches the unease of a worker who arrives at work to find his colleague, who got up much earlier, submerged in the hole he has already dug.[73] Rancière suggests that for Mallarmé these workmen are emblematic of proletarian existence. 'Confrontation' presents the holidaying poet's irritation at the worker who persists in cutting through his garden on his way to eat at midday; on his evening walk the poet's view of the horizon is spoiled by the sight of labourers collapsed in the fields in an inebriated heap as they celebrate the end of the working week.[74] Unlike the Saint-Simonians with their quasi-mystical glorification of manual labour, Mallarmé makes no attempt to redeem or explain the drudgery of the workers' lives: 'There is not and never will be glory in work.'[75] Both prose poems present the poet's encounter with the anonymous proletarian lives of workers caught in a circle which forces them to exchange labour for money, money for food, food for labour, and so on. Faced with the spectacle of this self-perpetuating circle, the poet's task is not to reinfuse the daily grind with glory, in Saint-Simonian or Stakhanovite fashion, but rather to step back from it and mark a distance. Paradoxically it is in this act of withdrawal, this strict separation of the poet's task from the circle of labour, that

his solidarity with the worker is supposed to lie: 'Any future relationship between the poet and the people must come about by way
of a decision, in the present, to opt for a separation which shields
the poet's task from the normal cycle of day and night and the
ordinary exchange of work for money.'[76] It is only by virtue of this
separation from the cycle of work in the present that the poet can
anticipate a better – more humane, less alienating – social order in
the future. Rather than a retreat into élitist aestheticism, Rancière
argues these prose poems suggest that Mallarmé marks a distance
from the ordinary world of labour and its language in the present
only to keep alive the promise of a better world in the future. Rancière asserts that the anticipatory character of the poet's work in
the 'interregnum' should not be seen as indifference to social
inequality but should rather be likened to the way Marx insisted
on the need to wait until the time for revolution is ripe.[77] Mallarmé's work, as Rancière reads it, is thus imbued with a certain mes-
sianism: 'He is working for the future celebration of a people which
the present social arrangement deprives of their glory.'[78] Its apparent aloofness from ordinary people and their language – its difficulty – is supposedly redeemed by its messianic anticipation of the
community of the future.

   Mallarmé specialists have objected that Rancière's reading is
insufficiently detailed and comprehensive.[79] There is certainly a
question of whether his reading of these two short prose poems
allows more general conclusions to be drawn about the poetry, or
indeed 'the poet's attitude', whatever exactly is understood by that
all-too-useful critical shorthand. Moreover, in the case of 'Conflit',
I would suggest that what Rancière presents as the poet's gesture
of solidarity-through-separation with the worker is perhaps more
equivocal than he makes out: 'I do not measure, from individual
to individual, a difference, in this moment, and I cannot manage
to not consider this maniac, staggering and vociferating as he is, a
man or to deny my resentment towards him' ('je ne mesure, individu à individu, de différence, en ce moment, et ne parviens à ne
pas considérer le forcené, titubant et vociférant, comme un homme
ou à nier le ressentiment à son endroit').[80] The recognition of shared
humanity, as the worker breaks through the makeshift barrier
erected by the poet to protect his garden, is here tempered syntacti-
cally by the double negative of 'I cannot manage to not consider
[. . .] as a man' ('ne parviens à ne pas considérer [. . .] comme un
homme'): hardly the most direct, or the warmest, of expressions of
human fellow-feeling.

Mallarmé presents a tough test to Rancière's theorization of the politics of literature, so vigorously does the poetry seem to struggle against ordinary language. At first glance it is far from clear – notwithstanding the anecdotal knowledge that the man himself was a democrat – how this most difficult, most rigorously conceived, poetry could be consistent with Rancière's theorization of literature as verbal art which carries with it the democratic waywardness of the ordinary language against which it struggles. Yet selective and sometimes gestural though it is, Rancière's reading, with its attention to the closely interrelated literary, religious and socio-political dimensions of Mallarmé's work and its emphasis on the 'interregnum', does provide an indication of how at least some of the work of even this purest exemplar of pure literature carries the democratic promise.

Rancière tries to save Mallarmé's work from the 'myth' of anti-democratic aloofness, both for the poet's own sake but also, let it be said, for that of the integrity of the philosopher's own overarching theorization of literature in its constitutive relationship to the principle of democracy. He does so by insisting on the anticipatory character of Mallarmé's work and the paradox of its solidarity-through-separation with the democratic community to which it looks forward. Not everyone will be satisfied with such a reading and some will have wanted one more consistent with established norms of literary-critical practice. Rancière's way of reading is certainly disarming, if judged by conventional standards, in the way it moves so freely between what are usually treated as different sources or levels of interpretation: historical context in a very broad sense, immanent textual meaning, authorial intention, the phenomenology of the reading encounter and the text's reception.

Rancière's work on literature leads directly into his wider investigation of art and aesthetics, which I discuss in the next chapter. As his inquiry broadens to embrace other artforms, the concept of literarity, which I have found to be problematic in this chapter, quietly fades into the background and a more nuanced understanding of the political meaning of the artwork begins to emerge.

5

Art and Aesthetics

Rancière's work in the 1990s on literature prepared the ground for his subsequent and much broader investigation of art and aesthetic experience over approximately the last two hundred years. This highly ambitious project, which is still ongoing at the time of writing, is nothing less than an attempt to analyse what art and aesthetic experience are today, as well as to defend and illustrate a non-reductive conception of the political meaning of the work of art. Before discussing what has emerged of the project to date I would like to say briefly how it follows on from Rancière's work on literature, covered in the previous chapter, as well as from his much earlier archival work on the worker-poets and worker-intellectuals. The transformation outlined in the previous chapter in the field of verbal art, when the conventions of representational poetics gave way to literature in the absolute sense, serves as a template for all the arts: the claim is that the concept of art, in the singular, with which we live today, like the concept of literature, first emerged in a seismic shift in discourse, practice and understanding some two hundred years ago. Rancière's term for the modern understanding of art which resulted, art in an absolute sense, is 'the aesthetic regime of art'.

Rancière's project distinguishes itself sharply and declaratively from much conventional and some less conventional wisdom about art and aesthetics. In particular, he rejects as misleading the notions of modernism and postmodernism; he also rejects as regressive what he has called the 'ethical turn' in aesthetics, a move he associates in particular with philosopher Jean-François Lyotard's rereading of Kant's work on the sublime. Modernism and post-modernism are rejected because they are judged to be falsely peri-odizing, indeed historicist: they misleadingly group into particular periods and movements tensions which are, Rancière argues, inher-ent in the aesthetic regime of art.[1] Although by no means alone in questioning the usefulness of modernism and postmodernism, Rancière's wholesale rejection of this way of thinking stands out in its decisive trenchancy. If modernism and postmodernism are dis-missed as falsely historicist, it will become clear as this chapter unfolds that Rancière's own conceptualization of the regimes of art reflects all of the careful ambivalence towards historical explana-tion derived, as I showed in Chapter 2, from his work in the archives and elaborated in his critique of the *Annales* school.

Rancière's own descriptions of his ongoing project on aesthetics suggest that he sees himself engaged in an analytical enterprise which aims to bring order to the enduring confusion surrounding the concepts of art and aesthetic experience. The aesthetic regime of art is, he says, 'already two centuries old yet still so obscure', and his is 'a long-term project that aims at re-establishing a debate's conditions of intelligibility'.[2] This clarificatory, or analytical, enter-prise is closely allied with his attempt to provide an account of the politics of art and aesthetic experience which does not reduce art to a mere epiphenomenon of the political. If the concern with art-works and discourse about them is a new departure at the end of the 1990s, his concern with the wider category of aesthetic experi-ence goes back almost as far as the break with Althusser.[3] Already in *The Nights of Labor* [1981], for example, the worker-artists and worker-intellectuals were found to be engaged in a new kind of disruptive politics when they stayed up into the night to write because their solitary and sometimes despair-inducing creative activity was in itself a challenge to an underlying principle of the inequitable social order, namely that workers are destined to do nothing but work and once the day is over to rest in order to work again. According to the new conception of politics which that anal-ysis implied, workers' cultural (aesthetic and intellectual) experi-ence can be thought of as directly political without there being a need to establish that it was conducive towards large-scale political change such as revolution.[4]

Rancière's own characterization of his work on aesthetics in disciplinary terms is also worth mentioning at the outset because it gives two accurate indications about the nature of his inquiry: 'I am not a historian of art, a philosopher of art, etc.; I work on aesthetic experience in so far is it is experience which opens a rift [*écart*] with ordinary forms of experience.'[5] This suggests first that we should expect an inquiry which will operate with a certain indifference to established disciplinary boundaries; it is a clue to expect an idiomatic, or singular, intervention and it is well given. It also signals that Rancière is concerned primarily with aesthetic experience, a category which includes but is not confined to the experience of artworks: aesthetic experience may also extend to the experience of natural beauty and of objects which were not made to be artworks. For Rancière, the rift (*écart*) which aesthetic experience opens up is first and foremost a space of equality, and I shall begin with an analysis of his defence of the egalitarian promise of aesthetic experience. This will lead to an examination of his theorization of the 'regimes' of art, and in particular of the aesthetic regime and its conflict with the representational regime, and from there to an analysis of his work on film. The last section will examine his discussion of political art in the light of some of his most recent work, which reappraises spectatorship and the spectacle.

Aesthetic experience and equality: with Kant and Gauny, against Bourdieu

The pre-history of Rancière's ongoing project on art and aesthetic experience can be located in his contestatory reading of the work of sociologist Pierre Bourdieu. This was first articulated in *The Philosopher and His Poor* [1983] and in his archival work on the worker-artists and worker-intellectuals, in particular Louis-Gabriel Gauny, the joiner-aesthete and intellectual who figured prominently in *The Nights of Labor* [1981] and an edition of whose selected writings Rancière published as *Louis-Gabriel Gauny: le philosophe plébéien* (1983).[6]

Bourdieu's *Distinction* [1979] presented, in some five hundred closely argued pages, a sociological case that the ability to appreciate art and express judgments of taste about artworks is part of the socio-cultural machinery with which ruling elites exert power over the oppressed and a key element in the legitimation and perpetuation of their hegemony. Only after this sociological case had been exhaustively put did Bourdieu turn, in a 'Postscript' of a mere fifteen pages, to engage with the main rival to, and implicit target of, his account: the tradition of philosophical aesthetics founded, in its modern form, by Kant in the *Critique of the Power of Judgment* [1790]. Bourdieu's 'Postscript', entitled 'Towards a "Vulgar" Critique of "Pure" Critiques', can hardly be considered a *reading* of Kant, or indeed of Derrida, whose work it also briefly mentions.[7] As Koenraad Geldof has suggested, in language which unwittingly echoes Rancière's own characterization of Bourdieu's ambitions in *The Philosopher and His Poor*, rather than a 'reading' it might better be described as a 'coup d'état' intended to signal that '[a]fter the dynasty of the philosophers follows – through a gesture of symbolic violence – the reign of the sociologists'.[8] Rancière takes Bourdieu's small but significant Postscript on Kant's aesthetics as his route into a contestatory reading of the sociologist's work, one which sees him defend and reassert aspects of Kantian aesthetics and reject Bourdieu's analysis of them.[9] So it will be necessary to say a little more now about both Kant's aesthetics and Bourdieu's attack on them before the nature of Rancière's own self-inscription within the Kantian tradition can be ascertained. Readers familiar with Kant may wish to skip the next two paragraphs.

In the *Critique of the Power of Judgment*, Kant distinguishes between the 'agreeable' and the 'beautiful'. He does so because he thinks that people often mistake aesthetic judgments, which he calls judgments about 'the beautiful', for another type of judgment, that something is, as he puts it, 'agreeable'; this confusion is problematic because, Kant thinks, although the two types of judgment look similar they mean very different things. The agreeable is 'that which pleases the senses in sensation' and the beautiful is 'that which, without concepts, is represented as the object of a *universal* satisfaction'.[10] The significance of the distinction for Kant is that 'the agreeable' is the category of pleasures which are judged to be pleasures for me but not necessarily for others; when I judge something to be beautiful, by contrast, I am saying it belongs to the category of pleasures which are pleasures for everyone. What is agreeable may be agreeable only to me, or to me and people relevantly similar to me, because it depends on the contingent state of my senses and on my situation: for example, a mountain pool may be agreeable to me if I happen to have come to the end of a long hot walk and fancy cooling off. If, however, I say the same pool is beautiful, then I am making a judgment that there is something about it which means it will be satisfying to everyone, for example its shape. Although only judgments about what Kant calls the beautiful are aesthetic judgments, there is no need for the person making the judgment actually to use the word 'beauty', or its cognates, in order for it to count as an aesthetic judgment; it suffices that the judgment in question be universal in its bearing, that it be a judgment about what everyone is expected to find pleasing.[11]

The universality of aesthetic judgments will be the point on which Rancière's disagreement with Bourdieu turns, so it is important to establish in what sense aesthetic judgments, or judgments about the beautiful, are universal for Kant. He is concerned in the *Critique of the Power of Judgment* not only to distinguish between aesthetic judgments and judgments about the merely agreeable but also to distinguish between aesthetic judgments and two other kinds of judgment – logical and moral judgments – which he thinks are also universal, but in a different sense, which he terms 'objective universality', because their universality is determined by the properties of the objects in question rather than the human subject apprehending them. By contrast, the universality of aesthetic judgments is 'subjective' in the sense that it refers to the subjects making the judgment rather than the object (the lake, for example) about which the judgment is being made. As Paul Guyer explains in his analysis of Kantian aesthetic experience, the condition of universality only applies to the second part of a 'duplex process' of reflection.[12] In the first half of this process there is a reflection on an object leading to a feeling of pleasure and in the second half there is further reflection on that experience itself in an attempt to establish whether the pleasure is aesthetic pleasure or pleasure of a different kind. In this 'duplex process', Guyer argues, 'These two forms of reflection are logically distinct, in that the latter both presupposes the former and is also subject to a condition – an express consideration of the communicability or intersubjective validity of experience – to which the former is not.'[13] It is in the second half of the 'duplex process' of reflection that consideration is given to whether or not the pleasure experienced in the first half is the result of an inclination of the senses (a matter of the 'agreeable'), or moral satisfaction (which would make it a different kind of universal judgment, an objectively universal judgment) or whether it really is aesthetic pleasure (in which case it is a subjectively universal judgment). To conclude that the pleasure in question is aesthetic pleasure means for Kant, as interpreted here by Guyer, that its origin lies in

> the harmonious and free play to which the perception of the object has inclined one's imagination and understanding. The attribution of the pleasure to such a state then licenses its imputation to anyone

else who is also in a position to respond to the object with a free play of the cognitive faculties because, unlike a physiological inclination, this state is the subjective condition of cognition in general and may thus itself be attributed to everyone.[14]

The universality of aesthetic judgment in Kant's account derives from the fact that the second half of the duplex process involves imputing the source of the pleasure in question to the 'free play' of the 'cognitive faculties', the imagination and the understanding. This 'free play' is, for Kant, the subjective source of cognition in general and so must be attributed to everyone; so aesthetic judgments are universal because any person (capable of cognition) will be expected to respond in the same way. This pleasure-inducing 'free play', on which the subjective universality of aesthetic judgments rests, is only possible in Kant's account if the object in question both invites and eludes interpretation: it must encourage the imagination and the understanding to work together to try to organize meanings while at the same time remaining resistant to any single meaning.[15] So for Kant aesthetic judgments are universal because when we make them we make them for everyone capable of cognition without exception and on an equal basis, without variation by any other irrelevant distinguishing factors such as wealth, sex, height, nationality, and so on. There is then something egalitarian about the capacity for aesthetic judgment in Kant's account and in the tradition of philosophical aesthetics which it founded; this egalitarian universalism is what Rancière seeks to defend against Bourdieu's reductive sociological analysis of it.

Bourdieu's attack on modern philosophical aesthetics argues that the universality with which it operates is 'illusory', a philosophical fiction which not only conceals inequitable social conditions but serves to perpetuate them. According to Bourdieu, the characterization of aesthetic experience by Kant and the whole tradition of philosophical aesthetics – that it is universal, disinterested, contemplative and cognitive – aligns it with the aristocratic social world of the court.[16] Kant may think his concern to distinguish aesthetic experience from that of the similar-seeming pleasures of the 'agreeable' originates in a demand for conceptually rigorous analysis, but, for Bourdieu, this fails to capture the full social reality of the process of distinguishing. The distinguishing process and the 'distinction' it produces, to which the title of Bourdieu's book refers, between pleasures of the senses and

aesthetic pleasure maps onto and reinforces an inequitable distribution of social goods; in common with other 'social critics' of
Kant, Bourdieu sees the distinction between pleasures which are
agreeable and pleasures which are properly aesthetic as far more
than merely typological.[17] Pleasures which are agreeable, Bourdieu
argues, are presented by Kant as inferior yet are precisely the kind
of 'visceral' pleasures associated with working-class, or 'vulgar',
enjoyment with its roots not in the distant contemplation of aesthetic experience but in immediate and bodily participation, for
example in football matches and carnivals.[18]

Rancière's response to Bourdieu begins by rejecting his claim
that Kant's account is entirely ahistorical. Rancière notes the date
of publication of the *Critique of the Power of Judgment*, 1790, one year
after the outbreak of the French Revolution. Although it is likely
that some of the text was written considerably before the Revolution, Rancière draws attention to Kant's attempt, in an Appendix,
broadly to situate his inquiry in relation to that historical event by
aligning it with the attempts of his contemporaries to reconcile
liberty and equality with respect and duty.[19] For Rancière, Kant's
insistence on the universality of aesthetic experience rooted in the
'free play' of the cognitive faculties cuts across social inequalities:
'In the formal universality of the judgment of taste (that is to say,
in the exigency of communication inherent to it), he seeks the
anticipation of the perceptible equality to come [*l'égalité sensible à
venir*].'[20] Rancière contends that Kant's very first example of an
object of aesthetic experience in the *Critique* is telling in this regard:
that of a palace, the form and beauty of which can be appreciated
by rich and poor alike.[21]

The problem with Rancière's response is that even if he and Kant
are right about the intrinsically egalitarian meaning of aesthetic
judgment, this does not necessarily imply that Bourdieu is wrong
about the social function played by judgments of taste. In other
words, the fact that the propositional meaning of judgments of
beauty necessarily involves a universal claim does not mean that
those same judgments, when articulated and circulated in a social
context, cannot serve precisely the kind of oppressive role which
Bourdieu and other 'social critics' claim they do. It may well be, as
Bourdieu claims, that the logic governing the social circulation of
such judgments and its effects is counterintuitive and so cannot be
deduced from the propositional meaning of the judgments as they
are made by individuals but can only be determined by rigorous
empirical investigation of the social field(s) in question. Bourdieu's

argument is precisely that the universal egalitarian meaning of aesthetic experience as analysed by Kant is confounded by the social functions which judgments about this experience actually perform.

Rancière never claims, however, that the universality inherent in aesthetic judgments, as Kant analyses them, has magically direct egalitarian social effects. Rather, he says that aesthetic experience contains something resembling a 'promise', or 'anticipation', of equality.[22] As I argued in Chapter 1, his position on Bourdieu's approach in *The Philosopher and His Poor* is not that the sociologist's analyses of oppression are incorrect but rather that his discourse is politically paralysing and self-serving, working first and foremost to enhance the position of the demystifying sociologist. Bourdieu's analysis offers no hope of a better future; instead, when translated into policy, his sociology offers only the mediocre hope of a future in which 'dumbed-down' cultural products are more equitably distributed. Rancière's philosophical alternative to the sociologist's calls for the legitimation of what he takes to be 'popular', or 'vulgar', pleasures is to defend and reassert the political potential inherent in Kant's severing of the link between social status and the capacity for aesthetic experience. This philosophical response is supplemented by a historical or archival illustration in which he gives as concrete examples of this severing the experience of a handful of exceptional worker-artists and worker-intellectuals, in particular the joiner-aesthete Louis-Gabriel Gauny. Gauny, he suggests, 'seems to be commenting on the *Critique of Judgment* when, from the room in which he lays a parquet floor, he offers the gaze of an aesthete on the décor of his servitude'.[23] It is unlikely that Gauny himself would have thought of his contemplation of the room and the gardens of the palatial abode in which he was working in these terms, but this is beside the point: Gauny's appreciation of the beauty of his surroundings testifies unwittingly to the promise of egalitarian universalism in Kant's theorization of aesthetic experience. Rather than denouncing this promise as 'illusory', as Bourdieu does, Rancière's conviction is that artists, critics and indeed everyone can and should work to give it effect. Whereas Bourdieu sees Kant's theorization of aesthetic experience as an ahistorical delusion which covers and perpetuates inequality, Rancière insists that its appeal to universality is part of Kant's broadly sympathetic response to the ideals of the French Revolution and that the equality of sentiment which it posits is an anticipation of a fairer society. Art and aesthetic experience, since the birth of modern aesthetics just over two hundred years ago, thus contain the 'promise' or 'anticipation' of equality in a way in which art and the appreciation of art in previous eras did not. Rancière's concept of the aesthetic regime of art is an attempt to spell out more clearly how this promise of equality is articulated.

The regimes of art

At the heart of Rancière's ongoing work on aesthetics is his concept of the regime of art. A regime of art is a network of relationships which informs the way an object, act, process or practice is understood as art. The relationships specified by a regime of art are between 'practices, forms of visibility and modes of intelligibility'.[24] In other words the regime of art specifies how certain practices are seen and how both these practices and the ways of seeing them are understood. After briefly summarizing Rancière's characterization of the regimes of art I shall evaluate the explanatory framework they together comprise and ask to what extent and in what sense it is historical.

There are three regimes.[25] Rancière explains in *Aesthetics and Its Discontents* [2004] that, depending on the regime in which it is apprehended, the same object – a statue of the goddess Juno, for example – may or may not be art, and if it is art, then it may be art in one of two very different ways. The first regime, which Rancière calls the ethical regime of images, is not strictly a regime of *art* at all. In this regime the statue is apprehended as an image of the goddess and the only questions which apprehension of the statue raises are of the following sort: Is it right to make images of deities? Is the deity in the image real? Is the image as it should be?[26] Rancière suggests that Plato's entire discussion of art, or what is usually taken to be a discussion of art, operates within the parameters defined by the ethical regime of images: in his discussion of poetry he is concerned to establish how the images of the poem affect the education of the audience and how poetry and theatre can interfere with or further the harmonious organization of the city.[27] In other words, he is concerned with the effect of the images under discussion on the 'ethos', or way of being, of individuals and the community; the image raises 'ethical' questions and is appreciated 'ethically' in this extended sense. Examples given by Rancière of practices apprehended under the ethical regime include dance as therapeutic technique, poetry as education and theatre as civic festival.[28]

The second regime, and the first which is properly a regime of *art*, is the representational regime of art. This was examined extensively, in the context of verbal art, in the preceding chapter and I shall briefly expand on that analysis here by outlining Rancière's understanding of the Aristotelian principle of mimesis. Representational art, in all its forms, is governed by this principle, which Rancière insists, contrary to what he says is a common misconception, is not first and foremost the demand that copies resemble their originals; the question of the accuracy of a resemblance to its original is a question which belongs in the ethical regime of images.[29] Rather, mimesis is above all the principle which allows certain practices to exist as arts by specifying that their products are to be seen as 'imitations' rather than as products in the ordinary sense, the sense in which, for example, a shoe is a product of the practice of shoemaking. The notion of mimesis implies that the norms by which these products are judged and appreciated are different from the pragmatic considerations which govern appreciation of the products of non-representational practices (shoes, for example) and different again from the 'ethical' considerations raised by images. Rancière insists that mimesis is to be understood in this way because Aristotle's elaboration of the concept was precisely an attempt to separate off a category of practices which could be judged in ways which were neither pragmatic nor 'ethical' and, by so doing, to find reason to lift Plato's exclusion of poets from the city; Rancière's insistence on this particular understanding of mimesis will also make more sense when we come to the aesthetic regime of art in a moment. When the products of a particular practice are seen as mimetic imitations, this means they are subject to codified normative conditions which are neither pragmatic nor ethical.[30] Thus the statue of Juno 'is viewed through an entire grid of expressive conventions'.[31]

The representational regime is intrinsically hierarchical: as outlined in the preceding chapter, its most basic demand is that the representation (its genre and language) be an appropriate match for the position in the social hierarchy of the represented subject. There is room to ask whether Rancière succeeds in sufficiently distinguishing this demand from the question raised under the ethical regime of images as to whether the statue is a good likeness of the deity and consequently whether the two regimes are really that different. Yet the important point about the representational regime is that the answer to the question of whether the representation is 'appropriate' can only be given by referring to a codified set of conventions; while the question of the accuracy of the resemblance does also arise in the ethical regime, it is answered there without reference to the codified system of norms which is a feature of the representational regime.

In the aesthetic regime of art there are no hierarchies of genre and there is no demand that the artwork be in any sense 'appropriate' to its subject, if indeed a 'subject' can be identified at all, which it need not be. It is the only regime in which it makes sense to speak of 'art', in the singular, rather than 'the arts'. In abandoning mimesis, it abandons the criterion by which, in the representational regime, certain practices were marked out as 'arts' and thereby exempted from evaluation in pragmatic and ethical terms; in the aesthetic regime *any* object can potentially be an artwork and *any* activity can potentially give rise to artworks.[32] Moreover, in the aesthetic regime of art there are no rules capable of determining whether and why objects are beautiful, and the implication of Rancière's analysis is, moreover, that beauty is a redundant notion.[33]

What, then, is the artwork in the aesthetic regime of art? In the most general terms an artwork in the aesthetic regime is an object of sense experience, part of the world, which has been transformed by being invested with thought in a singular way: this portion of the sensory realm (*ce sensible*) has been 'extricated from its ordinary connections and is inhabited by a heterogeneous power, the power of a form of thought that has become foreign to itself'.[34] This is unique to the aesthetic regime – in the ethical and representational regimes there is no question of thought investing matter in the artwork or indeed of matter alienated by thought – and incidentally it helps to explain why a philosopher might be particularly interested in aesthetics other than as a matter of personal predilection or bourgeois inclination: if artworks in the aesthetic regime are, in a significant sense, 'thought in exile', then a philosopher must presumably also be prepared, so to speak, to travel.

The statue apprehended under the aesthetic regime of art is neither an imitation which refers to a model nor the shaping of inert matter by the imposition of form. It transcends these and other dualities of ordinary sense experience: 'It is given in a specific experience, which suspends the ordinary connections not only between appearance and reality, but also beween form and matter, activity and passivity, understanding and sensibility.'[35] Rancière draws on the work of Schiller, the early German Romantic, to suggest that this quality of the artwork in the aesthetic regime means that it bears a particular political meaning: 'The power of "form" over "matter" is the power of the class of intelligence over the class of sensation.'[36] As interpreted by Schiller, the universalism of Kantian aesthetics and the suspension of the power of the under-standing over the imagination central to Kant's concept of the 'free play of the faculties' are bound up historically and conceptually with the new socio-political 'disorder' of the French Revolution: 'Aesthetics is the thought of the new disorder.'[37] Rancière's under-standing of the egalitarian political 'promise' of the artwork in the aesthetic regime of art is rooted in a reading of Kant mediated by Schiller. For Schiller the aesthetic has a political meaning: some-thing of the egalitarian spirit of the Revolution has, so to speak, rubbed off onto and suffuses aesthetics.[38] In the final section of this chapter, on art and politics, I discuss Rancière's incisive analysis of the two contrasting ways in which this political promise of the artwork in the aesthetic regime has been articulated in the aesthetic regime of art. First, however, I want to probe further his concep-tualization of the regimes of art and show how his work on film draws on this analytical framework.

Because the aesthetic regime of art came into being some two hundred years ago, it looks as though Rancière's framework of the regimes of art is broadly historical. He does indeed speak of the 'age of aesthetics', meaning the period since the inception of the aesthetic regime, yet it would be a mistake to think of the regimes as strong, overarching, historical paradigms which do con-ditioning work as forceful as Foucault's *episteme*.[39] The regime, as Rancière formulates it, is a weaker and more malleable concept; although the aesthetic regime of art came into being relatively recently, this does not mean that representational and indeed ethical artworks ceased suddenly to be possible when it did. In fact, Rancière's overall framework specifically allows for the persistence of, and reversion to, ethical and representational regimes alongside the aesthetic regime of art. There does, however, seem to be at least a falsifiable presumption that, in the last two hundred years, in the 'age of aesthetics', artworks conform to and are appreciated in terms of the aesthetic regime. The subtlety, in a positive sense, of Rancière's work on aesthetics derives, in large part, from the way in which his broadly historical analysis fights to avert a slide into historicism. This fine balance is not unexpected from a thinker who, as I showed in Chapter 2, has both engaged in historical work of his own and reflected extensively on the stifling effects of historicism and overcontextualization. The concept of the regime of art is informed, then, by Rancière's studied wariness of historical explanation.

The broadening of Rancière's field of inquiry from the aesthetic revolution in literature to the other arts is accompanied by an anti-historicist deepening of his analytical framework: the periodizing feel of his analysis of the transition from representation to aesthetics in verbal art, particularly in *La Parole muette*, gives way to a renewed emphasis on the concept of the *regime* of art. These 'regimes' can and do coexist, in productive tension, within single works and particular artforms; the regime of art is a concept both rooted in and uprooted from a historical analysis.[40] It could be termed a quasi-historical concept. The conflict between the representational and the aesthetic, which Rancière first found to be at work in Flaubert's writing, emerges as a more general feature of much of the art of the last two hundred years. No artform more fully exhibits this potential for conflict, or productive tension, between the representational and the aesthetic than film. Rancière's interest in film is not just a matter of personal predilection, though it is also this; it reflects his sense that central to film's meaning as an artform is its unrivalled potential to play the two regimes of art off against each other.[41]

Film and film theory

Rancière's most significant single publication on film, *Film Fables* [2001], is a collection of essays on work by a selection of mainly heavyweight twentieth-century directors, including Sergei Eisenstein, F.W. Murnau, Fritz Lang, Jean-Luc Godard, Chris Marker, Anthony Mann, Roberto Rossellini and Nicholas Ray, and also includes a piece on Gilles Deleuze's film theory. Yet it is more than just a collection of isolated engagements: through these analyses and in the dense and tightly argued introductory chapter, Rancière not only offers a magisterial demonstration of the analytical power of his theorization of the regimes of art but also sketches his own history of cinema and pays the homage of a true *amateur* to some of its singular achievements. As Tom Conley has noted, in their reach this text's conclusions extend well beyond the perimeters of film theory as it is conventionally understood; moreover, the essays

presuppose a certain familiarity with the broader terms of Rancière's inquiry into aesthetics.[42] Perhaps this is why one commenta-
tor has remarked that the collection is difficult to read: not because
the analyses of the detail of the films are especially hard to follow,
but rather because what may not be immediately apparent from
the book, approached in isolation, are the 'intentions which
motivate and sustain his analysis'.[43] In this section I outline the
view of cinema which the book presents and show how it draws
on Rancière's theorization of the regimes of art before examining
two of the discussions of particular works and associated prob-
lematics which, in my view, offer particularly revealing insights
into his distinctive approach to film: his chapters on F.W. Murnau's
Herr Tartüff (1925) and Chris Marker's *Le Tombeau d'Alexandre/The
Last Bolshevik* (1993). If in the main I have addressed Rancière's
work on literature and aesthetics directly, or frontally, I make no
apology for offering here a relatively oblique and selective approach
to Rancière's already oblique approach to film, one which recognizes that his excursus into film is driven in part by the pleasure
of the *amateur*. My coverage of *Film Fables* is not exhaustive; in
particular, the reader is referred elsewhere for a discussion of the
intricacies of Rancière's involved engagement with Deleuze's film
theory.[44]

   Rancière thinks of cinema as the artform with the greatest
potential to dramatize the interplay between the representational
and the aesthetic regimes of art: 'Cinema, the preeminently modern
art, experiences more than any other art the conflict of these two
poetics, though it is, by the same token, the art that most attempts
to combine them.'[45] Yet many programmatic declarations of what
cinema essentially is, or should be, fail to recognize this conflict,
and he begins his introductory chapter with one such manifesto
text, Jean Epstein's *Bonjour Cinéma* (1921). Epstein sets out a vision
of cinema as the artform which dispenses with fabulation, or
storytelling; fabulation, or fable-making, in the loosely Aristotelian
sense meaning an arrangement of human actions, is one of the
features which identifies the artwork in the representational
regime.

   Epstein's manifesto vision of what cinema essentially is, and
should strive as far as possible to be, is the artform which is the
apotheosis of the aesthetic regime of art, an artform which has
dispensed entirely with representational conventions. For Epstein,
cinema's mission is not, as in the representational regime, to show
the unfolding of a story of human endeavour, but rather to reveal

the texture of the world as it is, to record things 'as they come into being, in a state of waves and vibrations, before they can be qualified as intelligible objects, people, or events due to their descriptive and narrative properties'.[46] Epstein's purist vision of cinema is of a 'writing in light' which has abandoned the representational regime's concern for storytelling and which instead fully realizes the aesthetic regime's exile of thought in matter and corresponding alienation of matter by thought: 'In the writing of movement with light, fictional matter is reduced to sensible matter.'[47] Epstein's vision, Rancière observes, 'belongs to another time than our own', and cinema, in the main, far from abandoning the representational, has, in the years since Epstein's treatise, increasingly been the site of its resurgence.[48] Nostalgic purists lamenting cinema's failure, in its subsequent development, to embrace Epstein's vision would accordingly see cinema as a regressive artform:

> Cinema wasn't content just to use its visual power and experimental means to illustrate old stories of conflicting interests and romantic ordeals; it went further and put those at the service of restoring the entire representative order that literature, painting, and the theatre had so deeply damaged. It reinstated plots and typical characters, expressive codes and the old motivations of pathos, and even the strict division of genres.[49]

Rancière is not, however, a nostalgic purist and his vision of cinema is not Epstein's. While he recognizes the coexistence of codes and conventions from the representational regime – fabulation in particular – with those of the aesthetic regime, he does not think this makes cinema a regressive artform. Indeed not only is he not a nostalgic purist but the decisive move in the introductory essay comes when he scrutinizes the elements comprising Epstein's purist vision of cinema and reveals its decidedly 'impure' origins. In so doing, Rancière highlights what he thinks is a characteristic feature of most writing about film. He draws attention to the way in which Epstein's purist manifesto for a non-representational cinema is in fact constructed out of elements from 'impure' storytelling cinema. Epstein may well conclude that '[c]inema is true. A story is a lie', yet he only reaches that purist conclusion by 'sampling' or 'extracting' elements from a classic of representational, storytelling, cinema of his day, Thomas Harper Ince's melodrama, *The Honour of His House* (1918): 'He composes one film with the elements of another.'[50] This 'sampling' or 'extraction' (*prélèvement*) by Epstein of one film's fable to make a fable about film is, Rancière suggests, 'constitutive of the cinema as experience, art, and idea of art'.[51] This technique of Epstein's is one which Rancière finds replicated in two other seminal attempts to articulate the essence of the artform: Jean-Luc Godard's *Histoire(s) du cinéma* and the two volumes of philosopher Gilles Deleuze's film theory: 'they both extract, after the fact, the original essence of the cinematographic art [*l'essence originaire de l'art cinématographique est prélevée*] from the plots the art of cinema shares with the old art of telling stories.'[52]

Central to Rancière's analysis of film is the idea that its characteristics as an artform pre-existed the development of its particular technological apparatus and were already an established part of the meaning of the artwork in the age of aesthetics.[53] The same tension between the unfolding of the fable and the suspensive moments which frustrate that process is a characteristic of art in the age of aesthetics which Rancière also discerns in literature, most forcefully in Flaubert, in the theatre of Maeterlinck and others, as well as in the reinterpretation of earlier works by nineteenth-century art critics. Thus the Goncourt brothers, or Hegel, in reinterpreting paintings of an earlier age do a similar thing to Epstein, Deleuze and Godard: they 'sample' works which told a story, representational works of art, in such a way as to bring to the fore the aesthetic materiality of the works at the expense of their represented content, of their story. They, too, demonstrate that art in the aesthetic regime establishes itself by feeding off and disfiguring the storytelling conventions of the representational regime.

So, unlike the vision of Epstein and other cinematic purists, for whom cinema is the 'dream come true of this [the aesthetic] regime of art', Rancière sees film as, in essence, a dream or fable 'contrariée', thwarted, an artform which dreams of its purity as an apotheosis of the aesthetic yet which is constantly feeding off and falling back into the representational.[54] The essays which comprise *Film Fables* keep returning to the artform's rivennness and unearth countless examples of the friction between the two regimes. They also explore the relationships which particular films establish between cinema and other artforms, in particular literature, theatre and painting. At stake in the first of Rancière's readings of particular works I shall examine here, of Murnau's *Herr Tartüff* (1925), a filmic transposition of Molière's 1664 play, is both the relationship between the representational and aesthetic regimes of art and the dialogue initiated in the film between cinematic and theatrical art.

F.W. Murnau's Herr Tartüff *(1925)*

Most of the films which Rancière chooses to write about in *Film Fables* are ones which, as well as telling the story they are most obviously telling, are also taken to be saying something about the nature of the artform itself. In the case of *Herr Tartüff*, at issue is the relationship between film and theatre and the way in which the transposition from theatre to film of Molière's play intersects with the conflict between the representational and the aesthetic regimes of art. Rancière analyses this conflict by looking at the interplay between cinema, theatre and painting staged in the film.

The question of the transposition, as framed by Rancière, is that of how to represent cinematically, without recourse to spoken dialogue, the central notion of *Tartuffe*, hypocrisy. In Molière's play, he argues, the effect is achieved chiefly by exploiting the potential for ambiguity in the religious language of the day, an ambiguity which allows a seductive sexual undertone to be heard beneath apparent expressions of piety. Molière's play is the story of an impostor, Tartuffe, whose professed piety insinuates him into the esteem of wealthy householder Orgon but whose real ambition is to get his hands on Orgon's property. He is very nearly successful but, in the end, is unmasked by Orgon's wife Elmire, who lures Tartuffe into exposing himself by expressing his desire for her.

Murnau's adaptation cuts around half of Molière's characters and modifies the plot, refocusing the drama on the relationship between Orgon and Elmire rather than the machinations of Tartuffe. Murnau also frames the film of the play proper within a modern story of hypocrisy devised by Carl Mayer: a scheming housekeeper is seen first trying to get the master of the house to sign over all of his worldly goods to her in his will and then trying to poison him. The filmic adaptation of the play is projected in the living room of the house by the grandson, who is in disguise because the housekeeper has previously had him excluded from the house. The grandson's intention in showing the film of the play is to get the scheming housekeeper to confess, in an obvious parallel with the play-within-the-play in *Hamlet*. Just as in *Hamlet*, however, the performance of the play fails to elicit a public revelation of hypocrisy. In Carl Mayer's modern story of hypocrisy, which frames the adaptation, the moment of discovery comes when the grandson finds a bottle marked 'Poison' in the housekeeper's bag, drops from which he had previously seen her pour into the grandfather's drink: 'a poison flask taken directly from melodrama', as Rancière puts it.[55] Although he recognizes the sophistication of this framing technique, Rancière has surprisingly little to say about it, other than that its purpose is to function as 'an abstract signifier of modernity'.[56] I shall return to the framing tale in a moment. Rancière concentrates, for the remainder of the piece, on the way in which the middle section of the film, the filmic adaptation of the play, effects the transposition from play to film.[57]

Rancière focuses on the relationship between the film's use of shadow and the question of transposition. That Murnau and other German directors of his era exploited shadows and contrasts between light and shade is a critical commonplace.[58] Shadows are unquestionably a prominent feature in this film's visual repertoire and there is also evidence that Murnau went to great lengths to intensify their effect.[59] But what exactly is their effect? The originality of Rancière's analysis lies in the connections it effects between this visual technique, the thematics of this particular play and the question of the transposition from play to film. When he finally appears, Tartuffe (Emil Jannings) is not the active and mobile schemer of the play but a sinister, stiffly moving silhouette whose doubleness is suggested by the shadow his figure casts on the white walls of the staircase in Orgon's house. Rancière's analysis connects shadows in this literal sense to the idea of the shadow as a figure for the separation between Orgon and Elmire and the shadow as a metaphor for the cinematic itself. Figuring the separation between Orgon and Elmire, the shadow becomes an expression of the elsewhereness of Orgon's desire, which distracts his interest, indeed takes his love, away from Elmire: 'More than the falsely devout man who shows up to swindle the family, Tartuffe is the shadow that comes to separate Orgon and Elmire, the shadow that darkens Orgon's eyes [cette ombre qui est devant le regard d'Orgon] as he lowers Elmire's arms when she is about to embrace him.'[60] What is striking about this comment of Rancière's is that it effects, silently, a connection between shadow in the literal sense and shadow as a figure for separation and the 'elsewhereness' of Orgon's desire: for there is no shadow, in the literal sense, veiling Orgon's gaze, as is clearly shown in the still from the film included in La Fable cinématographique, but unfortunately not in the English translation, Film Fables.[61] The shadow has morphed, in Rancière's text, from a purely visual feature to a figure for the elsewhereness of Orgon's desire:

Still from F.W. Murnau's *Herr Tartüff* (1925), reproduced with kind permission of the Friedrich Wilhelm Murnau Stiftung.

> While she rejoices in her husband's return, he is dreaming of the new friend he made during his trip. This new friend is the shadow that comes between them, the one Elmire confronts again only a little later, when she goes to Orgon's room to try to win him back and the camera leaves us behind the door.[62]

Once again, however, close inspection of the scene to which the first part of the quotation refers reveals that there is in fact *no shadow* in a literal sense; the shadow to which Rancière is referring here can only be figurative, a figure for Orgon's distraction and Elmire's jealous sadness. How does this figurative shadow, projected as it is by the film onto the surface of Rancière's text, bear on the question of the transposition? Rancière's essay associates both the real and the figurative shadows cast by Tartuffe with cinema as an artform: 'The dark shadow outlined against the light of a white wall is a figure for cinema.'[63] Echoing Gorky's description of cinema as 'the kingdom of the shadows', cinema is said by

Rancière to be the artform which 'tells the story of substantial and beguiling shadows'.[64] So by the end of his essay there are three kinds of interconnected shadow in Rancière's account, one literal and two figurative: (i) the shadows cast on the wall by Tartuffe, (ii) the shadow figuring the elsewhereness of Orgon's desire and (iii) the shadow as metaphor for the artform itself.

In Murnau's film, as 'sampled' or 'remade' in Rancière's practice of *prélèvement*, the exposing of Tartuffe involves a simultaneous liquidation of the literal and the two figurative shadows: of the shadow cast by his figure on the white wall of the staircase, of the rift between Orgon and Elmire and of the cinematic itself. The scenes in which Tartuffe is exposed as a lecher are shot not against the white walls of the grand staircase and landing but in small rooms without (literal) shadows. Tartuffe's suddenly lustful and, Rancière adds, suddenly 'plebeian' face, together with the composition of the shots, indicates a reversion to the representational regime of genre painting and in particular to the paintings of Flemish students of Frans Hals, Adriaen Van Ostade (1610–85) and Adriaen Brouwer (c. 1605–38). While the painterliness of Murnau's room-scenes had been noted by Eisner, the new dimension Rancière brings is to observe that this reversion to painting is also a return to socially indexed representational hierarchies of genre and subject.[65] It is by way of this reference to the coded system of the representational regime that Tartuffe is suddenly revealed to be out of place in Orgon's aristocratic abode:

> To resolve the fictional problem, Murnau identifies Tartuffe with a pictorial figure, a character from genre painting. But this solution, to place the character in front of a figure from genre painting, means that cinema has in some ways renounced what had until then seemed its own way of imitating painting and substituting the theater, its own way of creating and dissipating shadows, its own immediate magic.[66]

The three kinds of shadow are entangled: to dispel the shadow which is the filmic transposition of Tartuffe's doubleness the film reverts to the representational regime in these references to genre painting. The story of revelation which these painterly scenes tell is a story which draws on the representational regime's coded interconnection between artistic and social hierarchies.

The most perplexing feature of Rancière's account of this film is his cursory treatment of the framing tale, for that tale allows the film of the transposition to figure within the film, thereby implying that the question or problem of transposition is already raised by the film and suggesting a degree of knowingness which goes unrecognized in Rancière's account. The cursory treatment of the framing tale is also surprising because it adds a class dimension to Molière's story of imposture and so supports one aspect of Rancière's reading of the adaptation proper: both are stories of individuals conspiring to elevate themselves above their social station.

In common with many of the other essays in *Film Fables*, Rancière's reading of Murnau's *Herr Tartüff* is by turns suggestive and exasperating: suggestive in the interconnections it manages to effect between the three different kinds of shadow and between these shadows and the question of the transposition, but frustrating in the way in which these connections are drawn, so to speak, 'silently', without explicit analytical commentary. One way of moderating this frustration would be to modify our expectations of Rancière's writing on film and think of it less as traditional discursive analysis of Murnau's *Herr Tartüff* and more as a 'sampled' remake of it, much as Epstein's account of the cinema samples and remakes *The Honour of His House*.

Chris Marker's Le Tombeau d'Alexandre/The Last Bolshevik *(1993)*

Chris Marker's film pays the homage of an artist and a friend to the obscure Russian film-director Alexander Medvedkin (1900–89). Its French title recalls the Renaissance form of the artistic *tombeau*, the posthumous tribute by one poet or musician to another's talent.[67] Medvedkin's life and his chequered career as a film-maker are explored by Marker both in their own right and as a way of reflecting upon the rise and fall of the utopian dream of Soviet Socialism and particularly upon the role of cinema in the elaboration of that dream: as Rancière rightly says, Marker's film presents 'the interwoven memory of communism and cinema'.[68] Medvedkin emerges as a paradoxical figure, a staunch Communist to the end, notwithstanding the fact that most of his films – entertainment and serious art alike – were either simply not shown or banned. Although he survived Stalin's purges, his daughter Chongara Medvedkina tells in the film of how the family used to listen anxiously at night to the footsteps of the NKVD in the corridor; but they never called for him.

Originally commissioned by French television, Marker's film comprises two hour-long parts, the first entitled 'The Kingdom of the Shadows', the second 'The Shadows of the Kingdom'. Echoing Gorky's characterization of cinema as the kingdom of the shadows, these symmetrical titles suggest both the interrelationship between cinema and Communism and the exploration of a utopian dream together with its sinister, shadowy, underside. Each part comprises three cinematic 'letters', from Marker to Medvedkin, which assemble and comment upon a remarkable range of material: interviews (with Medvedkin, with historians and former friends, with other directors, with Dziga Vertov's cameraman, Yakov Tolchan, with young Medvedkin enthusiasts and with Antonina Pirojkova, the widow of his contemporary, Isaac Babel); archival footage; clips from Medvedkin's work, in particular his film *Happiness* (1934) and rediscovered footage from his Cinema-Train project of the early thirties; new material shot in Russia in the early 1990s in the aftermath of the collapse of the USSR; as well as old material from earlier Marker films. The interviews paint a gently contradictory picture of Medvedkin. The film, even by Marker's standards, is an enchantingly complex work and I can only scratch at its surface here. I shall discuss it mainly through Rancière's reading before indicating a number of areas in which I think his account can productively be developed further.

Rancière's interest in the film lies mainly in its process of fabulation, in the way in which it tells its story by putting together the interlocking stories of Medvedkin and Soviet Russia. In this context fabulation means the way the film arranges visual material, sound, music and spoken commentary into sequences of events which make up a story, a 'fable' or a 'fiction', in the strict etymological sense of the latter, derived from the Latin verb *fingere* (to make), that is, a made object. Rancière claims that the documentary film as a genre, of which he asserts this is an example, offers a clearer insight into the way in which the process of fabulation occurs because it works with real materials which have simply to be arranged and does not, in addition, have to create the impression or illusion of reality, unlike the film which tells a made-up story. For Rancière, the approach to fabulation Marker will adopt is signalled in a sequence in the the first letter in which the narrator sets out to visit Medvedkin's tomb and encounters along the

way mourners laying flowers at the tomb of Alexander III, itself
thought to be symbolic of the entire Romanov dynasty. Rancière
comments:

> The relationship between these two tombs is more than simply a
> synonym for buried hope and for the vindication of the old world.
> It determines, from the start, the entire narrative structure of the
> film. Marker doesn't try to show a linear transition from Tsarist
> Russia to the Revolution, and from its collapse to the restoration of
> old values. Rather, he places three Russias together in our one
> present: the Russia of Nicholas II, of the Soviets, and of today.[69]

The memory constructed in Marker's film, as Rancière analyses it,
is of a nation torn between the nineteenth and the twenty-first
centuries. The contrast we see just after the visit to the graves,
between Medvedkin and the famous singer Ivan Kozlovski, both
born in 1900, as the narrator remarks, is the opposition between
Medvedkin the staunch Communist who experimented in the
1920s and 1930s with cinema as the progressive art of social and
individual transformation, only to find his works banned or
ignored, and the singer made famous by his performances of Rim-
sky-Korsakov's and Mussorgsky's settings of gloomy nineteenth-
century fables. As the film shows, Kozlovski starred in performances
of works such as Mussorgsky's opera *Boris Godunov*, based on the
Pushkin story, which showed 'every revolution as doomed from
the outset and [sang] the suffering of a people eternally condemned
to subjection and deceit', regressive musical fables which, as Rancière points out wryly, Party officials invariably preferred to the
forward-looking new music of the avant-garde.[70] This pair of 'dialectical' contrasts between the two tombs, Medvedkin's and Alexander III's, and the two exact contemporaries, Medvedkin and
Kozlovski, points to a process of fabulation based not on linear
progression but rather on the construction, in the present, of 'the
intertwining of two histories of the centuries'.[71]

Like Eisenstein, Marker has often been described as a 'dialectical'
film-maker.[72] Nora Alter, for her part, asserts categorically that '*The
Last Bolshevik* is a dialectical film.'[73] There are certainly a profusion
of contrasted pairings in the film, especially between Medvedkin
himself and other figures (Kozlovski, Vertov, Babel), as Catherine
Lupton has noted, yet what if its mode of fabulation were, as Rancière ultimately argues, less dialectical and more a matter of a
'pluralization of memory'?[74] As Rancière points out, the film is
engaging with not two but at least three Russias. This pluralization

is suggested, moreover, by the polysemic reference of the title: Alexander Medvedkin, Alexander III (and by extension the Romanovs) and Alexander Pushkin with his gloomy nineteenth-century prophecies of Russia's eternal suffering. And Rancière also speculates about a fourth Alexander concealed in the title: Alexander the Great, the conqueror whose tomb could famously not be located. It seems strangely appropriate that Marker, in a film which marks the end of the idea of utopia incarnated in the Soviet Union, should also move, albeit tentatively, beyond dialectic, beyond the official Marxist-Leninist philosophical mode and his own customary approach as a film-maker. The tentative move from dialectic towards 'pluralization', which Rancière correctly discerns, points forwards in Marker's own career to his CD-ROM *Immemory* (1997), which allows the user to explore the plethora of real documents which, the idea is, together comprise Marker's own memory, along plural interconnecting and diverging pathways.

Although Rancière's is a relatively short text and Marker's a dauntingly complex film, it seems to me curious that Rancière's account passes over some significant elements which have a bearing both on his own broader intellectual project and on that of the director concerned. Rancière's assumption that the film is a documentary is problematic and helps to explain some of these omissions. For not only has Marker expressed his aversion to the term, on account of the 'trail of sanctimonious boredom' it leaves behind it, but he was famously saluted by André Bazin in his assessment of Marker's *Letter from Siberia* (1958) as the pioneer of a new genre, the 'essay-film' or 'film-essay'.[75] The distinction is more than merely terminological, for as Michael Renov has noted, whereas the documentary film-maker strives mainly to account for a portion of the world out there, 'The essayist's gaze is drawn inward with equal intensity.'[76] This inward-looking, personalized, dimension to the essay-film sets it apart from the traditional documentary. As Laura Rascaroli argues, this influences not only the kinds of subject-matter included but also the nature of the presenting voice:

> an essay is the expression of a personal, critical reflection on a problem or set of problems. Such reflection does not propose itself as anonymous or collective, but as originating from a single authorial voice. [. . .] This authorial 'voice' approaches the subject matter not in order to present a factual report (the field of traditional documentary), but to offer an in-depth, personal, and thought-provoking reflection.[77]

As well as a documentary which explores the life of Medvedkin
and the Russia whose national animal, the bear (*Medved*), his name
contains, Marker's film-essay is also a reflection on his own involvement as a political film-maker with the utopian dream which died
with Soviet Russia. Rancière's piece misses this reflective dimension and, in so doing, mistakenly hears the voiceover as didacti-
cally pedagogical, wrongly accusing Marker of a tendency to
deliver 'a "lecture on memory"' and offer professorial explanation
of the sort which pre-empts the story told by the images themselves.[78] Rancière's assumption that the film is a traditional documentary, together perhaps with his acutely irritable sensitivity to
the pedagogical, leads him to mishear the voiceover as an authoritarian lecture.

Rancière's analysis of the intertwining of the centuries in Marker's portrait of Russia is spot-on. Yet by thinking of this as a documentary rather than a film-essay, he underplays the dimension of
the film which is an inward-looking reflection by Marker on the
intertwining of his own career as a film-maker with a certain idea
of political film-making associated with Medvedkin and in particular with his 'Film-Train' (*kino-poezd*). In 1931–2, Medvedkin toured
the Soviet Union in a train adapted to house everything needed
to make and project films. Medvedkin, his family and a team of
thirty-two toured the country from mining village to factory to
collective farm, making short films starring ordinary workers and
which he screened, typically, the following day. The official ratio-
nale for the project and the justification for its very substantial
funding had been to use film as a way of highlighting inefficient
working practices in the context of the first Five-Year Plan of 1928.
The story of the Film-Train was told by Marker in his 1971 film, *Le
Train en marche*, which features a long interview with Medvedkin,
filmed in Paris in January of that year, in the train depot at Noisy-
le-Sec, and clips from this interview are featured in *The Last Bolshevik*.[79] When Marker made that earlier film, however, it was thought
that all of the seventy films made by the Film-Train team had
been lost.[80]

Marker had been enthusiastic about the political premises of the
Film-Train decades before he saw any of the films it produced:
Medvedkin's idea of specatators who were also stars and his use
of film to intervene directly to improve social relationships was
reflected in Marker's own political film-making of the sixties and
in particular in his offering of finance and technical assistance to a
workers' film-making collective based at the Rhodiaceta Plant in

Besançon, a collective named the 'Medvedkin Group'.[81] Yet in *The Last Bolshevik*, Marker's enthusiasm for the egalitarian political premise of the Film-Train project, while still apparent, is tempered by his acknowledgement of its inscription in the sombre story of cinema's complicity in repressive political violence, notably in the show-trials which were to begin a few years later; the Film-Train project, as it is framed in *The Last Bolshevik*, appears indissociable from a history of persecution and censorship. In the third letter, a clip from the 1971 interview, in which Medvedkin declares of the Film-Train that 'we were all enthusiasts', is followed with footage from a Soviet film of the early 1930s accusing avant-garde composer Arthur Honegger of 'fetishism of technique'. The voiceover confirms Marker's newfound ambivalence in what I take to be a general verdict on his investment in the utopian dream sheltered, albeit as he says in 'amnesiac' fashion, by Soviet Russia: 'We were listening and we were dreaming.'

That Rancière's treatment of *The Last Bolshevik* passes over the side of this film which is a personal reflection by Marker on his own involvement in political film-making is curious. Marker and Rancière are similar in that each, in his different way, has produced some of the most thoughtful and original of any responses to May '68. It may be that Marker is too close a figure for Rancière to see entirely clearly: the egalitarian ideal of the Film-Train, as translated by Marker into the French context in his political film-making of the late 1960s, certainly has affinities with Rancière's own, non-reductive, conception of a political art capable of intervening to reconfigure social relations. In particular, the idea of an artform in which participants are, alternately, both stars and spectators, in which star and spectator are interchangeable positions, prefigures elements of his own argument in *The Emancipated Spectator*, which I examine in the next section.

Rancière's work on cinema as a whole develops his conceptualization of the representational and aesthetic regimes of art by showing how they coexist in productive tension in this artform. He resists purist definitions of the medium as the apotheosis of the aesthetic regime and shows how numerous films draw on representational devices and conventions. As was clear from the discussion of his treatment of Murnau's *Herr Tartüff*, however, some of this work is frustratingly elusive, indeed I am almost tempted to say 'thwarted' (*contrarié*), to echo the title of his introductory chapter, because key conceptual connections are effected so modestly, with so little fanfare, that they risk passing unnoticed. Perhaps this is an uncommon virtue. Rancière's writing in *Film Fables* may be initially disconcerting, but it is important to recognize that it is not and does not aspire to be straightforwardly analytical; as Geoffrey Whitehall has suggested, there is a sense in which it 're-partitions' the films it studies.[82] Rancière's writerly-cinematic art of 'sampling', or *prélèvement*, takes elements from these films and recombines them to make a new 'film', just as Epstein did in his manifesto.

Contemporary art, politics and community

Rancière's work on cinema, significant though it is in its own right and relying though it does on his theorization of the regimes of art, is also something of a detour away from what I take to be the two principal, interrelated, aims of his current and ongoing project: to bring analytical clarity to our understanding of art and aesthetics and to formulate a non-reductive account of the relationship between art and politics. In this final section I shall focus on the second of these objectives, but rather than attempting exhaustive coverage of the full range of his many interventions in this area over the last ten years, many of which have been written for very specific occasions, I shall select and discuss what I take to be the key theoretical insights.

As we saw in his reading of Kant through Schiller, inherent in the art of the aesthetic regime, as Rancière understands it, is what he calls a political 'promise' of equality. He argues that there are two alternative, 'apparently antithetical', ways in which this promise has been construed: either the work of art is taken to be a model or blueprint for a new form of life and community, or conversely its political promise is thought to lie in its self-sufficient separateness from ordinary sensory experience.[83] The first way of understanding art's political promise, which Rancière suggests is shared by numerous curators and artists who see their work as intervening modestly to reshape our understanding of community, involves it relinquishing its autonomous status as art: the work becomes something like a blueprint for a better state of things. The second, which Rancière associates with Adorno and avant-garde movements, by emphasizing art's aloof self-sufficiency, seems to leave no real room for its political effect: the work may contain an egalitarian political promise but it contains that promise so completely that nothing of it will ever spill over into the world at large.

Rancière suggests that this second understanding, which he names the 'politics of the resisting form', characterizes not only Lyotard's aesthetics of the sublime but also many works, or exhibitions, which seek to explore, emphasize or indeed contest the distinction between artworks and non-artworks.

Summing up these two visions of the politics of art in the aesthetic regime, Rancière writes of the contrast formed 'between a type of art that makes politics by eliminating itself as art and a type of art that is political on the proviso that it retains its purity, avoiding all forms of political intervention'.[84] Yet these two visions are only 'apparently' antithetical; two splintered fragments (*éclats*) of the same 'originary configuration' or 'initial kernel' on which the aesthetic regime stands.[85] Although this seldom happens, the same artist can, it seems, think of his or her own work in both ways alternately: Rancière cites Mallarmé as an example, for whom the same poem can be both 'a ceremonial of the community' (the first manner) and 'a heterogeneous sensory block' (the second).[86] The special place accorded to Mallarmé – no other single artist's work is the subject of so sustained a reading – can perhaps be explained by the fact that his writing comes closest to grasping both the splintered fragments of the aesthetic regime's 'originary configuration'. The clarificatory impulse of Rancière's project on aesthetics can be thought of as the drive, if not to piece back together the broken fragments of the original unity to which he refers, then to understand these fragments as complementary splinters of a lost and unrecoverable unity.

Political art or art as critique – art made with the intention of conveying a political message – is the site of negotiation between these two 'apparently antithetical' understandings of the politics of aesthetics. Rancière argues that such art opens up a middle way between them. If, in *Aesthetics and Its Discontents* [2004] and *The Future of the Image* [2003], this observation yields what is arguably rather a bourgeois survey of some recent works and exhibitions, *The Emancipated Spectator* [2008] presents a far more persuasive and more coherently theorized account of political art.[87] The new dimension this later account brings is, as the title of the book intimates, a critical reflection on what it means to be a spectator, an ordinary 'someone' who encounters art in the aesthetic regime, yet the book avoids the conclusion prevalent in much work on this question, namely that the spectator is necessarily duped by the work, or the spectacle, as s/he is duped by ambient images of consumerist society. Instead, Rancière's development of the concept of active or 'emancipated' spectatorship has affinities with and precursors in the liberating moment when literary theory discovered that there was something called 'reading' which was not the same as following, or 'appreciating', every turn and trope of the text and the recognition within film theory of the spectator's capacity to recombine and re-experience the work.[88] This relatively recent exploration of the autonomy and activity of the spectator is a significant and a welcome development in Rancière's project on aesthetics.

How does Rancière's interest in active, 'emancipated', spectatorship develop his work on aesthetics? Emancipated, active, spectatorship is the mode of engagement with the artwork which most fully realizes the egalitarian promise inherent in the aesthetic regime of art. However, Rancière thinks that this disposition of the spectator is invariably under threat from artists and curators who aspire to 'teach' their audience a particular political message or intervene in the world directly to reconfigure social relations. He suggests that many artists and exhibition curators who aspire to be political have an understanding of the artwork which owes more to the ethical or representational regimes than the aesthetic. Thus exhibitions which leave the confines of galleries and museums to intervene directly in the world outside may express a reversion to the ethical regime.[89] And distant though Molière's *Tartuffe* may seem from contemporary art, artworks or exhibitions which aspire to educate the spectator into a particular politics share the play's underlying mimetic-pedagogical intention: it sought to teach a seventeenth-century audience to recognize and abhor hypocrites, just as the collages and photomontages of John Heartfield or Martha Rosler aim to *teach* the viewer something about Nazi Germany or the state of the US during the Vietnam War. The implication of Rancière's analysis is that in their concern to convey a certain political message and elicit a certain response in the spectator they revert to the mimetic or representational regime and so produce something which not only falls short of art but which also fails to respect the interpretative autonomy of the spectator. Characteristic of the aesthetic regime is what Rancière calls a 'cut' or 'break' (*coupure*) which severs the intentions of the artist from the response of the spectator; it is this cut which allows for the autonomy of the spectator.[90] To be a spectator is certainly to watch passively, but it is also to interpret actively: the spectator 'observes, selects, compares, interprets. She links what she sees to a host of other things that she has seen on other stages, in other kinds of place. She composes her own poem with the elements of the poem before her.'[91] Art can allow people to see the world and their place in it differently, which may in turn lead them to intervene in it and change it by becoming political subjects, yet it can only do so *as art* by respecting their autonomy as spectators. It follows that artists and curators have to be wary of lapsing into the pedagogical position: 'An artist is not a teacher.'[92] It also follows, for Rancière at his most radically faithful to Jacotot's vision of the society of the emancipated as the society of artists, that the distinction between artist and spectator is, in the final analysis, positional or conventional.

Rancière is reluctant to be seen to be holding up particular works or artists as models of the kind of art to be imitated.[93] However, his broadly sympathetic analysis of one particular work in *The Emancipated Spectator*, a multifaceted three-year project (2003–6), entitled *Je et Nous* (*I and Us*), staged in the troubled Paris suburb of Sevran-Beaudottes by an artists' collective called Campement Urbain (Urban Encampment), provides an insight into his vision of the political possibilities of contemporary art and the concept of community which it implies. In his analysis Rancière clearly marks his distance from the conception of 'relational art' advanced by Nicolas Bourriaud and enthusiastically embraced by numerous politicians, artists and other curators. According to Bourriaud, the function of contemporary art is to create social relationships which remedy the brokenness of our increasingly fractured societies.[94] Rancière has spoken with considerable scepticism of this conception of art and the projects it has inspired, for example the sending of writers into deprived areas to run creative writing workshops and improve community cohesion.[95] The project undertaken by Campement Urbain, as Rancière analyses it, presents a critique of what he suggests is this complacement view of art's usefulness as a healer of social divisions. One of the ideas explored by the project is for a space, which the collective entitle *9m² au-dessus d'un jardin*, that could be seen by everyone but only occupied by one person at a time for solitary individual reflection:

> The possibility of being alone is seen to be the one form of social relation, the one dimension of social existence, which living conditions in these suburbs place beyond reach. By contrast, the empty space maps out a community of persons who are able to be alone. It points to the fact that members of a community are all equally capable of being an *I* whose judgment can be attributed to any other and it thus creates, along the universal lines of Kantian

9m² au-dessus d'un jardin, part of Campement Urbain's *Je et Nous* (2003–6), reproduced with kind permission of that collective.

aesthetic judgment, a new kind of *Us*, an aesthetic or dissensual community.[96]

The community which the artwork under the aesthetic regime envisages is one of individuals whose autonomous capacity to interpret the world in which they find themselves as spectators is recognized; this will necessarily be a 'dissensual' community, whose members reinterpret the works they encounter in the light of their own experiences and their knowledge of other works. The 'cut' of the aesthetic regime, which prevents the artist's political intentions being directly translated into political effects by manipulating the audience, is a 'cut' coextensive with the spectator's freedom, which allows the work to be misconstrued and which corresponds to a 'cut', or a series of 'cuts', between individual members of the dissensual community.

Rancière's reading of *Je et Nous* is certainly selective: there are others aspects of the project which are very much closer to Bourriaud's community-strengthening relational or 'consensual' view of art. One question that Rancière's reading of this work raises is how his renewed insistence in *The Emancipated Spectator* on the *dissensual* character of the community and the stress he places on individual singularization within that community, a stress which recalls themes in the work of Jean-Luc Nancy, coheres with his own broadly Kantian vision.[97] In Kant's work, especially as it is mediated by Schiller through his concept of 'aesthetic education', the promise of equality implicit in aesthetic judgment is connected to the establishment of a shared standard of taste, or in other words to the development of a *consensual* community.[98] In his haste to recognize in the design from *Je et Nous* a model for the dissensual community, Rancière seems to have jettisoned the idea of a shared standard of taste and retained only the disruptive promise of equality from Kant's vision and the promise of 'disorder' from Schiller's. The stark choice of dissensus over consensus, which Rancière makes in his analysis of this design, is not only a selective oversimplification of this artwork in particular but an unnecessarily extreme position which cannot easily be reconciled with the consensualist elements in a Kantian tradition on which he otherwise so strongly relies. An analysis of other artworks which are premised on the idea of an open and unforeseen community, for example Thomas Hirschhorn's installation *Bataille Monument* (2002), would perhaps more readily show how relationality, or consensuality, and dissensus can coexist or alternate.[99]

Rancière's commentary on the work of Campement Urbain has brought this chapter full circle, back to Kant. Rancière's non-reductive account of the politics of aesthetics, in the final analysis, allows only fairly modest room for the political effectivity of art *as art*. Politics, as he conceives of it, does not take place when people are manipulated or 'organized' – whether by those who govern them or by artists – and so it is not surprising that his account of the relationship between politics and art eventually marks a 'cut' between the two terms. The resulting account of the politics of art is more modest about art's capacity to intervene politically than perhaps many artists and critics would have hoped, but it does succeed in envisaging limited political possibilities for art, without reducing it in the process to an epiphenomenon of the political.

Is there any way of pushing Rancière's account further and describing in general terms how artworks can have political effects as art while still respecting the autonomy of the emancipated spectator? Rancière himself is hesitant on this point and sometimes seems almost to fall back on the idea that art broadens the mind, which of course it can: art can help to 'redraw the frame of our perception and redynamize our emotions' and in so doing to open up 'possible ways through to new forms of political subjectivation'.[100] Artworks can certainly propose, or model, a new 'division of the sensory' (*partage du sensible*), the key Rancierian term I first outlined in Chapter 3, but can they in any sense be said to be directly conducive to that new order of things or is it left to the autonomous spectator to take them up, or not, as a call to subjectivation and a blueprint for political action? In other words, does Rancière's later commitment to emancipated spectatorship block the direct political efficacy of the aesthetic theorized in his earlier concept of the division of the sensory?

In theoretical terms, what may be needed to reconcile emancipated spectatorship with the politicity of art provided for in the division of the sensory is, as Žižek has hinted in a somewhat different context, an anthropological or psychoanalytic concept of symbolic efficacy similar to that deployed by Lévi-Strauss.[101] Such a concept would elaborate on how, notwithstanding the 'cut' which exists in the aesthetic regime between the artist's intention and the spectator's autonomous response, the work acts on its spectators and, in so doing, opens new paths to political subjectivation. Given a theory of symbolic efficacy, or spectral influence, the embodiment in an artwork of a new political paradigm of community, of a new 'division of the sensory', would be rather more than merely anticipatory, one take-it-or-leave-it blueprint among others; in itself it would have disruptive and directly political effects. In other words, it would allow acknowledgement of the fact that to dream of (or write or read about, or paint, or sculpt, or film) new forms of community has an efficacy of its own:

> Political statements and literary locutions produce effects in reality. They define models of speech or action but also regimes of sensible intensity. They draft maps of the visible, trajectories between the visible and the sayable, relationships between modes of being, modes of saying, and modes of doing and making. [. . .] They thereby take hold of unspecified groups of people, they widen gaps, open up space for deviations, modify the speeds, the trajectories and the ways in which groups of people adhere to a condition, react to situations, recognize their images.[102]

If Rancière stops just short of entertaining the idea that the anticipatory character of the artwork itself has direct effects in the real, if he tends to eschew the question of the direct symbolic efficacy of its anticipatory dreaming, this must be because such a concept of symbolic efficacy would involve a form of unconscious 'rewiring' of the spectator which would be difficult to reconcile with the strong commitment to deliberate human agency in his historiographical work, his account of political subjectivation and his aesthetics of emancipated spectatorship.

Afterword

His encounter with the work of joiner-intellectual Louis-Gabriel Gauny moved Rancière to half-ventriloquize that

> [t]here is no point waiting for some moment in the future when everyone has the leisure to be by turns a shepherd, a fisherman and a critic at nightfall [. . .]. The time is now for us to break the chains of the working day in which and against which we struggle, the time to win for ourselves the body and soul of philosophical leisure.[1]

Gauny's self-emancipating decision to write actualizes Marx's humanist, egalitarian, vision of a life in which work fulfils rather than alienates, even as it rejects the procrastinating temporality of that vision by insisting that the time to live it is now. The decision to live Marx's dream in the present, to behave as though the leisure to think, to which he is as entitled as anyone else, had already been accorded to him, presupposed more than a little tenacious self-belief. Where does such life-changing and world-changing confidence come from?

Gauny and his ilk may have been exceptional, as professional historians have often pointed out. Along with the handful of other nineteenth-century worker-intellectuals whose performative enactments of their own equality have so captivated Rancière, Gauny is both an exceptional and an exemplary figure. Such is the suggestive singularity of his undertaking that we are invited to regard it not as a set of choices to be contemplated with dispassionate analytic interest but rather as an incitement and an invitation to follow,

albeit – and here is the paradox – in our own individual way. Rancière's own body of work can likewise be understood in terms of
its exemplary singularity: it voices a radically enabling and egalitarian call to intellectual, political and aesthetic exploration. Such
a conception of the exemplary life may seem to belong to another
age, even if its pale imitation, the 'role model', is sadly ubiquitous
in our own.[2] The decisive spacing, the *écart*, which distinguishes
Rancière's exemplary singularity from that brash interpellation,
from that demand to conform to type, lies in the openness of the
egalitarian appeal which Rancière voices: it is an incitement to all
– to anyone, to everyone – to pursue with application their own
autonomous intellectual-aesthetic-political path. The dangerously
anarchic and entirely seductive invitation voiced in Rossellini's
Europe 51, as Rancière analyses it, precisely captures the draw of
his own work's exemplary singularity: it is an egalitarian incitement to the kind of autonomous exploring which assumes confidently that 'the walker is always right to roam, that it is always
right to step outside, to go and see what is happening to one side,
to continue to walk wherever your footsteps – and not other people's – take you'.[3]

Notes

Preface

1 Where reference is made to the translation of a text, a date in square brackets refers to the date of publication of the first edition of the original, as opposed to the translation. Althusser et al., *Lire le Capital* (1st edn, Paris: Maspero, 1965).

2 Rancière, *Et tant pis pour les gens fatigués: entretiens* (Paris: Amsterdam, 2009). The translation given here is my own.

3 E.P. Thompson interviewed in MARHO [Mid-Atlantic Radical Historians' Organization], *Visions of History* (Manchester: Manchester University Press, 1976), 17.

4 Rancière, *The Ignorant Schoolmaster: Five Lessons in Intellectual Emancipation*, tr. by Kristin Ross (Stanford: Stanford University Press, 1991), 4–8.

5 Davis, 'Rancière and Queer Theory: On Irritable Attachment', *Borderlands* 8, 2 (2009), special issue: *Jacques Rancière on the Shores of Queer Theory*, ed. by Samuel Chambers and Michael O'Rourke (http://www.borderlands.net.au/issues/vol8no2.html). Rancière, *The Names of History: On the Poetics of Knowledge*, tr. by Hassan Melehy with a Foreword by Hayden White (Minneapolis: University of Minnesota Press, 1994), xviii. For two further attempts to characterize the specific challenges of Rancière's writing see Eric Méchoulan, 'Sophisticated Continuities and Historical Discontinuities, Or, Why Not Protagoras', in Gabriel Rockhill and Philip Watts (eds), *Jacques Rancière: History, Politics, Aesthetics* (Durham, NC: Duke University Press, 2009), 55–66, at 55 and James Swenson's excellent, 'Style Indirect Libre', in Rockhill and Watts (eds), *Jacques Rancière: History, Politics, Aesthetics*, 258–72.

6 Rancière, 'A Few Remarks on the Method of Jacques Rancière', in Paul Bowman and Richard Stamp (eds), *Parallax* 15, 3 (2009), 114–123, at 114.
7 In this notice, for example, written by a member of the ticket-counter staff on the Paris metro called away to attend to some unspecified but presumably pressing incident, the term 'intervention' refers in a general way to their act of responding: 'Désolé: un incident quelque part dans la station nécessite une intervention de ma part.'
8 Rancière, *Short Voyages to the Land of the People*, tr. by James Swenson (Stanford: Stanford University Press, 2003); Rancière, *Hatred of Democracy*, tr. by Steve Cocoran (London: Verso, 2006).

Chapter 1   The Early Politics: From Pedagogy to Equality

1 Althusser, 'On the Young Marx', in *For Marx*, tr. by Ben Brewster (London: Verso, 1990), 49–86, at 64.
2 Rancière, 'La philosophie en déplacement', in Marianne Alphant (ed.), *La Vocation philosophique* (Paris: Bayard, 2004), 11–36, at 18.
3 For a full discussion of Althusser's work see Gregory Elliott, *Althusser: The Detour of Theory* (2nd edn, Leiden and Boston: 2006); see also Rancière, 'Althusser', entry in Simon Critchley and William Schroeder (eds), *A Companion to Continental Philosophy* (Oxford: Blackwell, 1998), 530–6.
4 Althusser readily acknowledged this borrowing from Bachelard, for example in the Introduction to *For Marx*, 32.
5 Althusser, 'From *Capital* to Marx's Philosophy', in Althusser and Étienne Balibar, *Reading Capital*, tr. by Ben Brewster (London: New Left Books, 1970), 13–69, at 17.
6 *Karl Marx: Selected Writings*, ed. by David McLellan (Oxford: Oxford University Press, 1977), 80.
7 Marx, *Capital*, vol. 1, ed. by Ernest Mandel (London: Penguin, 1990).
8 Althusser, 'From *Capital* to Marx's Philosophy', 14.
9 Althusser, 'From *Capital* to Marx's Philosophy', 19–21.
10 Althusser tends to oversimplify psychoanalysis as he borrows from it: the symptom can only really be 'read' by a psychoanalyst in the temporally extended and transference-laden context of the session or cure. Althusser's notion of the 'symptomatic' reading was one of a number of theoretical appropriations of psychoanalysis, displacements which arguably stood in place of the proper analysis of his own array of symptoms.
11 At least it did in the first edition of 1965. The textual history of Rancière's piece reflected the vicissitudes of his relationship with Althusser: the second French edition at the end of 1968 contained only Althusser's and Balibar's contributions. In his preface to that edition, Althusser remarks rather insultingly that the new edition is

'improved' ('améliorée') (p. xii), and that the omissions in no way damage the integrity of the interpretation of Marx's work being put forward. In 1973 Althusser and his publisher Maspero wanted to reprint the 1965 volume in its entirety; Rancière asked for his contribution to be preceded by a prefatory *autocritique* but Althusser refused. The *autocritique* was published separately as Rancière, 'Mode d'emploi pour une réédition de "Lire le Capital"', *Les Temps Modernes* 328 (Nov. 1973), 788–807.

12 The translation is my own. Rancière, 'Le concept de critique et la critique de l'économie politique des *Manuscrits de 1844* au *Capital*', in Althusser et al., *Lire le Capital* (1st edn, Paris: Maspero, 1965), 81–199.

13 Rancière, 'Le concept de critique', 87–8.

14 Rancière, 'Le concept de critique', 123. This and all subsequent translations from this text are my own.

15 Rancière, 'Le concept de critique', 126, emphasis in original.

16 Rancière, 'Althusser', 530.

17 Althusser, 'On the Materialist Dialectic', in *For Marx*, 161–218, at 177, n. 7, emphasis in original.

18 Rancière, *La Leçon d'Althusser* (Paris: Gallimard, 1974), 89, emphasis in original. This and all subsequent translations from this work are my own.

19 Maurice Larkin, *France since the Popular Front, 1936–1996* (2nd edn, Oxford: Oxford University Press, 1997), 258.

20 Rancière, *La Leçon d'Althusser*, 97, emphasis in original.

21 See also Rancière, 'Althusser, Don Quixote, and the Stage of the Text', in *The Flesh of Words: The Politics of Writing*, tr. by Charlotte Mandell (Stanford: Stanford University Press, 2004), 129–45, at 129–30. Rancière rightly notes that there is a lot more to be said about the way in which Althusser defined his approach negatively against a caricaturally oversimplified understanding of what 'religious reading' involved. The religious in Althusser's case is overdetermined, for not only does the church often stand in for the Party he would not publicly criticize but the church is also the church, or metonymically the fervent religious belief of Althusser's youth, with which he 'broke' into atheist Marxism.

22 Althusser, 'From *Capital* to Marx's Philosophy', 27, translation adapted, emphasis in orginal. Brewster gives 'an *informed* gaze' for 'un regard *instruit*', yet *instruit* also means 'trained' or 'instructed', and these pedagogical overtones are particularly important in the context of Rancière's argument.

23 Rancière, *La Leçon d'Althusser*, 104.

24 Rancière, *La Leçon d'Althusser*, 109.

25 Alain Badiou, 'Les leçons de Jacques Rancière: savoir et pouvoir après la tempête', in Laurence Cornu and Patrice Vermeren (eds), *La Philosophie déplacée: autour de Jacques Rancière* (Paris: Horlieu, 2006), 131–54, at 142, my translation.

26   Michel de Certeau, *The Capture of Speech and Other Political Writings*,
     tr. by Tom Conley (Minneapolis: University of Minnesota Press,
     1997), 22, translation adapted.
27   Rancière, *La Leçon d'Althusser*, 10.
28   Rancière, 'Sobre la teoria de la ideologia (la politica de Althusser)',
     in *Lectura de Althusser* (Buenos Aires: Galerna, 1970), published in
     French as 'Sur la théorie de l'idéologie politique d'Althusser',
     *L'Homme et la Société: revue internationale de recherches et de syntheses
     sociologiques* (Jan.–Mar. 1973), 31–61. Rancière, 'Mode d'emploi pour
     une réédition de "Lire le Capital"', 789–90.
29   Rancière, *La Leçon d'Althusser*, 11.
30   On Althusser's concept of ideology see Michael Sprinker, 'The Lega-
     cies of Althusser', *Yale French Studies*, 88 (1995), special issue:
     Althusser, Balibar, Macherey, and the Labor of Reading, 201–25, at 217.
31   Nicholas Hewlett, *Badiou, Balibar, Rancière: Re-thinking Emancipation*
     (London: Continuum, 2007), 113.
32   Rancière, 'La méthode de l'égalité', in Cornu and Vermeren (eds),
     La Philosophie déplacée, 507–23, at 522–3, my translation.
33   The term 'indiscipline' is derived from a reference, in the editors'
     preface to the proceedings of the 2005 Cerisy conference, to Ran-
     cière's 'indisciplinarité' and to those influenced by his thought as
     his 'indisciples'. Cornu and Vermeren (eds), *La Philosophie déplacée*,
     14.
34   Alain Badiou, 'Louis Althusser', in *Petit panthéon portatif* (Paris: La
     Fabrique, 2008), 57–87, at 67.
35   See also Badiou, 'Louis Althusser', 68.
36   Étienne Balibar, 'Althusser's Object', tr. by Margaret Cohen and
     Bruce Robbins, *Social Text* 39 (Summer 1994), 157–88, at 158.
37   See Yann Moulier-Boutang, *Althusser: une biographie* (Paris: Flam-
     marion, 1992). See also Colin Davis, 'After Hope: Althusser on
     Reading and Self-Reading', in *After Poststructuralism: Reading, Stories
     and Theory* (London: Routledge, 2004), 102–28.
38   Elliott, *Althusser: The Detour of Theory*, 322–3.
39   Rancière, 'Althusser, Don Quixote, and the Stage of the Text', 145.
40   Rancière, 'Althusser, Don Quixote, and the Stage of the Text', 134.
41   Rancière, 'Althusser, Don Quixote, and the Stage of the Text', 142.
42   Rancière's approach in this careful but direct essay is entirely differ-
     ent from similarly themed vilificatory pieces by Althusser's detrac-
     tors all too eager to pour invective on the 'madness' of his work. E.P.
     Thompson, for example, described Althusser's work as a series of
     '*imaginary* revolutionary psycho-dramas'. Thompson, *The Poverty of
     Theory: Or an Orrery of Errors* (2nd edn, London: Merlin, 1995), 4,
     emphasis in original.
43   The question of melancholy in Rancière's work is raised by Andrew
     Gibson in 'The Unfinished Song: Intermittency and Melancholy in
     Rancière', *Paragraph* 28, 1 (March 2005), special issue: *Jacques Ran-
     cière: Aesthetic, Politics, Philosophy*, ed. by Mark Robson, 61–76.

44 Winnicott, 'True and False Self', in *The Maturational Processes and the Facilitating Environment* (London: Karnac, 1990), 140–52, at 147; see also Winnicott, *Playing and Reality* (London: Routledge Classics edn, 2005), 87–114.

45 Rancière, 'Althusser, Don Quixote, and the Stage of the Text', 145.

46 Rancière, *La Leçon d'Althusser*, 34.

47 In 'Sobre la teoria de la ideologia (la politica de Althusser)', 'Mode d'emploi pour une réédition de "Lire le Capital"' and *La Leçon d'Althusser*.

48 See Rancière et al., *Les Révoltes Logiques*, special issue on May '68: *Les Lauriers de Mai ou les chemins du pouvoir 1968–1978* (February 1978), 6. The collective are asserting, in their opening presentation, their wish to remain, in fidelity to May, '"épidermiquement" sensible' to privilege and hierarchy. See my 'Rancière and Queer Theory: On Irritable Attachment', *Borderlands* 8, 2 (2009), special issue: *Jacques Rancière on the Shores of Queer Theory*, ed. by Samuel Chambers and Michael O'Rourke (http://www.borderlands.net.au/issues/vol8no2.html).

49 Rancière, *La Leçon d'Althusser*, 97.

50 Dick Geary, *Karl Kautsky* (New York: St Martin's Press, 1987), 12.

51 Marx, *1844 Manuscripts*, 72.

52 Elliott, *Althusser: The Detour of Theory*, 96.

53 Slavoj Žižek, *The Ticklish Subject: The Absent Centre of Political Ontology* (London: Verso, 1999), 127–8.

54 Rancière, *La Leçon d'Althusser*, 35, emphasis in original.

55 Rancière, *La Leçon d'Althusser*, 29, emphasis in original.

56 Rancière, *The Philosopher and His Poor*, tr. by John Drury, Corinne Oster and Andrew Parker (Durham, NC: Duke University Press, 2003).

57 Rancière, *Le Philosophe et ses pauvres* (1st edn, Paris: Fayard, 1983; 2nd edn, Paris: Flammarion, 2007), Preface to Second Edition, viii, my translation.

58 Rancière, *The Philosopher and His Poor*, 87.

59 Rancière, *The Philosopher and His Poor*, 85–7.

60 Rancière, *The Philosopher and His Poor*, 75.

61 Rancière has been careful to distinguish between his critique of Marxism and the anti-Marxism of the 'Nouveaux philosophes'. See Jacques and Danièle Rancière, 'La légende des philosophes (les intellectuels et la traversée du gauchisme)', *Les Révoltes Logiques*, special issue (February 1978): *Les Lauriers de Mai ou Les chemins du pouvoir (1968–1978)*, 7–25.

62 I borrow the term from the title of Kristin Ross's inspiring and concertedly Rancierian analysis, *May '68 and its Afterlives* (Chicago: University of Chicago Press, 2002).

63 Even though his subsequent argument tends in a very different direction from Rancière's, Karl Popper also takes Plato's model of

the ideal city state in *Republic* as his negative point of departure in *The Open Society and Its Enemies* (4th edn, London: Routledge, 1962).

64   Irving M. Zeitlin, *Plato's Vision: The Classical Origins of Social and Political Thought* (Englewood Cliffs, NJ: Prentice-Hall, 1993), 92.

65   Rancière, *The Philosopher and His Poor*, 31.

66   Zeitlin, *Plato's Vision*, 107–9.

67   The principle of specialization bears more strongly on classes than individuals. As George Klosko notes: 'Plato does not believe that each individual is able to perform only one task in the state. [. . .] Indeed, he says that no great harm comes from a carpenter doing the work of a cobbler or a cobbler that of a carpenter (434a).' Klosko, *The Development of Plato's Political Theory* (London: Methuen, 1986), 138.

68   Rancière, *The Philosopher and His Poor*, 17.

69   Zeitlin, *Plato's Vision*, 96.

70   Rancière, *The Philosopher and His Poor*, 137, emphasis in original.

71   Rancière, *The Philosopher and His Poor*, 132.

72   Rancière, *The Philosopher and His Poor*, 165.

73   Rancière, *The Philosopher and His Poor*, 146.

74   Rancière, *The Philosopher and His Poor*, 147, translation adapted.

75   Rancière, *The Philosopher and His Poor*, 147.

76   Rancière, *The Philosopher and His Poor*, 151.

77   Rancière, *The Philosopher and His Poor*, 121, emphasis in original.

78   Rancière, *Le Philosophe et ses pauvres*, ix.

79   Charlotte Nordmann, *Bourdieu/Rancière: la Politique entre sociologie et philosophie* (Paris: Amsterdam, 2006), 102–3.

80   Rancière, *The Philosopher and His Poor*, 189.

81   Pierre Bourdieu and Jean-Claude Passeron, *The Inheritors: French Students and their Relation to Culture*, tr. by Richard Nice (Chicago: University of Chicago Press, 1979). Bourdieu and Passeron, *Reproduction in Education, Society and Culture*, tr. by Richard Nice (London: Sage, 1990), 162.

82   Rancière, *The Philosopher and His Poor*, 176.

83   Richard Jenkins, *Pierre Bourdieu* (London: Routledge, 1992), 91. See also 97.

84   Terry Lovell, 'Thinking Feminism with and against Bourdieu', in Bridget Fowler (ed.), *Reading Bourdieu on Society and Culture* (Oxford: Blackwell, 2000), 27–48.

85   Rancière, *The Philosopher and His Poor*, 180.

86   Rancière, *The Philosopher and His Poor*, 181.

87   Rancière, *The Philosopher and His Poor*, 179–80.

88   Rancière, *The Ignorant Schoolmaster: Five Lessons in Intellectual Emancipation*, tr. by Kristin Ross (Stanford: Stanford University Press, 1991), 1–4.

89   Rancière, *The Ignorant Schoolmaster*, 6.

90   Rancière, *The Ignorant Schoolmaster*, 38.

91 Rancière, *The Ignorant Schoolmaster*, 24, translation adapted.
92 Badiou, 'Les leçons de Jacques Rancière', 143, my translation.
93 Rancière, *The Ignorant Schoolmaster*, 68.
94 Badiou, 'Les leçons de Jacques Rancière', 143. May, *The Political Thought of Jacques Rancière: Creating Equality* (Edinbugh: Edinburgh University Press, 2008), 2.
95 Geneviève Fraisse's general observation on the enchanting quality of Rancière's writing is particularly apt in the case of *The Ignorant Schoolmaster*: 'His [Rancière's] readers have all, at some time, experienced his magic art, the art of someone who leads us somewhere we did not know we were going, to a place we do not know how we found.' Fraisse, 'À l'impossible on est tenu', in Cornu and Vermeren (eds), *La Philosophie déplacée*, 71–7, at 72, my translation.
96 Rancière, *The Ignorant Schoolmaster*, 4, 34–5, 108, emphasis in original.
97 The egalitarian dream of the 'society of artists' (Rancière, *The Ignorant Schoomaster*, 71–3) is dispelled by the narrative event of a knock at Jacotot's door (75).
98 Rancière, *The Ignorant Schoolmaster*, 105.
99 Rancière, *The Ignorant Schoolmaster*, 105.
100 Rancière, *The Ignorant Schoolmaster*, 96.
101 Rancière, *The Ignorant Schoolmaster*, 105, emphasis in original.
102 Rancière, *The Ignorant Schoolmaster*, 134, emphasis in original.
103 See Kristin Ross, 'Rancière and the Practice of Equality', *Social Text* 29 (1991), 57–71, at 62–4. See also Rancière interviewed by Davide Panagia, 'Dissenting Words: A Conversation with Jacques Rancière', *diacritics* 30, 2 (Summer 2000), 113–26, at 121 and Oliver Davis, 'The Radical Pedagogies of François Bon and Jacques Rancière', *French Studies* 64, 2 (April 2010), 178–91.
104 Rancière, *Le Philosophe et ses pauvres*, 'Preface' to 2007 edition, ix–x.
105 Rancière, *Le Philosophe et ses pauvres*, 'Preface' to 2007 edition, xi, my translation.
106 Joel Spring, *Wheels in the Head: Educational Philosophies of Authority, Freedom, and Culture from Socrates to Paulo Freire* (New York: McGraw-Hill, 1994), 38–43, at 38.
107 See also Ivan Illich, *Deschooling Society* (New York: Harper & Row, 1971).
108 Goodman, *Compulsory Miseducation* (New York: Horizon, 1962), 20.
109 Aronowitz, *Against Schooling* (Boulder, CO: Paradigm, 2008), 26.
110 Dewey, *Democracy and Education: An Introduction to the Philosophy of Education* (London: Macmillan, 1916, reprinted 1966), 79.
111 Goodman, *Compulsory Miseducation*, 41.
112 Davis, 'The Radical Pedagogies of François Bon and Jacques Rancière'. Independently, Kristin Ross has noted the resemblance between Rancière's Jacotot on the one hand and Freire and Illich on the other in her 'Historicizing Untimeliness', in Gabriel Rockhill

and Philip Watts (eds), *Jacques Rancière: History, Politics, Aesthetics* (Durham, NC: Duke University Press, 2009), 15–29, at 16.

113 Colin Ward and Anthony Fyson, *Streetwork: The Exploding School* (London: Routledge, 1973), 16.

114 For a fuller discussion of Rancière–Jacotot in relation to other examples of egalitarian pedagogy, see Davis, 'The Radical Pedagogies of François Bon and Jacques Rancière'.

115 Paulo Freire, *Pedagogy of Hope: Reliving Pedagogy of the Oppressed*, tr. by Robert R. Barr (London: Continuum, 2006), 30.

Chapter 2   History and Historiography

1 Most of Rancière's 'historical' work is also intensely 'historiographical' so, for the sake of brevity and leaning heavily on its etymology, I shall normally use just the term 'historiography' to refer to both.

2 Adrian Rifkin's Rancierian rejoinder to the anticipated calumnies of methodology fetishists in his compelling *Street Noises: Parisian Pleasure, 1900–40* (Manchester: Manchester University Press, 1993), 11.

3 Yves Michaud, 'Les pauvres et leur philosophe. La philosophie de Jacques Rancière', *Critique* 601–2 (June–July 1997), special issue: *Autour de Jacques Rancière*, 421–2.

4 Raphael Samuel refers to 'the Workshop's growing – if tense – association with the women's movement' in the editorial introduction to Samuel (ed.), *History Workshop: A Collectanea 1967–1991: Documents, Memoirs, Critique and Cumulative Index to History Workshop Journal* (Oxford: History Workshop, 1991), 2.

5 Rancière, *Les Scènes du peuple (Les Révoltes logiques, 1975–1985)* (Lyon: Horlieu, 2003); Adrian Rifkin and Roger Thomas (eds), *Voices of the People: The Politics and Life of 'la Sociale' at the End of the Second Empire*, tr. by John Moore (London: Routledge, 1987).

6 Ross, *May '68 and Its Afterlives* (Chicago: University of Chicago Press, 2002), 116.

7 Rancière, *Les Scènes du peuple*, 12. This and all subsequent translations from this work are my own.

8 Rancière, 'Postface' to the new 2007 edition of Rancière and Alain Faure, *La Parole ouvrière 1830–1851* (Paris: La Fabrique, 2007), 332–42, at 339, my translation.

9 Ross, *May '68 and Its Afterlives*, 126; Annie Cohen-Solal, *Sartre* (Paris: Gallimard, 1985), 641.

10 Ross, *May '68 and Its Afterlives*, 125. See also Philippe Artières, Laurent Quéro and Michelle Zancarini-Fournel, *Le Groupe d'Information sur les Prisons: Archives d'une lutte, 1970–1972* (Paris: Imec, 2003), 13–19.

11 Rancière, *Les Scènes du peuple*, 10.

12 Rancière, *Les Scènes du peuple*, 10.

13 Ross, *May '68 and Its Afterlives*, 125. Sartre, Gavi and Victor, *On a raison de se révolter: discussions* (Paris: Gallimard, 1974).

14 Rancière, *Les Scènes du peuple*, 10.

15 'Ce premier numéro', *Les Révoltes Logiques* 1 (Winter 1975), 2–3, at 2. This and all subsequent translations from *Les Révoltes Logiques*, except where they are taken from articles already translated in Rifkin and Thomas, are my own.

16 *Les Révoltes Logiques* 7 (Spring–Summer 1978), 2; 'Mutineries à Clairvaux', documents presented by Stéphane Douailler and Patrice Vermeren, *Les Révoltes Logiques* 6 (Autumn–Winter 1977), 77–95; Olivier Roy, 'Afghanistan, la guerre des paysans', *Les Révoltes Logiques* 13 (Winter 1980–1), 50–64; Jean Borreil, 'Un été irlandais', *Les Révoltes Logiques* 14–15 (Summer 1981), 136–50.

17 *Les Révoltes Logiques* 1 (Winter 1975), inside back cover.

18 *Les Révoltes Logiques* 1 (Winter 1975), inside back cover.

19 Rancière, 'Postface' to *La Parole ouvrière 1830–1851*, 335.

20 Rancière, *Les Scènes du peuple*, 11.

21 Rancière, *Les Scènes du peuple*, 13. Rancière also signals his departure from this assumption of *La Parole ouvrière* in his 2007 'Postface', Rancière and Faure, *La Parole ouvrière*, 340–1.

22 *Les Révoltes Logiques* 1 (Winter 1975), inside front cover.

23 The film presented an indulgent portrait of one young working-class collaborator and was roundly criticized by Foucault and the *Cahiers du cinéma* group for epitomizing the Giscardist attempt to efface the memory of popular resistance.

24 Burguière, *Bretons de Plozévet* (Paris: Flammarion, 1975), Le Roy Ladurie, *Montaillou, village occitan* (Paris: Gallimard, 1976).

25 Borreil, 'Des politiques nostalgiques', *Les Révoltes Logiques* 3 (Autumn 1976), 87–105, at 105.

26 Rancière, 'L'usine nostalgique', *Les Révoltes Logiques* 13 (Winter 1980–1), 89–97.

27 Rancière, 'De Pelloutier à Hitler: syndicalisme et collaboration', *Les Révoltes Logiques* 4 (Winter 1976), 23–61. Fernand Pelloutier (1867–1901) was one of the founding fathers of the French trade union movement.

28 See Olivier Lalieu, 'L'invention du "devoir de mémoire"', *Vingtième Siècle* 69 (2001), 83–94. Rancière, 'De Pelloutier à Hitler', 23.

29 Rancière and Vauday, 'Going to the Expo: The Worker, His Wife, and Machines', in Rifkin and Thomas (eds), *Voices of the People*, 23–44.

30 'Ce premier numéro', 2. Rancière and Vauday, 'Going to the Expo', 23.

31 Rancière and Vauday, 'Going to the Expo', 41.

32 Rancière and Vauday, 'Going to the Expo', 33.

33 Fraisse and Elhadad, '"L'AFFRANCHISSEMENT DE NOTRE SEXE": À propos des textes de Claire Demar réédité par Valentin Pelosse', *Les Révoltes Logiques* 2 (Spring–Summer 1976), 105–20.

34 Rancière, 'Une femme encombrante (à propos de Suzanne Voilquin)', *Les Révoltes Logiques* 8–9 (Winter 1979), 116–22, at 118.
35 Rancière, 'Une femme encombrante', 118.
36 Fraisse, 'Des femmes présentes (Notes sur l'article précédent)', *Les Révoltes Logiques* 8–9 (Winter 1979), 123–5, at 125.
37 Derrida asked: 'Is the choice of period – the period in which Marxism was being elaborated – a necessary one?' and Rancière responded: 'There is no privileging of a particular period. However, in this period, the problem of how to "articulate oneself" left traces, indeed this was the moment in which problems of identification arose.' Discussion reported by the editors after Rancière's, 'La représentation de l'ouvrier ou la classe impossible', in Philippe Lacoue-Labarthe and Jean-Luc Nancy (eds), *Le Retrait du politique* (Paris: Galilée, 1983), 89–111, at 111, my translation.
38 Nor indeed is Fraisse's position in her defence of Elhadad exactly representative of Fraisse's own work, which tends to be closer to the materialist tradition. She may have felt called upon to exercise in the present the sort of solidarity with Elhadad which Rancière accused her, perhaps wrongly, of failing to exercise in relation to Voilquin.
39 Rancière, 'Le bon temps ou la barrière des plaisirs', *Les Révoltes Logiques* 7 (Spring–Summer 1978), 25–66. Reprinted in Rancière, *Les Scènes du peuple*, 203–52 and in English translation as 'Good Times or Pleasure at the Barriers', in Rifkin and Thomas (eds), *Voices of the People*, 45–94.
40 Rancière, *Les Scènes du peuple*, 12.
41 Rancière, 'Good Times or Pleasure at the Barriers', 47.
42 Rancière, 'Good Times or Pleasure at the Barriers', 50.
43 Rancière, 'Good Times or Pleasure at the Barriers', 50.
44 Rancière, 'Good Times or Pleasure at the Barriers', 49.
45 Ross, *May '68 and Its Afterlives*, 136.
46 Donald Reid, 'Introduction' to *The Nights of Labor: The Workers' Dream in Nineteenth-Century France*, tr. by John Drury, introduced by Donald Reid (Philadelphia: Temple University Press, 1989), xv–xxxvii; Nicholas Hewlett, *Badiou, Balibar, Rancière: Re-thinking Emancipation* (London: Continuum, 2007), 87–90.
47 Benjamin, 'Saint-Simon, Railroads', in *The Arcades Project*, tr. by Howard Eiland and Kevin McLaughlin (Cambridge, MA: Harvard University Press, 1999), 571–602.
48 Rancière, *The Nights of Labor*, vii.
49 Rancière, *The Nights of Labor*, 17.
50 May, *The Political Thought of Jacques Rancière: Creating Equality* (Edinbugh: Edinburgh University Press, 2008).
51 Rancière, *The Nights of Labor*, ix, translation adapted.
52 Rancière, *The Nights of Labor*, viii, emphasis added.
53 Rancière, *The Nights of Labor*, 27, emphasis added. The original is: 'Dans cette socialisation nocturne des vanités individuelles *se sont*

préparées ces trois journées glorieuses auxquelles ont succédé les nuits sans pain ni feu de l'hiver 1830–1831'. Rancière, *La Nuit des prolétaires: archives du rêve ouvrier* (Paris: Fayard, 1981), 39, emphasis added.

54 Rancière, *The Nights of Labor*, 15.
55 Rancière, *The Nights of Labor*, 60.
56 Rancière, *The Nights of Labor*, 124.
57 Christophe Prochasson, *Saint-Simon ou l'anti-Marx: figures du saint-simonisme français XIXe–XXe siècles* (Paris: Perrin, 2005), 17.
58 Pierre Musso, *Le Vocabulaire de Saint-Simon* (Paris: Ellipses, 2005), 3.
59 See Paul Bénichou, *Le Temps des prophètes: doctrines de l'âge romantique* (Paris: Gallimard, 1977), especially Ch. 2 on Simon Ballanche, another important figure in Rancière's work, 74–102.
60 Prochasson, *Saint-Simon ou l'anti-Marx*, 135.
61 Prochasson, *Saint-Simon ou l'anti-Marx*, 143.
62 Prochasson, *Saint-Simon ou l'anti-Marx*, 150.
63 Rancière, *Louis-Gabriel Gauny: le philosophe plébéien*, texts by Gauny selected and introduced by Rancière (Paris: La Découverte/Maspero and Presses Universitaires de Vincennes, 1983), 9, emphasis in original, my translation.
64 See also Francis Damier, 'Les Saint-Simoniens à la rencontre des ouvriers parisiens au tournant des années 1830', in Pierre Musso (ed.) *Actualité du Saint-Simonisme: Colloque de Cerisy* (Paris: Presses Universitaires de France, 2004), 115–47, at 125.
65 See also Neil McWilliam, 'Peripheral Visions: Class, Cultural Aspiration, and the Artisan Community in Mid-Nineteenth-Century France', in Salim Kemal and Ivan Gaskell (eds), *Politics and Aesthetics in the Arts* (Cambridge: Cambridge University Press, 2000), 140–73, at 151–2.
66 Farge, 'L'Histoire comme avènement', in *Critique* 601–2 (June–July 1997), special issue: *Autour de Jacques Rancière*, 461–6 at 461, my translation. In issues 13–15, Farge is also listed as a member of the journal's collective.
67 For reliable accounts of the *Annales* school see Peter Burke, *The French Historical Revolution: The Annales School, 1929–89* (Cambridge: Polity, 1990), and Robert Gildea, *The Past in French History* (New Haven: Yale University Press, 1994). See also Jean-Pierre Hérubel's very useful bibliography, but treat with caution his 'theoretical' commentary, which, after a reading of *The Names of History*, cannot but seem complacent. Hérubel, *Annales Historiography and Theory: A Selective and Annotated Bibliography* (London: Greenwood, 1994).
68 See Burke, *The French Historical Revolution*, 2.
69 Rancière, *The Names of History: On the Poetics of Knowledge*, tr. by Hassan Melehy with a Foreword by Hayden White (Minneapolis: University of Minnesota Press, 1994), 107, n. 1.

70 Barthes, *Michelet*, tr. by Richard Howard (Oxford: Blackwell, 1987). Barthes, 'The Discourse of History', in Barthes, *The Rustle of Language*, tr. by Richard Howard (London: Farrar, Straus and Giroux, 1986), 127–54. Hartog, *Évidence de l'histoire* (2nd edn, Paris: Gallimard, 2007), 207, my translation.

71 Barthes, 'The Discourse of History', 139.

72 Rancière is explict about this in *The Politics of Aesthetics*, where he says of his thesis in *The Names of History* that '[t]his has nothing whatsoever to do with a thesis on the reality or unreality of things'. Rancière, *The Politics of Aesthetics: The Distribution of the Sensible*, tr. and introduced by Gabriel Rockhill, with an Afterword by Slavoj Žižek (London: Continuum, 2004), 38.

73 Rancière, *The Names of History*, 8, translation adapted.

74 Farge's comments on the work's reception are supported by Martyne Perrot and Martin de la Soudière, in Perrot and de la Soudière, interview with Rancière, 'Histoire des mots, mots de l'histoire', *Communications* 58 (1994), 87–101, at 100.

75 Paul Ricoeur notes that Aron's text was a key moment in this history of institutional and intellectual friction in *Temps et récit I: l'intrigue et le récit historique* (Paris: Seuil, 1983), 174.

76 Certeau, *L'Écriture de l'histoire* (Paris: Gallimard, 1975), 80.

77 Louis Althusser and Étienne Balibar, *Reading Capital*, tr. by Ben Brewster (London: New Left Books, 1970), 96.

78 Derrida, 'Politics and Friendship', interview with Michael Sprinker, in Michael Sprinker and E. Ann Kaplan (eds), *The Althusserian Legacy* (London: Verso, 1993), 183–231, at 197 and 187.

79 Farge, 'L'Histoire comme avènement', 464.

80 Perrot and de la Soudière, 'Histoire des mots, mots de l'histoire', 97.

81 Peter Schöttler draws attention to three points of convergence between early Althusser and the *Annales* school in 'Althusser and Annales Historiography – An Impossible Dialogue', in Sprinker and Kaplan (eds), *The Althusserian Legacy*, 81–98.

82 Rancière, *The Names of History*, 2.

83 Chartier's reaction is reported in Farge, 'L'Histoire comme avènement', 464 n. 4. Furet, *In the Workshop of History*, tr. by Jonathan Mandelbaum (Chicago: Chicago University Press, 1984), 54–74, at 56.

84 Veyne, *Comment on écrit l'histoire* (Paris: Seuil, 1971), 10; White, *Metahistory: The Historical Imagination in Nineteenth-Century Europe* (Baltimore: Johns Hopkins University Press, 1973); Ricoeur's *Temps et récit I*; Carrard, *Poetics of the New History: French Historical Discourse from Braudel to Chartier* (Baltimore: Johns Hopkins University Press, 1992). White prefaced the English translation of *Les Noms de l'histoire*. Carrard's book, published in the same year as *The Names*, is a workmanlike narratological analysis of key texts by *Annales*-school historians.

85 Ricoeur, *Temps et récit I*, 184, 186.

86   See Ricoeur, *Temps et récit I*, 382. Hartog insists that the interest of Ricoeur's reading lies not in the fact that he catches Braudel out unwittingly writing narrative but rather in the way he shows that Braudel invented a new kind of narrative. Hartog, *Evidence de l'histoire*, 214.

87   Rancière, *The Names of History*, 14; *Les Noms de l'histoire*, 33.

88   Braudel, cited in Rancière, *The Names of History*, 17.

89   Rancière, *The Names of History*, 18.

90   Rancière, *The Names of History*, 23.

91   Rancière, *The Names of History*, 45.

92   Rancière, *The Names of History*, 46, emphasis in original.

93   Michelet, cited in Rancière, *The Names of History*, 49.

94   Rancière, *The Names of History*, 49, emphasis in original.

95   Febvre, *The Problem of Unbelief in the Sixteenth Century: The Religion of Rabelais*, tr. by Beatrice Gottlieb (Boston: Harvard University Press, 1982), 5.

96   Rancière is not alone in taking this view of Febvre's study. See Burke, *The French Historical Revolution*, 30.

97   Rancière, 'Le concept d'anachronisme et la vérité de l'historien', *L'Inactuel* 6 (Autumn 1996), 53–68, at 66.

98   Furet, *Interpreting the French Revolution*, tr. by Elborg Forster (Cambridge: Cambridge University Press, 1981).

99   Rancière, *The Names of History*, 39, translation adapted.

100 Rancière, *The Names of History*, 44, translation substantially adapted. It may not be obvious why Rancière claims that speaking beings are temporally different from themselves. I take him to mean that with language comes a sense of different temporal moments (past, present, future) and the necessity – apparent in hoping or regretting, for example – of living simultaneously in more than one of these, which prevents us from ever fully coinciding with ourselves in temporal terms. There are well-established variations on this theme within the phenomenological tradition, particularly in the work of Husserl, Heidegger and the early Sartre.

101 White, Foreword to Rancière, *The Names of History*, x.

102 Rancière, *The Names of History*, 19.

103 Rancière, *The Names of History*, 20.

104 Hobbes, *Leviathan*, ed. by J. Gaskin (Oxford: Oxford University Press/World's Classics, 2008 edition), Ch. 29 § 14 [170–2], 216–17.

105 Hobbes, *Leviathan*, Ch. 29 § 14 [170–2], 216–17, underlining added, italic emphasis in original.

106 Hobbes, *Behemoth or The History of the Causes of the Civil Wars of England*, in *English Works of Thomas Hobbes*, vol. vi, ed. by Robert Molesworth (London, 1839), 192–3. Cited in Gaskin's Introduction to *Leviathan*, xiv.

107 E.P. Thompson, *The Making of the English Working Class* (1st edn, London: Victor Gollancz, 1963; reprinted London: Penguin, 1991), 24.

108 Rifkin, 'JR Cinéphile, or the Philosopher Who Loved Things', *Parallax* 15, 3 (2009), 81–7, at 82.

109 Gabriel Rockhill argues that there is a similar disjunction between Rancière's transhistorical analysis of politics and his profoundly historicizing approach to aesthetics. See Rockhill, 'La démocratie dans l'histoire des cultures politiques', in Jérôme Game and Aliocha Wald Lasowski (eds), *Jacques Rancière et la politique de l'esthétique* (Paris: Éditions des Archives Contemporaines, 2009), 55–71, at 65.

Chapter 3   The Mature Politics: From Policing to Democracy

1 Rancière, 'Ten Theses on Politics', *Theory & Event* 5, 3 (2001), Thesis 1 (available online from http://muse.jhu.edu/login?uri=/journals/theory_and_event/v005/5.3ranciere.html).

2 Rancière, *The Ignorant Schoolmaster: Five Lessons in Intellectual Emancipation*, tr. by Kristin Ross (Stanford: Stanford University Press, 1991), 105, emphasis in original.

3 Rancière, *The Ignorant Schoolmaster*, 76–80.

4 Rancière, *Disagreement: Politics and Philosophy*, tr. by Julie Rose (Minneapolis: University of Minnesota Press, 1999), 29.

5 Rancière, *Disagreement*, 28.

6 Rancière, *Disagreement*, 28.

7 Which is what Gabriel Rockhill does when he considers Rancière's use of the term 'police' a particularly flagrant example of his tendency to forge transhistorical concepts from selectively historicized examples. Rockhill, 'La démocratie dans l'histoire des cultures politiques', in Jérôme Game and Aliocha Wald Lasowski, *Jacques Rancière et la politique de l'esthétique* (Paris: Éditions des Archives Contemporaines, 2009), 55–71, at 59. See also n. 18, below.

8 Rancière, 'Sur la théorie de l'idéologie politique d'Althusser', *L'Homme et la Société: revue internationale de recherches et de synthèses sociologiques* (Jan.–Mar. 1973), 31–61, at 34, my translation, emphasis in original. The first version of this essay was written in 1969.

9 Jean-Pierre Le Goff, *Mai 68: l'héritage impossible* (Paris: La Découverte, 2002).

10 Althusser, 'Ideology and Ideological State Apparatuses', in *Lenin and Philosophy, and Other Essays*, tr. by Ben Brewster (London: New Left Books, 1971), 121–76.

11 Rancière, 'Ten Theses', Thesis 7, translation adapted.

12 Rancière, *Disagreement*, 31.

13 Rancière, *Disagreement*, 16, emphasis in original.

14 See Rancière's comments in the interview with Arrous and Costanzo, 'Questions à Jacques Rancière', *Drôle d'époque* 14 (Spring 2004), 15–29, at 16.

15 See Rancière, *Disagreement*, 32.

16 Rancière, 'Ten Theses', Thesis 10.

17 Slavoj Žižek, *The Ticklish Subject: The Absent Centre of Political Ontology* (London: Verso, 1999), 199, italics in original.
18 For Rockhill, Rancière's treatment of Athenian democracy is another example of what he calls his 'conceptual transcendentalism' (see also n. 7, above), the detaching of concepts from particular situations and concrete contexts in order to derive abstract transhistorical meanings which can then be re-projected back onto different particular situations. For Rockhill, the approach is problematic both because it is at odds with the historicizing bent of Rancière's work on aesthetics and because it is 'anti-democratic' in the sense that it tends towards an idiolect which leaves Rancière himself the sole arbiter of the legitimate meaning of his concepts. See Rockhill, 'La démocratie dans l'histoire des cultures politiques', 61. While Rockhill is correct to discern a tension in Rancière's work between the urge to historicize and the critique of historicism, it is possible to see this as a productive tension rather than an inconsistency. Moreover, in analysing Athenian democracy in *Disagreement*, Rancière is not assuming that the concept is transhistorically valid simply because it is historically prior to other examples of politics which he considers. Rather, he simply sees a common structural process at work in Athenian democracy and other examples of what he wants to call politics which just happen to occur later.
19 See Gilles Labelle, 'Two Refoundation Projects of Democracy in Contemporary French Philosophy: Cornelius Castoriadis and Jacques Rancière', *Philosophy and Social Criticism* 27, 4 (July 2001), 75–103, at 78. Granted, this 'sociological' way of explaining the emergence of Athenian democracy already presupposes a certain conception of politics, as Rancière notes. See Rancière, *Disagreement*, 7.
20 Rancière, *Disagreement*, 9.
21 Rancière, *Disagreement*, 9.
22 Rancière, *Disagreement*, 9.
23 Rancière in an interview with Davide Panagia, 'Dissenting Words: A Conversation with Jacques Rancière', *diacritics* 30, 2 (Summer 2000), 113–26, at 124.
24 Rancière, *Disagreement*, 14; Rancière, *La Mésentente: politique et philosophie* (Paris: Galilée, 1995), 34.
25 Rancière, *Disagreement*, 38.
26 Rancière, *Disagreement*, 39.
27 Rancière, *La Mésentente*, 64: 'le litige politique révèle un inconciliable qui est pourtant traitable.' The translation given is my own. Cf. Rancière, *Disagreement*, 39.
28 Rancière, *Disagreement*, 39, translation adapted; Rancière, *La Mésentente*, 64.
29 I have opted for 'subjectivation' as the most straightforward translation of Rancière's 'subjectivation', though it has also been rendered with both 'subjectification', notably by Rose in *Disagreement*, and

'subjectivization'. See also Sam Chambers, 'The Politics of Literarity', *Theory & Event* 8, 3 (2005), n. 2 (available online from http://muse.jhu.edu/login?uri=/journals/theory_and_event/v008/8.3chambers.html).

30 Rancière, *On the Shores of Politics*, tr. by Liz Heron (London: Verso, 1995), 45–52. Note that this is a translation of the first, Osiris, edition from 1992 of *Aux bords du politique*. The second, Gallimard/La Fabrique edition of the French text (1998) contains additional material not included in the Verso translation. In some cases this is because the material in question had already appeared in English.

31 This is an example cited by Rancière in 'Politics, Identification, and Subjectivization', *October* 61 (1992), 58–64, at 62.

32 Rancière has been careful to distinguish his account of politics from Habermas's theory of politics as communicative action (see, in particular, Rancière, *Disagreement*, 55–60). Yet his discussion tends to overlook the fact that for Habermas the idea that the parties to a rational dispute are fully recognized as participants in the negotiating process is only ever the *ideal* scenario: it is the ideal communicative community which is 'an undamaged intersubjectivity that allows both for unconstrained mutual understanding among individuals and for the identities of individuals who come to an unconstrained understanding with themselves'. Habermas, *The Theory of Communicative Action*, vol. 2, *Lifeworld and System: A Critique of Functionalist Reason*, tr. by Thomas McCarthy (Cambridge: Polity, 1987), 2. Although this in principle allows for other communicative communities which fall short of that ideal, Habermas thinks that where they do, the political process is one which still tends towards that ideal: 'In communicative action participants pursue their plans cooperatively on the basis of a shared definition of the situation. If a shared definition of the situation has first to be negotiated, or if efforts to come to some agreement within the framework of shared situation definitions fail, the attainment of consensus, which is normally a condition for pursuing goals, can itself become an end. In any case, the *success* achieved by teleological action and the *consensus* brought about by acts of reaching understanding are the criteria for whether a situation has been dealt with successfully or not.' Habermas, *The Theory of Communicative Action*, vol. 2, 127, emphasis in original. For Rancière, of course, politics tends in exactly the opposite direction, towards dissensus rather than consensus, and consists in disagreement rather than negotiation.

33 Rancière, 'Ten Theses', Thesis 8.

34 Hallward, 'Jacques Rancière et la théâtrocratie ou Les limites de l'égalité improvisée', in Laurence Cornu and PatriceVermeren (eds), *La Philosophie déplacée: autour de Jacques Rancière* (Paris: Horlieu, 2006), 481–96. Hallward is also alluding to Rancière's use of the term 'theatocracy', after Plato, in *The Philosopher and His Poor*, tr. by John

Drury, Corinne Oster and Andrew Parker (Durham, NC: Duke University Press, 2003), 45–7.

35 Hallward, 'Jacques Rancière et la théâtrocratie', 483.

36 Rancière, *Disagreement*, 52, emphasis in orginal.

37 Rancière, 'Politics, Identification, and Subjectivization', 62, emphasis in original.

38 For more on the source of the texts see Rancière, *Aux Bords du politique* (2nd edn, Paris: Gallimard/Folio, 1998), 255–6. 'La Cause de l'autre' is reprinted in *Aux Bords*, 202–20.

39 Rancière, 'Politics, Identification, and Subjectivization', 61.

40 Rancière, 'Politics, Identification, and Subjectivization', 61. The definitive account of the October 1961 massacre is Jim House and Neil MacMaster, *Paris 1961: Algerians, State Terror, and Memory* (Oxford: Oxford University Press, 2006). For their discussion of Rancière's response to it see pp. 200–1.

41 Rancière, 'Politics, Identification, and Subjectivization', 61. It is a shame Rancière has not said more about exactly how this is an example of heterologic disidentification. As Nicholas Hewlett notes, the slogan first arose in response to xenophobic and anti-Semitic remarks directed against one of the most prominent figures in the movement, Daniel Cohn-Bendit. Hewlett, *Badiou, Balibar, Rancière: Re-thinking Emancipation* (London: Continuum, 2007), 98. Clearly it also resonated with the Holocaust and perhaps also with the preparatory measures enacted by the Nazis during the 1930s to deprive Jews living in Germany of full citizenship, such that the subject-position of a 'German Jew' was itself in legal terms 'impossible' at the end of that decade.

42 Rancière, 'Politics, Identification, and Subjectivization', 62.

43 Joy Sorman, *Boys, boys, boys* (Paris: Gallimard, 2005), 19, my translation.

44 For example, Rancière, *Disagreement*, 123–4. This pejorative commonplace of mainstream French political discourse denotes any conception of politics suspected of privileging the rights of particular segments of society, especially those marked by their particularity of race or ethnicity, religion or sexuality, in a manner presumed to be inconsistent with the universal values of the French republican tradition.

45 On the relationship between Rancière and queer theory more generally, see my own 'Rancière and Queer Theory: On Irritable Attachment' and the other articles in a recent special issue, *Borderlands* 8, 2 (2009), *Jacques Rancière on the Shores of Queer Theory*, ed. by Samuel Chambers and Michael O'Rourke (http://www.borderlands.net.au/issues/vol8no2.html).

46 See also Lisa Duggan's analysis of the emergence of a 'neoliberal "equality" politics' in the gay and lesbian movement in 1990s in the US in her *The Twilight of Equality? Neoliberalism, Cultural Politics, and*

the Attack on Democracy (Boston: Beacon, 2003), Ch. 3. For this 'new homonormativity', as she calls it (p. 50), ' "equality" becomes narrow, formal access to a few conservatizing institutions, "freedom" becomes immunity for bigotry and vast inequalities in commercial life and civil society, the "right to privacy" becomes domestic confinement, and democratic politics itself becomes something to be escaped' (pp. 65–6).

47 Weeks, *The World We Have Won: The Remaking of Erotic and Intimate Life* (London: Routledge, 2007). Fassin, *L'Inversion de la question homosexuelle* (2nd edn, Paris: Amsterdam, 2008), 105–14.

48 Clifford, 'Taking Identity Politics Seriously: The Contradictory, Stony Ground . . .', in Paul Gilroy, Lawrence Grossberg and Angela McRobbie (eds), *Without Guarantees: In Honour of Stuart Hall* (London: Verso, 2000), 94–11. Halberstam, *In a Queer Time and Place: Transgender Bodies, Subcultural Lives* (New York: New York University Press, 2005), 19–21.

49 And if 'cannot be allowed to mean' implies a limited endorsement of 'policing', so be it.

50 Rancière, *Disagreement*, 36.

51 This is a legitimate understanding of the term 'aesthetics' and not another example of Rancierian 'twisting'. It is common in eighteenth-century philosophical writing, for example in Kant, though is no longer the most usual meaning of the term.

52 Rancière, *Disagreement*, 36, emphasis in original.

53 Rancière, *Disagreement*, 36.

54 The consensus among translators of Rancière seems to be that 'le partage du sensible' has to be translated as the division or distribution of 'the sensible' rather than 'the sensory', but, after careful consideration, I have opted in this book for 'the sensory'. Rancière's own attempt to distinguish between the two terms is perplexing: see his interview with Jan Völker and Frank Ruda, 'Politique de l'indétermination esthétique', in Game and Wald Lasowski (eds), *Jacques Rancière et la politique de l'esthétique*, 157–75, at 159. He says there that '[t]he sensible is distributed meaning, meaning brought into relation with one of the senses, the visible articulated as the sayable, interpreted, evaluated, etc.' ('Le sensible, c'est du sens distribué: du sens mis en rapport avec le sens, du visible qui est articulté en dicible, qui est interprété, évalué, etc.'). According to Rancière's gloss here then, *le partage du sensible* would be 'the distribution of distributed meaning'. I understand his reason for insisting on the distinction between the sensible and the sensory and for preferring the former to be because he wants to insist that the point of the concept of *le partage du sensible* and of his thinking on the relationship between politics and aesthetics more generally is that at any given moment this totality of possible meaningful sensory experience is *not* all available to all equally and in the same way, precisely because

it is shared out or carved up in ways which privilege some rather than others. So the point I understand him to be trying to make is that everything that could, in principle, be available to sensation never actually is because it is restricted and mediated in the carving-up and sharing-out which *le partage du sensible* designates. Yet it seems to me that as a matter of logic this restrictive work is already performed, in the expression *le partage du sensible* and the concept it designates, by the noun *le partage* (or its verb *partager*), such that to try to perform it again by opting for 'sensible' over 'sensory' is to try to say the same thing twice, as I did above in the light of his gloss. My objection is not to the concept of *le partage du sensible* but to the way it is being expressed and to the way it has been translated. This is a separate issue from the obvious confusion which rendering *le sensible* with 'the sensible' in English risks generating.

55   Rancière, *The Politics of Aesthetics: The Distribution of the Sensible*, tr. and introduced by Gabriel Rockhill with an Afterword by Slavoj Žižek (London: Continuum, 2004), 13. Rancière is presumably thinking here of Foucault's concept of the *episteme*, the historically specific conditions which determine what can be meant, seen and experienced.

56   Rancière, *The Politics of Aesthetics*, 13. This way of formulating the concept supports my argument in n. 54, above.

57   Rancière, *Disagreement*, 35.

58   Élie During, 'Politiques de l'accent: Rancière entre Deleuze et Derrida', in Game and Wald Lasowski (eds), *Jacques Rancière et la politique de l'esthétique*, 74–92.

59   Rancière, *Disagreement*, 31.

60   May, *The Political Thought of Jacques Rancière: Creating Equality* (Edinbugh: Edinburgh University Press, 2008), 118.

61   Žižek, *The Ticklish Subject: The Absent Centre of Political Ontology* (London: Verso, 1999), 238.

62   Žižek, *In Defense of Lost Causes* (London: Verso, 2008), 418–19.

63   Žižek, *The Ticklish Subject*, 233–4, emphasis in original.

64   Žižek, *The Ticklish Subject*, 238. I say derisive mainly because neither 'game' nor 'provocation' in this context carries especially positive connotations but also because I suspect 'hysterical' is being used pejoratively as well as technically.

65   Žižek, *In Defense of Lost Causes*, 418–19.

66   Badiou, *L'Être et l'événement* (Paris: Seuil, 1988), particularly 361.

67   E.P. Thompson interviewed by Mike Merrill, in MARHO [Mid-Atlantic Radical Historians' Organization], *Visions of History* (Manchester: Manchester University Press, 1976), 22.

68   My argument here echoes some of the concerns expressed by Peter Hallward in his 'Jacques Rancière et la théâtrocratie'.

69   Rancière, *Aux Bords*, 72–3.

70   Jean-Philippe Deranty has suggested Rancière and Honneth are both advancing versions of a 'politics of recognition'. Deranty, 'Rancière

and Contemporary Political Ontology', *Theory & Event* 6, 4 (2003) (available online from http://muse.jhu.edu/login?uri=/journals/ theory_and_event/v006/6.4deranty.html). See also Deranty et al., *Recognition, Work, Politics: New Directions in French Critical Theory* (Leiden: Brill, 2007), Ch. 7. While in a sense Deranty is right to say that Rancière's is a politics of recognition, in that Rancière is concerned with the miscount and the wrong, one major difference is that Honneth is far more interested in the affective dimension to (non-)recognition than the socio-structural. This is why I suggest that, rather than their being merely similar, as Deranty does, Honneth's account can usefully supplement Rancière's in the affective sphere.

71 Honneth, *The Struggle for Recognition: The Moral Grammar of Social Conflicts*, tr. by Joel Anderson (Cambridge: Polity, 1995), xi.
72 Honneth, *The Struggle for Recognition*, 131.
73 Honneth, *The Struggle for Recognition*, 163.
74 Žižek, *In Defense of Lost Causes*, 418–19.
75 Here again is the crux of Rancière's disagreement with Habermas's theory of politics as communicative action: whereas for Habermas politics involves rational debate between fully constituted subjects over particular issues, for Rancière the very existence of at least one of the parties and the status of their discourse is in question.
76 Rancière, *On the Shores of Politics*, 49.
77 It could be argued that 1789 is shorthand for the Revolution in its entirety, but why not say 'the Revolution' in that case?
78 In the other examples of subjectivation he gives in the mature politics, violence is even less present than it is here.
79 For a useful sociological discussion of this trend in another context, the US, see Steven Brint, *In an Age of Experts: The Changing Role of Professionals in Politics and Public Life* (Princeton: Princeton University Press, 1994).
80 Rancière, *Disagreement*, 14.
81 Labelle, 'Two Refoundation Projects of Democracy in Contemporary French Philosophy', 93.

Chapter 4   Literature

1 Rancière, *La Parole muette: essai sur les contradictions de la littérature* (Paris: Hachette, 1998), 5, 175. Ann Jefferson concurs in her argument that 'literature be seen primarily as a question [. . .] a site of repeated contestations from within'. Jefferson, *Biography and the Question of Literature* (Oxford: Oxford University Press, 2007), 10.
2 The term 'paradigm shift', with its echoes of Bachelard's and Kuhn's philosophies of science, is used by Rancière in *La Parole muette*, 13.
3 Williams, *Marxism and Literature* (Oxford: Oxford University Press, 1977), 45–54. Pierre Macherey and Étienne Balibar, 'Literature as an

Ideological Form: Some Marxist Propositions', *Oxford Literary Review* 3 (1978), 4–12.

4 Nancy and Lacoue-Labarthe, *The Literary Absolute: The Theory of Literature in German Romanticism*, tr. by Philip Barnard and Cheryl Lester (Albany: State University of New York Press, 1988).

5 Rancière, *La Parole muette*, 22. This and all subsequent translations from *La Parole muette* are my own.

6 Rancière, *La Parole muette*, 22.

7 Rancière, *La Parole muette*, 26.

8 Rancière, *La Parole muette*, 28.

9 Rancière, *La Parole muette*, 29.

10 Rancière, *The Politics of Aesthetics: The Distribution of the Sensible*, tr. and introduced by Gabriel Rockhill, with an Afterword by Slavoj Žižek (London: Continuum, 2004), 23.

11 Rancière, *La Parole muette*, 32.

12 Rancière, *La Parole muette*, 27.

13 Rancière, *La Parole muette*, 33.

14 Rancière, *La Parole muette*, 71.

15 Rancière, *La Parole muette*, 71, 28 (quotation).

16 Kollias, 'Taking Sides: Jacques Rancière and Agonistic Literature', *Paragraph* 30, 2 (2007), 82–97.

17 Rancière, *La Parole muette*, 87.

18 Derrida, 'Plato's Pharmacy', in *Dissemination*, tr. by Barbara Johnson (London: Athlone, 1981), 61–171.

19 Plato, *Phaedrus* [275 d], tr. by Robin Waterfield (Oxford: Oxford University Press, 2002), 70.

20 Derrida, 'Plato's Pharmacy', 149; Rancière, *La Parole muette*, 82.

21 David Bell, 'Writing, Movement/Space, Democracy: On Jacques Rancière's Literary History', *SubStance* 103 (2004), 126–40.

22 Rancière, *La Parole muette*, 82.

23 Insisting that there is more to the contrast than first meets the eye, he argues that 'writing is not merely the tracing of signs as opposed to vocalization' (Rancière, *La Parole muette*, 82). He seems to allow for spoken language which functions as writing does in a dual passing reference to writing 'entrusted to transient breath or to fragile paper' (Rancière, *La Parole muette*, 95).

24 Rancière, *La Parole muette*, 82.

25 Rancière, *La Chair des mots: politiques de l'écriture* (Paris: Galilée, 1998), 125, 132. Kollias renders *littérarité* with 'literariness' in his 'Taking Sides', 83.

26 Rancière, *The Politics of Aesthetics*, 39.

27 Rancière's conviction, expressed forcefully in *The Politics of Aesthetics* (pp. 39–40) and somewhat more forcefully in *Le Partage du sensible: esthétique et politique* (Paris: La Fabrique, 2000, 63), is that the effects of literarity on communities are more often disturbing or disincorporating than homogenizing: 'Instead [*bien plutôt*], they

introduce lines of fracture and disincorporation into imaginary collective bodies.'

28 Rancière explicitly differentiates the Russian Formalists' conception of *literaturnost* from his *littérarité* in *Politique de la littérature* (Paris: Galilée, 2007), 22. Although his use of the same term is unfortunate, it is unlikely that an attentive reader of *La Parole muette* would have confused the two underlying concepts. See *La Parole muette*, 8.

29 Rancière, 'Balzac and the Island of the Book', in *The Flesh of Words: The Politics of Writing*, tr. by Charlotte Mandell (Stanford: Stanford University Press, 2004), 94–112, 103. See also *La Parole muette*, 94, where Rancière's personification of the written word is more than usually pronounced when he writes of '[t]he trace of the mute letter, of *Paul and Virginie* or any other book which roams randomly through the world before going to sleep on a fairground stall where it lies available to all those men and women who have no business to be reading books'.

30 Rancière, *Politique de la littérature*, 21–2. This and all subsequent translations from this work are my own. An English translation is forthcoming from Polity in 2011, but was not available at the time of going to press.

31 Vernant, cited in Derrida, 'Plato's Pharmacy', 144, n. 68.

32 Rancière, *La Parole muette*, 83.

33 Nancy, 'Jacques Rancière et la métaphysique', in Laurence Cornu and Patrice Vermeren (eds), *La Philosophie déplacée: autour de Jacques Rancière* (Paris: Horlieu, 2006), 155–67.

34 Rancière, *The Politics of Aesthetics*, 39.

35 Rancière, *Politique de la littérature*, 51.

36 Rancière, *Politique de la littérature*, 22.

37 As will become clear in Chapter 5, however, Rancière will refine his position by saying that this notion of the work of art as a 'blueprint' for a new form of community is one of two seemingly antithetical ways in which the political meaning of the artwork in the age of aesthetics (or under the aesthetic regime) has been understood.

38 Solange Guénoun and John Kavanagh, 'Literature, Politics, Aesthetics: Approaches to Democratic Disagreement', tr. by R. Lapidus, *SubStance* 92 (2000), 3–24, at 17.

39 Rancière, *The Politics of Aesthetics*, 29.

40 Rancière, *Politique de la littérature*, 17.

41 See Barthes, 'The Reality Effect' in Barthes, *The Rustle of Language*, tr. by Richard Howard (London: Farrar, Straus and Giroux, 1986), 141–8. Barthes, however, starts out in this essay from the conviction that the barometer *cannot* be a useless object.

42 Rancière, *La Parole muette*, 117.

43 Rancière, *Politique de la littérature*, 49.

44 Rancière, *The Politics of Aesthetics*, 14.

45 Rancière, *La Parole muette*, 106.

46 Rancière, *Politique de la littérature*, 156.
47 Rancière, *La Parole muette*, 114. No Nietzschean reference is intended in the use here of the term 'sub-personal'. I am simply referring to a level of explanation or experience which lies beneath that of the fully formed person. Emotions and perceptions, for example, can be thought of as operating, in this sense, at a sub-personal level.
48 Rancière, *Politique de la littérature*, 158.
49 Rancière, *Politique de la littérature*, 73.
50 Rancière, *Politique de la littérature*, 74.
51 Rancière, 'La mise à mort d'Emma Bovary: littérature, démocratie et médecine', in *Politique de la littérature*, 59–83.
52 Rancière interviewed by Adrien Arrous and Alexandre Costanzo, 'Questions à Jacques Rancière', *Drôle d'époque* 14 (Spring 2004), 15–29, at 25–6, my translation.
53 Rancière, *Mallarmé: la politique de la sirène* (Paris: Hachette, 1996), my translation of the title.
54 For Rancière's categorical rejection of this reading, or 'myth', see *Mallarmé*, 64.
55 On Mallarmé's writings for *La Dernière Mode* and the history of their reception see Damian Catani, *The Poet in Society: Art, Consumerism, and Politics in Mallarmé* (New York: Peter Lang, 2003).
56 Catani, *The Poet in Society*, 1.
57 For a useful overview of recent trends see Roger Pearson, *Mallarmé and Circumstance: The Translation of Silence* (Oxford: Oxford University Press, 2004), 1–6.
58 Rancière, *Mallarmé*, 12–13. This and all subsequent translations from this work are my own.
59 Catani, *The Poet in Society*, 5, 261.
60 Rancière, *Mallarmé*, 25.
61 Rancière, *Mallarmé*, 17.
62 Rancière, *Mallarmé*, 30. See also Rancière, 'La rime et le conflit: la politique du poème', in Bertrand Marchal and Jean-Luc Steinmetz (eds), *Mallarmé ou l'obscurité lumineuse* (Paris: Hermann, 1999), 115–41, at 117.
63 Rancière, *Mallarmé*, 32.
64 Mallarmé, 'Un spectacle interrompu', *Oeuvres complètes*, vol. 2, ed. by Bertrand Marchal (Paris: Gallimard, 2003), 90–2.
65 Rancière, *Mallarmé*, 36.
66 Rancière, *Mallarmé*, 32. On Mallarmé and the surface see also Rancière, 'The Surface of Design', in *The Future of the Image*, tr. by Gregory Elliott (London: Verso, 2007), 91–107.
67 Rancière, *Mallarmé*, 47–8.
68 Rancière, *Mallarmé*, 54–5.
69 Rancière, *Mallarmé*, 59.
70 Rancière, *Mallarmé*, 80. ('Le poème n'est pas seulement une "oeuvre d'art". La fiction n'est pas seulement le travail de l'imagination. Elle est proprement ce qui doit assumer la succession de la religion

comme élévation de l'humain à son grandeur et principe d'une communauté accordée à cette grandeur.')
71 Catani, *The Poet in Society*, 6.
72 Rancière, *Mallarmé*, 53.
73 Mallarmé, 'Conflit', *Oeuvres complètes*, vol. 2, 104–9.
74 Mallarmé, 'Confrontation', *Oeuvres complètes*, vol. 2, 260–4.
75 Rancière, *Mallarmé*, 62.
76 Rancière, *Mallarmé*, 63.
77 Rancière, *Mallarmé*, 64.
78 Rancière, *Mallarmé*, 107.
79 Catani, for example, although he is enthusiastic about Rancière's attention to popular cultural forms in Mallarmé's work objects that 'the "democratic" side to Rancière's argument promises more than it delivers' (Catani, *The Poet in Society*, 5). Granted, Rancière's approach, here as elsewhere, is far from being laboriously comprehensive, but nor does it preclude others from working on the detail.
80 Mallarmé, 'Conflit', 107, my translation.

Chapter 5   Art and Aesthetics

1 Rancière, *Aesthetics and Its Discontents*, tr. by Steven Cocoran (Cambridge: Polity, 2009), 36.
2 Rancière, 'Existe-t-il une esthétique deleuzienne?', in Eric Alliez (ed.), *Gilles Deleuze: une vie philosophique* (Paris: Synthélabo, 1998), 525–36, at 526, my translation. Rancière, *The Politics of Aesthetics: The Distribution of the Sensible*, tr. and introduced by Gabriel Rockhill, with an Afterword by Slavoj Žižek (London: Continuum, 2004), 10.
3 A point made in Sudeep Dasgupta's very useful analysis, 'Jacques Rancière en de spiraal van het denken over politiek en esthetiek', Afterword to Jacques Rancière, *Het Esthetische Denken*, the Dutch translation of *Le Partage du sensible* (Amsterdam: Valiz, 2007). I am very grateful to Sudeep Dasgupta for providing me with an English version of this piece.
4 Although, as I noted in Chapter 2, above, sometimes such claims are made in addition, by implication, but the important point is that this is a conception of the intrinsically political character of aesthetic experience which is, in principle, independent of such claims for influence over governmental structures and institutions.
5 Rancière, interview by Jérôme Game, 'Critique de la critique du "spectacle"', *La Revue internationale des livres et des idées* 12 (July 2009) (http://revuedeslivres.net/articles.php?id=360), my translation. Here the operator 'etc.' expresses a principled scepticism towards the whole question of self-definition in disciplinary or institutional terms, which can also be traced back to his critique of the *Annales* school.

6 At a time in the 1970s and 1980s when Bourdieu's work was increasingly influential, both in academic and, increasingly after the Socialists' victory in 1981, in political circles, Rancière and other members
   of the *Révoltes Logiques* collective were among the few voices on the
   Left in France to question the premises of its sociological analysis of
   inequality. See, in particular, their highly polemical *L'Empire du
   sociologue* (Paris: La Découverte, 1984). On Rancière's archival work
   on Gauny and other worker-artists and worker-intellectuals see
   Chapter 2, above.

7 Bourdieu, *Distinction: A Social Critique of the Judgement of Taste*, tr. by
   Richard Nice (London: Routledge, 1984), 485–500.

8 Geldof, 'Authority, Reading, Reflexivity: Pierre Bourdieu and the
   Aesthetic Judgment of Kant', *Diacritics* 27, 1 (1997), 20–43, at 30.

9 On Rancière's characteristic mode of operating through polemical
   critique or 'intervention', which I have described elewhere as 'irritable attachment', see the Preface, above, and my 'Rancière and
   Queer Theory: On Irritable Attachment', *Borderlands* 8, 2 (2009),
   special issue: *Jacques Rancière on the Shores of Queer Theory*, ed. by
   Samuel Chambers and Michael O'Rourke (http://www.border-
   lands.net.au/issues/vol8no2.html).

10 Kant, *Critique of the Power of Judgment*, ed. by Paul Guyer, tr. by Paul
   Guyer and Eric Matthews (Cambridge: Cambridge University Press,
   2000), § 2 (p. 91) and § 6 (p. 96), emphasis in original.

11 Indeed some would argue that the language of beauty is an unhelp-
   ful indicator of aesthetic judgments.

12 Guyer, 'Pleasure and Society in Kant's Theory of Taste', in Ted
   Cohen and Paul Guyer (eds), *Essays in Kant's Aesthetics* (Chicago:
   University of Chicago Press, 1982), 21–54, at 22.

13 Guyer, 'Pleasure and Society in Kant's Theory of Taste', 22.

14 Guyer, 'Pleasure and Society in Kant's Theory of Taste', 24.

15 See Robert Gero, 'The Border of the Aesthetic', in James Elkins (ed.),
   Art History versus Aesthetics (London: Routledge, 2006), 3–18, at 5.

16 Bourdieu, *Distinction*, 493–4.

17 See Thomas Hove, 'Communicative Implications of Kant's Aesthetic
   Theory', *Philosophy and Rhetoric* 42, 2 (2009), 103–14, at 103.

18 The examples are Bourdieu's own.

19 Rancière, *The Philosopher and His Poor*, tr. by John Drury, Corinne
   Oster and Andrew Parker (Durham, NC: Duke University Press,
   2003), 197–8. Guyer, in his Editor's Introduction to Kant's *Critique of
   the Power of Judgment*, suggests that there is evidence that Kant had
   envisaged writing a 'Critique of Taste' as early as 1772, but asserts
   that it was not until 1787 that he actually began writing. Guyer,
   'Editor's Introduction' to Kant, *Critique of the Power of Judgment*, xviii.
   The Appendix in question is at § 60.

20 Rancière, *The Philosopher and His Poor*, 198.

21 Kant, *Critique of the Power of Judgment*, § 2.

22 Rancière, *Louis-Gabriel Gauny: le philosophe plébéien* (Paris: La Décou-
    verte/Maspero and Presses Universitaires de Vincennes, 1983), 15;
    Rancière, *The Philosopher and His Poor*, 198.
23 Rancière, *The Philosopher and His Poor*, 199.
24 Rancière, *Aesthetics and Its Discontents*, 28. See also Rancière, *The
    Politics of Aesthetics*, 20–1.
25 Or three 'within the Western tradition'. Rancière, *The Politics of Aes-
    thetics*, 20. He does not elaborate further, however, on the extent to
    which his analyses are culturally, ethnically or geographically
    specific.
26 Rancière, *Aesthetics and Its Discontents*, 28.
27 Rancière, *The Politics of Aesthetics*, 27–8.
28 Rancière, interviewed by Jan Völker and Frank Ruda, 'Politique de
    l'indétermination esthétique', in Jérôme Game and Aliocha Wald
    Lasowski (eds), *Jacques Rancière et la politique de l'esthétique* (Paris:
    Éditions des Archives Contemporaines, 2009), 157–75, at 158.
29 Rancière, *The Politics of Aesthetics*, 21–2. Rancière, *The Future of the
    Image*, tr. by Gregory Elliott (London: Verso, 2007), 73.
30 Rancière, *The Politics of Aesthetics*, 21–2.
31 Rancière, *The Politics of Aesthetics*, 29.
32 Rancière, *The Politics of Aesthetics*, 23. See also Rancière's interview
    with Völker and Ruda, 'Politique de l'indétermination esthétique',
    158.
33 Rancière interviewed by Völker and Ruda, 'Politique de
    l'indétermination esthétique', 158.
34 Rancière, *The Politics of Aesthetics*, 23.
35 Rancière, *Aesthetics and Its Discontents*, 30.
36 Rancière, *Aesthetics and Its Discontents*, 31.
37 Rancière, *Aesthetics and Its Discontents*, 13.
38 Rancière's approach to aesthetics clearly presupposes that 'thinking
    has a history', to use Joseph Margolis's expression. While I am con-
    cerned to inquire here about the precise nature of the historical
    conditionality implied in Rancière's analysis, this book is not the
    place to question that general presupposition, which I am assuming
    for the sake of argument to be true. See Margolis, 'Exorcising the
    Dreariness of Aesthetics', in Elkins (ed.), *Art History versus Aesthetics*,
    21–38, at 25–6.
39 See Michel Foucault, *The Order of Things: An Archaeology of the Human
    Sciences* (London: Tavistock, 1970), Ch. 10.
40 See Rancière's interview with Völker and Ruda, 'Politique de
    l'indétermination esthétique', 165.
41 On Rancière's cinephilia see Adrian Rifkin, 'JR Cinéphile, or the
    Philosopher Who Loved Things', *Parallax* 15, 3 (2009), 81–7.
42 Tom Conley, 'Fabulation and Contradiction: Jacques Rancière on
    Cinema', in Temenuga Trifonova (ed.), *European Film Theory* (New
    York: Routledge, 2009), 137–50, at 149.

43 Jean-Clet Martin, *Constellation de la philosophie* (Paris: Kimé, 2007), 163.

44 Tom Conley, 'Cinema and Its Discontents', in Gabriel Rockhill and Philip Watts (eds.), *Jacques Rancière: History, Politics, Aesthetics* (Durham, NC: Duke University Press, 2009), 216–28.

45 Rancière, *Film Fables*, tr. by Emiliano Battista (Oxford: Berg, 2006), 161.

46 Rancière, *Film Fables*, 2.

47 Rancière, *Film Fables*, 2, translation adapted.

48 Rancière, *Film Fables*, 3.

49 Rancière, *Film Fables*, 3.

50 Rancière, *Film Fables*, 5.

51 Rancière, *Film Fables*, 5, translation adapted.

52 Rancière, *Film Fables*, 6.

53 Rancière, *Film Fables*, 6.

54 Rancière, *Film Fables*, 9, 10.

55 Rancière, *Film Fables*, 36.

56 Rancière, *Film Fables*, 36.

57 Rancière is not alone in dismissing the frame tale: Lotte Eisner describes it as 'faintly ridiculous'. Eisner, *The Haunted Screen: Expressionism in the German Cinema and the Influence of Max Reinhardt* (London: Thames and Hudson, 1969), 269.

58 Jo Leslie Collier, *From Wagner to Murnau: The Transposition of Romanticism from Stage to Screen* (Ann Arbor, MI/London: UMI Research Press, 1988), 5. Lotte Eisner, *Murnau* (London: Secker & Warburg, 1973), 60.

59 Lotte Eisner reports Robert Herlth, one of the set-designers, with Walter Röhrig, saying that 'In *Tartuffe* everything was done to heighten the black-and-white effects'. Eisner, *Murnau*, 60.

60 Rancière, *Film Fables*, 39.

61 Rancière, *La Fable cinématographique* (Paris: Seuil, 2001), 53.

62 Rancière, *Film Fables*, 39.

63 Rancière, *La Fable cinématographique*, 59, my translation. Cf. *Film Fables*, 42.

64 Rancière, *Film Fables*, 40.

65 Eisner, *The Haunted Screen*, 273–4.

66 Rancière, *Film Fables*, 43.

67 For example, Marin Marais's 'Tombeau de M. de Ste. Colombe', Mallarmé's 'Le Tombeau d'Edgar Poe' and 'Tombeau de Charles Baudelaire', Ravel's 'Le Tombeau de Couperin'.

68 Rancière, *Film Fables*, 168.

69 Rancière, *Film Fables*, 164, translation adapted.

70 Rancière, *Film Fables*, 163.

71 Rancière, *Film Fables*, 165, translation adapted.

72 For example, William F. Van Wert, 'Chris Marker: the SLON Films', *Film Quarterly* 32, 3 (1979), 38–46, at 44.

73 Alter, *Chris Marker* (Urbana and Chicago: University of Illinois Press, 2006), 48.
74 Catherine Lupton, *Chris Marker: Memories of the Future* (London: Reaktion, 2005), 191; Rancière, *Film Fables*, 164.
75 Marker cited in Lupton, *Chris Marker*, 49; Lupton, *Chris Marker*, 55. *Letter from Siberia*, like *The Last Bolshevik*, was a portrayal of part of the Soviet Union torn between 'the Middle Ages and the 21st century', as the closing lines of the commentary put it. Cited in Lupton, *Chris Marker*, 57.
76 Renov, *The Subject of the Documentary* (Minneapolis: University of Minnesota Press, 2004), 70.
77 Rascaroli, 'The Essay Film: Problems, Definitions, Textual Commitments', *Framework: The Journal of Cinema & Media* 49, 2 (2008), 24–47, at 35.
78 Rancière, *La Fable cinématographique*, 213, my translation.
79 Alter, *Chris Marker*, 84; Lupton, *Chris Marker*, 128.
80 Lupton, *Chris Marker*, 130.
81 Alter, *Chris Marker*, 83; Natasha Synessios, 'The Last Bolshevik (*Le Tombeau d'Alexandre*)', *The Slavonic and East European Review* 72, 4 (1994), 792–4, at 792.
82 Whitehall, 'Jacques Rancière, *Film Fables*', *Theory & Event* 11, 3 (2008) (available online from http://muse.jhu.edu/journals/theory_and_event/summary/v011/11.3.whitehall.html).
83 Rancière, *Aesthetics and Its Discontents*, 29.
84 Rancière, *Aesthetics and Its Discontents*, 40.
85 Rancière, *Aesthetics and Its Discontents* 25, 34.
86 Rancière, *Aesthetics and Its Discontents*, 34.
87 Rancière, 'Problems and Transformations of Critical Art', in *Aesthetics and Its Discontents*, 45–60; Rancière, 'Les paradoxes de l'art politique', in *Le Spectateur émancipé* (Paris: La Fabrique, 2008), 56–92, a substantially reworked version of which is translated as 'Aesthetic Separation, Aesthetic Community', in *The Emancipated Spectator*, tr. by Gregory Elliott (London: Verso, 2010), Ch. 3, 51–82.
88 The concept of active spectatorship has been well established in film theory since the 1970s. See Jan Campbell, *Film and Cinema Spectatorship: Melodrama and Mimesis* (Cambridge: Polity, 2005).
89 Rancière, *Le Spectateur émancipé*, 62. This reference is to the French edition; the third chapter of *The Emancipated Spectator* is a translation of a substantially reworked version of the third chapter of *Le Spectateur émancipé*, 'Les paradoxes de l'art politique'.
90 Rancière, *Le Spectateur émancipé*, 91; Rancière, *The Emancipated Spectator*, 74–5.
91 Rancière, *Le Spectateur émancipé*, 19.
92 Rancière in conversation with Adrian Rifkin and Andrea Philips at the Whitechapel Gallery, London, 4 February 2010.

93 See his antepenultimate response in a recent interview by Jérôme Game, 'Critique de la critique du "spectacle"'.

94 Bourriaud, *Relational Aesthetics* (Paris: Les Presses du Réel, 1998).

95 See Jacques Lévy, Juliette Rennes and David Zerbib, 'Jacques Rancière: "Les territoires de la pensée partagée". Entretien', January 2007 (http://espacestemps.net/document2142.html).

96 Rancière, *Le Spectateur émancipé*, 70.

97 See Nancy, *La Communauté désoeuvrée* (Paris: Christian Bourgois, 1986) and Beth Hinderleiter et al. (eds), *Communities of Sense: Rethinking Aesthetics and Politics* (Durham, NC: Duke University Press, 2009), 2.

98 Rancière, *Aesthetics and Its Discontents*, 32. On the concept of aesthetic education see Andrew Bowie, *Aesthetics and Subjectivity: From Kant to Nietzsche* (2nd edn, Manchester: Manchester University Press, 2003), 36.

99 See Carlos Basualdo and Reinaldo Laddaga, 'Experimental Communities', in Hinderleiter et al. (eds.), *Communities of Sense*, 197–214, at 202–6.

100 Rancière, *Le Spectateur émancipé*, 91.

101 Žižek, *The Ticklish Subject: The Absent Centre of Political Ontology* (London: Verso, 1999), 195.

102 Rancière, *The Politics of Aesthetics*, 39.

Afterword

1 Rancière, *Louis-Gabriel Gauny: le philosophe plébéien*, texts by Gabriel Gauny selected and introduced by Rancière (Paris: La Découverte/ Maspero and Presses Universitaires de Vincennes, 1983), 17, my translation.

2 And especially to an understanding of biography from another age.

3 Rancière, *Courts Voyages au pays du peuple* (Paris: Seuil, 1990), 157, my translation. See also Rancière, *Short Voyages to the Land of the People*, tr. by James Swenson (Stanford: Stanford University Press, 2003), 122. No criticism is implied of Swenson's translation.

References

Unless otherwise stated, page references in the notes are to the most recent editions and to English translations where these exist. The bibliography of works by and interviews with Rancière is not exhaustive and contains only those referred to in this book. In the case of articles, lectures and the many other shorter pieces by Rancière which he has subsequently reworked and published in book form, the reference to the book will normally be the only one given. Interviews with Rancière are mainly listed under the name of the interviewer in the second section. Works in French and English are indexed throughout by the first letter of their first word, except where that is a definite or indefinite article. There is some repetition, particularly within and across sections three to five, which is intended purely to facilitate location of material.

I Books, articles, book chapters and shorter pieces authored singly or jointly by Rancière, in French

Arrêt sur histoire, with Jean-Louis Comolli (Paris: Centre Pompidou, 1997).
Aux Bords du politique (1st edn, Paris: La Fabrique, 1998; 2nd edn, Paris: Gallimard/Folio, 1998).
'Le bon temps ou la barrière des plaisirs', *Les Révoltes Logiques* 7 (Spring–Summer 1978), 25–66; reprinted in *Les Scènes du peuple (Les Révoltes logiques, 1975–1985)* (Lyon: Horlieu, 2003), 203–52.
La Chair des mots: politiques de l'écriture (Paris: Galilée, 1998).

'Le concept d'anachronisme et la vérité de l'historien', *L'Inactuel* 6 (Autumn 1996), 53–68.

'Le concept de critique et la critique de l'économie politique des *Manuscrits de 1844* au *Capital*', in Louis Althusser et al., *Lire le Capital* (1st edn, Paris: Maspero, 1965; 3rd edn, Paris: Presses Universitaires de France/Quadrige, 1996).

'Les confidences du monument: Deleuze et la "résistance" de l'art', in Bruno Gelas and Hervé Micolet (eds), *Deleuze et les écrivains: littérature et philosophie* (Nantes: Cécile Defaut, 2007), 479–91.

Courts Voyages au pays du peuple (Paris: Seuil, 1990).

Le Destin des images (Paris: La Fabrique, 2003).

L'Empire du sociologue, with the other members of the *Révoltes Logiques* collective (Paris: La Découverte, 1984).

'En allant à l'Expo: l'ouvrier, sa femme et les machines', co-authored with Patrick Vauday, *Les Révoltes Logiques* 1, 5–22.

Esthétiques du peuple, with the other members of the *Révoltes Logiques* collective (Paris: La Découverte/Presses Universitaires de Vincennes, 1985).

'Existe-t-il une esthétique deleuzienne?', in Eric Alliez (ed.), *Gilles Deleuze: une vie philosophique* (Paris: Synthélabo, 1998), 525–36.

La Fable cinématographique (Paris: Seuil, 2001).

'Une femme encombrante (à propos de Suzanne Voilquin)', *Les Révoltes Logiques* 8–9 (Winter 1979), 116–22.

'La fiction de mémoire: à propos du *Tombeau d'Alexandre*', *Trafic: revue de cinéma* 29 (Spring 1999), 36–47.

La Haine de la démocratie (Paris: La Fabrique, 2005).

'L'Historicité du cinéma', in Antoine de Baecque and Christian Delage (eds), *De l'histoire au cinéma* (Paris: Complexe, 1998), 45–60.

L'Inconscient esthétique (Paris: Galilée, 2001).

Les Lauriers de Mai ou les chemins du pouvoir 1968–1978, Rancière et al., *Les Révoltes Logiques*, special issue on May '68 (February 1978).

La Leçon d'Althusser (Paris: Gallimard, 1974).

'La légende des philosophes (les intellectuels et la traversée du gauchisme)', with Danièle Rancière, *Les Révoltes Logiques*, special issue (February 1978): *Les Lauriers de Mai ou Les chemins du pouvoir (1968–1978)*, 7–25.

Louis-Gabriel Gauny: le philosophe plébéien, texts by Gabriel Gauny selected and introduced by Rancière (Paris: La Découverte/ Maspero and Presses Universitaires de Vincennes, 1983).

Le Maître ignorant: cinq leçons sur l'émancipation intellectuelle (Paris: Fayard, 1987).

Mallarmé: la politique de la sirène (Paris: Hachette, 1996).

Malaise dans l'esthétique (Paris: Galilée, 2004).

La Mésentente: politique et philosophie (Paris: Galilée, 1995).

'La méthode de l'égalité', in Laurence Cornu and Patrice Vermeren (eds), *La Philosophie déplacée: autour de Jacques Rancière* (Paris: Horlieu, 2006), 507–23.

'Mode d'emploi pour une réédition de "Lire le Capital"', *Les Temps Modernes* 328 (Nov. 1973), 788–807.

Moments politiques: interventions 1977–2009 (Paris: La Fabrique, 2009).

Les Noms de l'histoire: essai de poétique du savoir (Paris: Seuil, 1992).

La Nuit des prolétaires: archives du rêve ouvrier (Paris: Fayard, 1981).

La Parole muette: essai sur les contradictions de la littérature (Paris: Hachette, 1998).

La Parole ouvrière 1830–1851, with Alain Faure (Paris: La Fabrique, 2007)

Le Partage du sensible: esthétique et politique (Paris: La Fabrique, 2000).

'De Pelloutier à Hitler: syndicalisme et collaboration', *Les Révoltes Logiques* 4 (Winter 1976), 23–61; reprinted in *Les Scènes du peuple (Les Révoltes logiques, 1975–1985)* (Lyon: Horlieu, 2003), 117–63.

Le Philosophe et ses pauvres (1st edn, Paris: Fayard, 1983; 2nd edn, Paris: Flammarion, 2007).

'La philosophie en déplacement', in Marianne Alphant (ed.), *La Vocation philosophique* (Paris: Bayard, 2004), 11–36.

'Les pieds du héros', *Trafic: revue de cinéma* 56 (Winter 2005), special issue: *Politique(s) de John Ford*, 26–32.

Politique de la littérature (Paris: Galilée, 2007).

'La représentation de l'ouvrier ou la classe impossible', in Philippe Lacoue-Labarthe and Jean-Luc Nancy (eds), *Le Retrait du politique* (Paris: Galilée, 1983), 89–111.

'La rime et le conflit: la politique du poème', in Betrand Marchal and Jean-Luc Steinmetz (eds), *Mallarmé ou l'obscurité lumineuse* (Paris: Hermann, 1999), 115–41.

'Ronds de fumée (Les poètes ouvriers dans la France de Louis-Philippe', *Revue des sciences humaines* (Lille 3) 190 (April–June 1983), 31–47.

'Savoirs hérétiques et émancipation du pauvre', in *Les Sauvages dans la cité: auto-émancipation du peuple et instruction des prolétaires au XIXe siècle* (Seyssel: Champ Vallon, 1985), 34–53; reprinted in *Les Scènes du peuple (Les Révoltes logiques, 1975–1985)* (Lyon: Horlieu, 2003), 35–54.

Les Scènes du peuple (Les Révoltes logiques, 1975–1985) (Lyon: Horlieu, 2003).

'Sobre la teoria de la ideologia (la politica de Althusser)', in *Lectura de Althusser* (Buenos Aires: Galerna, 1970), subsequently published in French as 'Sur la théorie de l'idéologie politique d'Althusser', *L'Homme et la Société: revue internationale de recherches et de synthèses sociologiques* (Jan.–Mar. 1973), 31–61.

Le Spectateur émancipé (Paris: La Fabrique, 2008).

'Sur la théorie de l'idéologie politique d'Althusser', *L'Homme et la Société: revue internationale de recherches et de synthèses sociologiques* (Jan.–Mar. 1973), 31–61

'L'usine nostalgique', *Les Révoltes Logiques* 13 (Winter 1980–1), 89–97.

II   Work in English by Rancière (including translations, books, articles, book chapters and shorter pieces authored singly or jointly)

Aesthetics and Its Discontents, tr. by Steven Cocoran (Cambridge: Polity, 2009).

'Althusser', in Simon Critchley and William Schroeder (eds), *Blackwell Companion to Continental Philosophy* (Oxford: Blackwell, 1998), 530–6.

Disagreement: Politics and Philosophy, tr. by Julie Rose (Minneapolis: University of Minnesota Press, 1999).

Dissensus: On Politics and Aesthetics, ed. by Steven Cocoran (London: Continuum, 2009).

The Emancipated Spectator, tr. by Gregory Elliott (London: Verso, 2009).

'A Few Remarks on the Method of Jacques Rancière', in Paul Bowman and Richard Stamp (eds), *Parallax* 15, 3 (2009), 114–23.

Film Fables, tr. by Emiliano Battista (Oxford: Berg, 2006).

The Flesh of Words: The Politics of Writing, tr. by Charlotte Mandell (Stanford: Stanford University Press, 2004).

The Future of the Image, tr. by Gregory Elliott (London: Verso, 2007).

'Going to the Expo: The Worker, His Wife, and Machines', in Adrian Rifkin and Roger Thomas (eds), *Voices of the People: The Politics and Life of 'la Sociale' at the End of the Second Empire*, tr. by John Moore (London: Routledge, 1987), 23–44.

'Good Times or Pleasure at the Barricades', in Adrian Rifkin and Roger Thomas (eds), *Voices of the People: The Politics and Life of 'la*

Sociale' at the End of the Second Empire, tr. by John Moore (London: Routledge, 1987), 45–94.

Hatred of Democracy, tr. by Steven Cocoran (London: Verso, 2006).

The Ignorant Schoolmaster: Five Lessons in Intellectual Emancipation, tr. by Kristin Ross (Stanford: Stanford University Press, 1991).

The Names of History: On the Poetics of Knowledge, tr. by Hassan Melehy with a Foreword by Hayden White (Minneapolis: University of Minnesota Press, 1994).

The Nights of Labor: The Workers' Dream in Nineteenth-Century France, tr. by John Drury, introduced by Donald Reid (Philadelphia: Temple University Press, 1989).

On the Shores of Politics, tr. by Liz Heron (London: Verso, 1995).

The Philosopher and His Poor, tr. by John Drury, Corinne Oster and Andrew Parker (Durham, NC: Duke University Press, 2003).

'Politics, Identification, and Subjectivization', *October* 61 (1992), 58–64.

The Politics of Aesthetics: The Distribution of the Sensible, tr. and introduced by Gabriel Rockhill, with an Afterword by Slavoj Žižek (London: Continuum, 2004).

The Politics of Literature, tr. by Julie Rose (Cambridge: Polity, 2011).

Short Voyages to the Land of the People, tr. by James Swenson (Stanford: Stanford University Press, 2003).

'Ten Theses on Politics', *Theory & Event* 5, 3 (2001) (available online from http://muse.jhu.edu/login?uri=/journals/theory_and_event/v005/5.3ranciere.html).

III Interviews with Rancière in French and English

Arrous, Adrien and Costanzo, Alexandre, 'Questions à Jacques Rancière', *Drôle d'époque* 14 (Spring 2004), 15–29.

Game, Jérôme, 'Critique de la critique du "spectacle"', *La Revue internationale des livres et des idées* 12 (July 2009) (http://revuedeslivres.net/articles.php?id=360).

Guénoun, Solange and Kavanagh, John, 'Literature, Politics, Aesthetics: Approaches to Democratic Disagreement', tr. by R. Lapidus, *SubStance* 92 (2000), 3–24.

Lévy, Jacques, Rennes, Juliette and Zerbib, David, 'Jacques Rancière: "Les territoires de la pensée partagée". Entretien', January 2007 (http://espacestemps.net/document2142.html).

Panagia, Davide, 'Dissenting Words: A Conversation with Jacques Rancière', *diacritics* 30, 2 (Summer 2000), 113–26.

Perrot, Martyne and de la Soudière, Martin, 'Histoire des mots, mots de l'histoire', *Communications* 58 (1994), 87–101.

Rancière, Jacques, *Et tant pis pour les gens fatigués: entretiens* (Paris: Amsterdam, 2009) [a collection of selected interviews in French including some of those listed separately here].

Völker, Jan and Ruda, Frank, 'Politique de l'indétermination esthétique', in Jérôme Game and Aliocha Wald Lasowski (eds), *Jacques Rancière et la politique de l'esthétique* (Paris: Éditions des Archives Contemporaines, 2009), 157–75.

IV Books and special issues of journals devoted to Rancière's work, in French and English

Bowman, Paul and Stamp, Richard (eds), *Parallax* 15, 3 (2009), special issue on Rancière.

Chambers, Samuel and O'Rourke, Michael (eds), *Borderlands* 8, 2 (2009), special issue: *Jacques Rancière on the Shores of Queer Theory* (http://www.borderlands.net.au/issues/vol8no2.html).

Cornu, Laurence and Vermeren, Patrice (eds), *La Philosophie déplacée: autour de Jacques Rancière* (Paris: Horlieu, 2006), proceedings of the 2005 Cerisy conference.

Critique special issue: *Autour de Jacques Rancière*, 601–2 (June–July 1997).

Déotte, Jean-Louis, *Qu'est-ce qu'un appareil? Benjamin, Lyotard, Rancière* (Paris: L'Harmattan, 2007).

Game, Jérôme and Wald Lasowski, Aliocha (eds), *Jacques Rancière et la politique de l'esthétique* (Paris: Éditions des Archives Contemporaines, 2009).

Greco, Maria Beatriz, *Rancière et Jacotot: une critique du concept d'autorité* (Paris: L'Harmattan, 2007).

Hewlett, Nicholas, *Badiou, Balibar, Rancière: Re-thinking Emancipation* (London: Continuum, 2007).

Hinderleiter, Beth et al. (eds), *Communities of Sense: Rethinking Aesthetics and Politics* (Durham, NC: Duke University Press, 2009).

May, Todd, *The Political Thought of Jacques Rancière: Creating Equality* (Edinbugh: Edinburgh University Press, 2008).

Méchoulan, Eric (ed.), *SubStance* 33, 1 (2004), special issue: *Contemporary Thinker: Jacques Rancière*.

Pasquier, Renaud (ed.), *Labyrinthe: atelier interdisciplinaire* 17, 1 (2004), special issue: *Jacques Rancière: l'indiscipliné* (http://labyrinthe.revues.org/index85.html).

Robson, Mark (ed.), *Paragraph* 28, 1 (March 2005), special issue: *Jacques Rancière: Aesthetics, Politics, Philosophy.*

Rockhill, Gabriel and Watts, Philip (eds), *Jacques Rancière: History, Politics, Aesthetics* (Durham, NC: Duke University Press, 2009).

Ruby, Christian, *L'Interruption: Jacques Rancière et la politique* (Paris: La Fabrique, 2009).

Le Télémaque 27 (2005), special issue devoted to *Le Maître ignorant.*

Theory & Event 6, 4 (2003), symposium section on Rancière (available online from http://muse.jhu.edu/journals/theory_and_event/toc/tae6.4.html).

V   Other works cited

Alter, Nora M., *Chris Marker* (Urbana and Chicago: University of Illinois Press, 2006).

Althusser, Louis, *Lenin and Philosophy, and Other Essays*, tr. by Ben Brewster (London: New Left Books, 1971).

Althusser, Louis, *Réponse à John Lewis* (Paris: Maspero, 1973).

Althusser, Louis, *For Marx*, tr. by Ben Brewster (London: Verso, 1990).

Althusser, Louis and Balibar, Étienne, *Reading Capital*, tr. by Ben Brewster (London: NLB, 1970).

Althusser, Louis et al., *Lire le Capital* (1st edn, Paris: Maspero, 1965; 3rd edn, Paris: Presses Universitaires de France/Quadrige, 1996).

Aron, Raymond, *Introduction à la philosophie de l'histoire: essai sur les limites de l'objectivité historique*, ed. revised with notes by Sylvie Mesure (Paris: Gallimard, 1991).

Aronowitz, Stanley, *Against Schooling* (Boulder, CO: Paradigm, 2008).

Artières, Philippe, Laurent Quéro and Michelle Zancarini-Fournel, *Le Groupe d'Information sur les Prisons: Archives d'une lutte, 1970–1972* (Paris: Imec, 2003).

Badiou, Alain, *L'Être et l'événement* (Paris: Seuil, 1988).

Badiou, Alain, 'Les leçons de Jacques Rancière: savoir et pouvoir après la tempête', in Laurence Cornu and Patrice Vermeren (eds), *La Philosophie déplacée: autour de Jacques Rancière* (Paris: Horlieu, 2006), 131–54.

Badiou, Alain, 'Louis Althusser', in *Petit panthéon portatif* (Paris: La Fabrique, 2008), 57–87.

Balibar, Étienne, 'Althusser's Object', tr. by Margaret Cohen and Bruce Robbins, *Social Text* 39 (Summer 1994), 157–88.

Barthes, Roland, 'The Discourse of History', in *The Rustle of Language*, tr. by Richard Howard (London: Farrar, Straus and Giroux, 1986), 127–54.

Barthes, Roland, 'The Reality Effect', in *The Rustle of Language*, tr. by Richard Howard (London: Farrar, Straus and Giroux, 1986), 141–8.

Barthes, Roland, *Michelet*, tr. by Richard Howard (Oxford: Blackwell, 1987).

Basualdo, Carlos and Laddaga, Reinaldo, 'Experimental Communities', in Beth Hinderleiter et al. (eds), *Communities of Sense: Rethinking Aesthetics and Politics* (Durham, NC: Duke University Press, 2009), 197–214.

Bell, David, 'Writing, Movement/Space, Democracy: On Jacques Rancière's Literary History', *SubStance* 103 (2004), 126–40.

Bénichou, Paul, *Le Temps des prophètes: doctrines de l'âge romantique* (Paris: Gallimard, 1977).

Benjamin, Walter, *The Arcades Project*, tr. by Howard Eiland and Kevin McLaughlin (Cambridge, MA: Harvard University Press, 1999).

Borreil, Jean, 'Des politiques nostalgiques', *Les Révoltes Logiques* 3 (Autumn 1976), 87–105.

Borreil, Jean, 'Un été irlandais', *Les Révoltes Logiques* 14–15 (Summer 1981), 136–50.

Bourdieu, Pierre, *Distinction: A Social Critique of the Judgement of Taste*, tr. by Richard Nice (London: Routledge, 1984).

Bourdieu, Pierre and Passeron, Jean-Claude, *The Inheritors: French Students and Their Relation to Culture*, tr. by Richard Nice (Chicago: University of Chicago Press, 1979).

Bourdieu, Pierre and Passeron, Jean-Claude, *Reproduction in Education, Society and Culture*, tr. by Richard Nice (London: Sage, 1990).

Bourriaud, Nicolas, *Relational Aesthetics* (Paris: Les Presses du Réel, 1998).

Bowie, Andrew, *Aesthetics and Subjectivity: From Kant to Nietzsche* (2nd edn, Manchester: Manchester University Press, 2003).

Braudel, Fernand, *The Mediterranean and the Mediterranean World in the Age of Phillip II*, tr. by Siân Reynolds (London: Collins, 1972).

Brint, Steven, *In an Age of Experts: The Changing Role of Professionals in Politics and Public Life* (Princeton, NJ: Princeton University Press, 1994).

Burguière, André, *Bretons de Plozévet* (Paris: Flammarion, 1975).

Burke, Peter, *The French Historical Revolution: The Annales School, 1929–89* (Cambridge: Polity, 1990).

Campbell, Jan, *Film and Cinema Spectatorship: Melodrama and Mimesis* (Cambridge: Polity, 2005).

Carrard, Philippe, *Poetics of the New History: French Historical Discourse from Braudel to Chartier* (Baltimore, MD: Johns Hopkins University Press, 1992).

Catani, Damian, *The Poet in Society: Art, Consumerism, and Politics in Mallarmé* (New York: Peter Lang, 2003).

Certeau, Michel de, *L'Écriture de l'histoire* (Paris: Gallimard, 1975).

Certeau, Michel de, *The Capture of Speech and Other Political Writings*, tr. by Tom Conley (Minneapolis: University of Minnesota Press, 1997).

Chambers, Samuel, 'The Politics of Literarity', *Theory & Event* 8, 3 (2005) (available online from http://muse.jhu.edu/login?uri=/journals/theory_and_event/v008/8.3chambers.html).

Clifford, James, 'Taking Identity Politics Seriously: The Contradictory, Stony Ground . . .', in Paul Gilroy, Lawrence Grossberg and Angela McRobbie (eds), *Without Guarantees: In Honour of Stuart Hall* (London: Verso, 2000), 94–11.

Cohen-Solal, Annie, *Sartre* (Paris: Gallimard, 1985).

Collier, Jo Leslie, *From Wagner to Murnau: The Transposition of Romanticism from Stage to Screen* (Ann Arbor, MI/London: UMI Research Press, 1988).

Conley, Tom, 'Cinema and its Discontents', in Gabriel Rockhill and Philip Watts (eds), *Jacques Rancière: History, Politics, Aesthetics* (Durham NC: Duke University Press, 2009), 216–28.

Conley, Tom, 'Fabulation and Contradiction: Jacques Rancière on Cinema', in Temenuga Trifonova (ed.), *European Film Theory* (New York: Routledge, 2009), 137–50.

Cornu, Laurence and Vermeren, Patrice (eds), *La Philosophie déplacée: autour de Jacques Rancière* (Paris: Horlieu, 2006).

Damier, Francis, 'Les Saint-simoniens à la rencontre des ouvriers parisiens au tournant des années 1830', in Pierre Musso (ed.), *Actualité du Saint-Simonisme: Colloque de Cerisy* (Paris: Presses Universitaires de France, 2004), 115–47.

Dasgupta, Sudeep, 'Jacques Rancière en de spiraal van het denken over politiek en esthetiek', Afterword to Jacques Rancière, *Het*

Esthetische Denken [Dutch translation of *Le Partage du sensible*] (Amsterdam: Valiz, 2007).

Davis, Colin, *After Post-structuralism: Reading, Stories and Theory* (London: Routledge, 2004).

Davis, Oliver, 'Rancière and Queer Theory: On Irritable Attachment', *Borderlands* 8, 2 (2009), special issue: *Jacques Rancière on the Shores of Queer Theory*, ed. by Samuel Chambers and Michael O'Rourke (http://www.borderlands.net.au/issues/vol8no2.html).

Davis, Oliver, 'The Radical Pedagogies of François Bon and Jacques Rancière', *French Studies* 64, 2 (April 2010), 178–91.

Deranty, Jean-Philippe, 'Rancière and Contemporary Political Ontology', *Theory & Event* 6, 4 (2003) (available online from http://muse.jhu.edu/login?uri=/journals/theory_and_event/v006/6.4deranty.html).

Deranty, Jean-Philippe et al., *Recognition, Work, Politics: New Directions in French Critical Theory* (Leiden: Brill, 2007).

Derrida, Jacques, 'Plato's Pharmacy', in *Dissemination*, tr. by Barbara Johnson (London: Athlone, 1981), 61–171.

Derrida, Jacques, 'Politics and Friendship', interview with Michael Sprinker, in Michael Sprinker and E. Ann Kaplan (eds), *The Althusserian Legacy* (London: Verso, 1993), 183–231.

Dewey, John, *Democracy and Education: An Introduction to the Philosophy of Education* (London: Macmillan, 1916, reprinted 1966).

Douailler, Stéphane and Vermeren, Patrice, 'Mutineries à Clairvaux', documents presented in *Les Révoltes Logiques* 6 (Autumn–Winter 1977), 77–95.

Duggan, Lisa, *The Twilight of Equality? Neoliberalism, Cultural Politics, and the Attack on Democracy* (Boston: Beacon, 2003).

During, Élie, 'Politiques de l'accent: Rancière entre Deleuze et Derrida', in Jérôme Game and Aliocha Wald Lasowski (eds), *Jacques Rancière et la politique de l'esthétique* (Paris: Éditions des Archives Contemporaines, 2009), 74–92.

Eisner, Lotte, *The Haunted Screen: Expressionism in the German Cinema and the Influence of Max Reinhardt* (London: Thames and Hudson, 1969).

Eisner, Lotte, *Murnau* (London: Secker & Warburg, 1973).

Elkins, James (ed.), *Art History versus Aesthetics* (London: Routledge, 2006).

Elliott, Gregory, *Althusser: The Detour of Theory* (2nd edn, Leiden and Boston: Brill, 2006).

Farge, Arlette, 'L'Histoire comme avènement', in *Critique* 601–2 (June–July 1997), special issue: *Autour de Jacques Rancière*, 461–6.

Fassin, Eric, *L'Inversion de la question homosexuelle* (2nd edn, Paris: Amsterdam, 2008).

Febvre, Lucien, *The Problem of Unbelief in the Sixteenth Century: The Religion of Rabelais*, tr. by Beatrice Gottlieb (Boston: Harvard University Press, 1982).

Foucault, Michel, *The Order of Things: An Archaeology of the Human Sciences* (London: Tavistock, 1970).

Fraisse, Geneviève and Elhadad, Lydia, ' "L'AFFRANCHISSEMENT DE NOTRE SEXE": à propos des textes de Claire Demar réédité par Valentin Pelosse', *Les Révoltes Logiques* 2 (Spring–Summer 1976), 105–20.

Fraisse, Geneviève and Elhadad, Lydia, 'Des femmes présentes (Notes sur l'article précédent)', in *Les Révoltes Logiques* 8–9 (Winter 1979), 123–5.

Fraisse, Geneviève and Elhadad, Lydia, 'À l'impossible on est tenu', in Laurence Cornu and Patrice Vermeren (eds), *La Philosophie déplacée: autour de Jacques Rancière* (Paris: Horlieu, 2006), 71–7.

Freire, Paulo, *Pedagogy of Hope: Reliving Pedagogy of the Oppressed*, tr. by Robert R. Barr (London: Continuum, 2006).

Furet, François, *Interpreting the French Revolution*, tr. by Elborg Forster (Cambridge: Cambridge University Press, 1981).

Geary, Dick, *Karl Kautsky* (New York: St Martin's Press, 1987).

Geldof, Koenraad, 'Authority, Reading, Reflexivity: Pierre Bourdieu and the Aesthetic Judgment of Kant', *Diacritics* 27, 1 (1997), 20–43.

Gero, Robert, 'The Border of the Aesthetic', in James Elkins (ed.), *Art History versus Aesthetics* (London: Routledge, 2006), 3–18.

Gibson, Andrew, 'The Unfinished Song: Intermittency and Melancholy in Rancière', in Mark Robson (ed.), *Paragraph* 28, 1 (March 2005), special issue: *Jacques Rancière: Aesthetics, Politics, Philosophy*, 61–76.

Gildea, Robert, *The Past in French History* (New Haven: Yale University Press, 1994).

Goodman, Paul, *Compulsory Miseducation* (New York: Horizon, 1962).

Guyer, Paul, 'Pleasure and Society in Kant's Theory of Taste', in Ted Cohen and Paul Guyer (eds), *Essays in Kant's Aesthetics* (Chicago: University of Chicago Press, 1982), 21–54.

Habermas, Jürgen, *The Theory of Communicative Action*, vol. 2, *Life-world and System: A Critique of Functionalist Reason*, tr. by Thomas McCarthy (Cambridge: Polity, 1987).

Halberstam, Judith, *In a Queer Time and Place: Transgender Bodies, Subcultural Lives* (New York: New York University Press, 2005).

Hallward, Peter, 'Jacques Rancière et la théâtocratie ou Les limites de l'égalité improvisée', in Laurence Cornu and Patrice Verme-ren (eds), *La Philosophie déplacée: autour de Jacques Rancière* (Paris: Horlieu, 2006), 481–96.

Hartog, François, *Evidence de l'histoire* (2nd edn, Paris: Gallimard, 2007).

Hérubel, Jean-Pierre, *Annales Historiography and Theory: A Selective and Annotated Bibliography* (London: Greenwood, 1994).

Hewlett, Nicholas, *Badiou, Balibar, Rancière: Re-thinking Emancipa-tion* (London: Continuum, 2007).

Hinderleiter, Beth et al. (eds), *Communities of Sense: Rethinking Aes-thetics and Politics* (Durham, NC: Duke University Press, 2009).

Hobbes, Thomas, *Behemoth or The History of the Causes of the Civil Wars of England*, in *English Works of Thomas Hobbes*, vol. vi, ed. by Robert Molesworth (London, 1839).

Hobbes, Thomas, *Leviathan*, ed. by J. Gaskin (Oxford: Oxford Uni-versity Press/World's Classics, 2008 edn).

Honneth, Axel, *The Struggle for Recognition: The Moral Grammar of Social Conflicts*, tr. by Joel Anderson (Cambridge: Polity, 1995).

House, Jim, and MacMaster, Neil, *Paris 1961: Algerians, State Terror, and Memory* (Oxford: Oxford University Press, 2006).

Hove, Thomas, 'Communicative Implications of Kant's Aesthetic Theory', *Philosophy and Rhetoric* 42, 2 (2009), 103–14.

Jefferson, Ann, *Biography and the Question of Literature* (Oxford: Oxford University Press, 2007).

Jenkins, Richard, *Pierre Bourdieu* (London: Routledge, 1992).

Kant, Immanuel, *Critique of the Power of Judgment*, ed. by Paul Guyer, tr. by Paul Guyer and Eric Matthews (Cambridge: Cam-bridge University Press, 2000).

Klosko, George, *The Development of Plato's Political Theory* (London: Methuen, 1986).

Kollias, Hector, 'Taking Sides: Jacques Rancière and Agonistic Lit-erature', *Paragraph* 30, 2 (2007), 82–97.

Labelle, Gilles, 'Two Refoundation Projects of Democracy in Contemporary French Philosophy: Cornelius Castoriadis and Jacques Rancière', *Philosophy and Social Criticism* 27, 4 (July 2001), 75–103.

Lalieu, Olivier, 'L'invention du "devoir de mémoire"', *Vingtième Siècle* 69 (2001), 83–94.

Larkin, Maurice, *France since the Popular Front, 1936–1996* (2nd edn, Oxford: Oxford University Press, 1997).

Le Goff, Jean-Pierre, *Mai 68: l'héritage impossible* (Paris: La Découverte, 2002).

Le Roy Ladurie, Emmanuel, *Montaillou, village occitan* (Paris: Gallimard, 1976).

Lovell, Terry, 'Thinking Feminism with and against Bourdieu', in Bridget Fowler (ed.), *Reading Bourdieu on Society and Culture* (Oxford: Blackwell, 2000), 27–48.

Lupton, Catherine, *Chris Marker: Memories of the Future* (London: Reaktion, 2005).

Macherey, Pierre and Balibar, Étienne, 'Literature as an Ideological Form: Some Marxist Propositions', *Oxford Literary Review* 3 (1978), 4–12.

McWilliam, Neil, 'Peripheral Visions: Class, Cultural Aspiration, and the Artisan Community in Mid-Nineteenth-Century France', in Salim Kemal and Ivan Gaskell (eds), *Politics and Aesthetics in the Arts* (Cambridge: Cambridge University Press, 2000), 140–73.

Mallarmé, Stéphane, *Oeuvres complètes*, vol. 2, ed. by Bertrand Marchal (Paris: Gallimard, 2003).

Margolis, Joseph, 'Exorcising the Dreariness of Aesthetics', in James Elkins (ed.), *Art History versus Aesthetics* (London: Routledge, 2006), 21–38.

MARHO [Mid-Atlantic Radical Historians' Organization], *Visions of History* (Manchester: Manchester University Press, 1976).

Martin, Jean-Clet, *Constellation de la philosophie* (Paris: Kimé, 2007).

Marx, Karl, *Karl Marx: Selected Writings*, ed. by David McLellan (Oxford: Oxford University Press, 1977).

Marx, Karl, *Capital*, vol. 1, ed. by Ernest Mandel (London: Penguin, 1990).

Méchoulan, Eric, 'Sophisticated Continuities and Historical Discontinuities, Or, Why Not Protagoras', in Gabriel Rockhill and Philip Watts (eds), *Jacques Rancière: History, Politics, Aesthetics* (Durham NC: Duke University Press, 2009), 55–66.

Moulier-Boutang, Yann, *Althusser: une biographie* (Paris: Flammarion, 1992).

Musso, Pierre (ed.), *Actualité du Saint-Simonisme: Colloque de Cerisy* (Paris: Presses Universitaires de France, 2004).

Musso, Pierre, *Le Vocabulaire de Saint-Simon* (Paris: Ellipses, 2005).

Nancy, *La Communauté désoeuvrée* (Paris: Christian Bourgois, 1986).

Nancy, Jean-Luc, 'Jacques Rancière et la métaphysique', in Laurence Cornu and Patrice Vermeren (eds), *La Philosophie déplacée: autour de Jacques Rancière* (Paris: Horlieu, 2006), 155–67.

Nancy, Jean-Luc and Lacoue-Labarthe, Philippe, *The Literary Absolute: The Theory of Literature in German Romanticism*, tr. by Philip Barnard and Cheryl Lester (Albany, NY: State University of New York Press, 1988).

Nordmann, Charlotte, *Bourdieu/Rancière: la Politique entre sociologie et philosophie* (Paris: Amsterdam, 2006).

Pearson, Roger, *Mallarmé and Circumstance: The Translation of Silence* (Oxford: Oxford University Press, 2004).

Plato, *Phaedrus*, tr. by Robin Waterfield (Oxford: Oxford University Press, 2002).

Popper, Karl, *The Open Society and Its Enemies* (4th edn, London: Routledge, 1962).

Prochasson, Christophe, *Saint-Simon ou l'anti-Marx: figures du saint-simonisme français XIXe–XXe siècles* (Paris: Perrin, 2005).

Rascaroli, Laura, 'The Essay Film: Problems, Definitions, Textual Commitments', *Framework: The Journal of Cinema & Media* 49, 2 (2008), 24–47.

Renov, Michael,*The Subject of the Documentary* (Minneapolis: University of Minnesota Press, 2004).

Ricoeur, Paul, *Temps et récit I: l'intrigue et le récit historique* (Paris: Seuil, 1983).

Rifkin, Adrian, *Street Noises: Parisian Pleasure, 1900–40* (Manchester: Manchester University Press, 1993).

Rifkin, Adrian, 'JR Cinéphile, or the Philosopher Who Loved Things', *Parallax* 15, 3 (2009), 81–7.

Rifkin, Adrian and Thomas, Roger (eds), *Voices of the People: The Politics and Life of 'la Sociale' at the End of the Second Empire*, tr. by John Moore (London: Routledge, 1987).

Rockhill, Gabriel, 'La démocratie dans l'histoire des cultures politiques', in Jérôme Game and Aliocha Wald Lasowski (eds), *Jacques Rancière et la politique de l'esthétique* (Paris: Éditions des Archives Contemporaines, 2009), 55–71.

Ross, Kristin, 'Rancière and the Practice of Equality', *Social Text* 29 (1991), 57–71.

Ross, Kristin, *May '68 and its Afterlives* (Chicago: University of Chicago Press, 2002).

Ross, Kristin, 'Historicizing Untimeliness', in Gabriel Rockhill and Philip Watts (eds), *Jacques Rancière: History, Politics, Aesthetics* (Durham, NC: Duke University Press, 2009), 15–29.

Samuel, Raphael (ed.), *History Workshop: A Collectanea 1967–1991: Documents, Memoirs, Critique and Cumulative Index to History Workshop Journal* (Oxford: History Workshop, 1991).

Sartre, Jean-Paul, Gavi, Philippe, and Victor, Pierre, *On a raison de se révolter: discussions* (Paris: Gallimard, 1974).

Schöttler, Peter, 'Althusser and Annales Historiography – An Impossible Dialogue', in Michael Sprinker and E. Ann Kaplan (eds), *The Althusserian Legacy* (London: Verso, 1993), 81–98.

Sorman, Joy, *Boys, boys, boys* (Paris: Gallimard, 2005).

Spring, Joel, *Wheels in the Head: Educational Philosophies of Authority, Freedom, and Culture from Socrates to Paulo Freire* (New York: McGraw-Hill, 1994).

Sprinker, Michael, 'The Legacies of Althusser', *Yale French Studies* 88 (1995), special issue: *Althusser, Balibar, Macherey, and the Labor of Reading*, 201–25.

Sprinker, Michael and Kaplan, E. Ann (eds), *The Althusserian Legacy* (London: Verso, 1993).

Swenson, James, 'Style Indirect Libre', in Gabriel Rockhill and Philip Watts (eds), *Jacques Rancière: History, Politics, Aesthetics* (Durham, NC: Duke University Press, 2009), 258–72.

Synessios, Natasha, '*The Last Bolshevik (Le Tombeau d'Alexandre)*', *The Slavonic and East European Review* 72, 4 (1994), 792–4.

Thompson, E.P., *The Making of the English Working Class* (1st edn, London: Victor Gollancz, 1963).

Thompson, E.P. *The Poverty of Theory: Or an Orrery of Errors* (2nd edn, London: Merlin, 1995).

Van Wert, William F., 'Chris Marker: The SLON Films', *Film Quarterly* 32, 3 (1979), 38–46.

Veyne, Paul, *Comment on écrit l'histoire* (Paris: Seuil, 1971).

Ward, Colin and Fyson, Anthony, *Streetwork: The Exploding School* (London: Routledge, 1973).

Weeks, Jeffrey, *The World We Have Won: The Remaking of Erotic and Intimate Life* (London: Routledge, 2007).

White, Hayden, *Metahistory: The Historical Imagination in Nineteenth-Century Europe* (Baltimore: Johns Hopkins University Press, 1973).

Whitehall, Geoffrey, 'Jacques Rancière, *Film Fables*', *Theory & Event* 11, 3 (2008) (available online from http://muse.jhu.edu/journals/theory_and_event/summary/v011/11.3.whitehall.html).

Williams, Raymond, *Marxism and Literature* (Oxford: Oxford University Press, 1977).

Winnicott, Donald, 'True and False Self', in *The Maturational Processes and the Facilitating Environment* (London: Karnac, 1990), 140–52.

Winnicott, Donald, *Playing and Reality* (London: Routledge Classics edn, 2005).

Zeitlin, Irving, *Plato's Vision: The Classical Origins of Social and Political Thought* (Englewood Cliffs NJ: Prentice-Hall, 1993).

Žižek, Slavoj, *The Ticklish Subject: The Absent Centre of Political Ontology* (London: Verso, 1999).

Žižek, Slavoj, *In Defense of Lost Causes* (London: Verso, 2008).

Index